1999

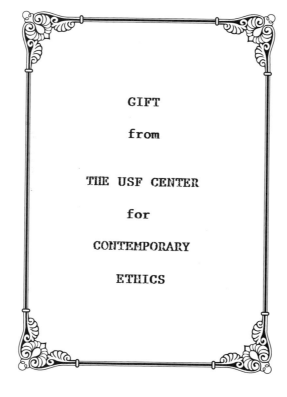

FINANCE
ETHICS

FINANCE
ETHICS
The Rationality of Virtue

John Dobson

ROWMAN & LITTLEFIELD PUBLISHERS, INC.
Lanham • Boulder • New York • Oxford

ROWMAN & LITTLEFIELD PUBLISHERS, INC.

Published in the United States of America
by Rowman & Littlefield Publishers, Inc.
4720 Boston Way, Lanham, Maryland 20706

12 Hid's Copse Road
Cummor Hill, Oxford OX2 9JJ, England

British Cataloging in Publication Information Available

Library of Congress Cataloging-in-Publication Data

Finance ethics :   the rationality of virtue / John Dobson.
        p.   cm.
    Includes bibliographical references and index.
    ISBN 0-8476-8401-6 (cloth: alk. paper). — ISBN 0-8476-8402-4
(paper: alk. paper)
    1. Business ethics.   2. Finance—Moral and ethical aspects.
I. Title.
HF5387.D63   1997
174'.4—dc20
                                                            96-41422
                                                            CIP

Printed in the United States of America

♾ ™ The paper used in this publication meets the minimum requirements of
American National Standard for Information Sciences—Permanence of Paper for Printed Library Materials, ANSI Z39.48-1984.

To Sharon

Contents

Preface

The theory of the firm, as it has evolved in financial-economic theory, is premised on a single narrow concept of rationality. Within this 'finance paradigm', a rational agent is simply one who pursues personal material advantage *ad infinitum*. In essence, to be rational in finance is to be individualistic, materialistic, and competitive. Business is a game played by individuals, as with all games the object is to win, and winning is measured in terms solely of material wealth. Within the discipline this rationality concept is never questioned, and has indeed become the theory-of-the-firm's *sine qua non*.

Beyond the monastic cloisters of financial economics, however, it is generally recognized that there is no single 'right' concept of rationality. Within the human milieu there are rationalities rather than rationality. This book proposes an alternative rationality premise for financial economics, a premise that is broader and more morally inclusive than the existing 'wealth-maximization' paradigm.

If this book were merely a moral critique of the finance paradigm, it would provide nothing particularly new. The business ethics literature is now replete with such critiques, and the moral shortcomings of the financial-economic concept of rationality are well known. What distinguishes this book, however, is the nature of the critique. Previous criticisms have invariably been by moral philosophers or business ethicists; in other words, by people from the outside looking in. Consequently their critiques are invariably based on some moral perspective that highlights the moral shortcomings of finance.

The distinguishing characteristic of this book is that I critique the finance paradigm from *within* the paradigm. Unlike other authors in this area, my professional background is financial economics. Thus, I view the finance paradigm from the inside, looking out. In part I, I begin with a critique of the paradigm on its own terms, from *within*. I show that even in economic terms, the paradigm has a serious flaw. It views the firm, and financial markets in general, as a contractual nexus, yet it fails to supply any adequate mechanism for the enforcement of these contractual relations.

This lack of an efficient contractual enforcement mechanism in financial markets provides an economic justification for the introduction of some form of ethic. In short, participants in financial markets need to be able to trust one another if these markets are to function efficiently. In part II, a challenge to the existing paradigm, I review the implications of this need for trust, and evaluate some of the conventional ways of imbuing the finance paradigm with some ethic.

These conventional ways have generally taken the form of adding ethics as some form of constraint on the individual's wealth-maximization objective. An obvious practical example would be a corporate credo that lists a set of dos and don'ts. Alternatively, business ethicists have attempted to 'sell' ethics as good for business: ethics is viewed as a means to strategic advantage.

I conclude that these attempts have failed, particularly in the context of international finance. In the final part of the text, therefore, I move beyond the finance paradigm by suggesting a new approach to modeling rational behavior in finance. This approach does not attempt to add on ethics as some form of appendage or constraint to the existing theory; rather it goes right to the heart of the theory: to the finance paradigm's very notion of rationality. I draw on the moral philosophy of virtue ethics to provide an alternative rationality premise for financial economics. This alternative premise brings notions of ethical behavior within the rationality rubric. Thus, such actions as 'honoring trust' become rational in and of themselves, and do not have to be justified in material terms.

The book's central argument is therefore taken full circle. In addition to its moral appeal, this new finance paradigm also enables trust to become a rational contractual enforcement mechanism. So, whether viewed from the perspective of ethics or economics, the new virtue-based paradigm dominates the old.

In a formal educational context, I have found that this book makes an excellent supplementary text in both finance and business ethics courses at the upper-level undergraduate and graduate levels.[1] In the case of finance, because the subject of financial ethics is so new, there is really nothing available in this area and finance texts themselves give ethics—at most—a cursory mention. In the case of business ethics, although there are now several business ethics texts available, these texts cover all areas of business and generally tend to focus on the management function since the authors, if not moral philosophers, tend to be in the management area. In a finance course, therefore, this book is a valuable supplementary text because it covers the financial aspects of business enterprise from the latest theoretical perspective, namely that of agency theory. It also gives a detailed overview of virtue-ethics theory, which is often inadequately addressed in existing business ethics texts.

I am indebted to the work of many authors. I build from a concept of the firm that finds its origin in Adam Smith's *The Wealth of Nations*, published originally in 1776, and more recently in the work of R.H. Coase (1937), "The Nature of the Firm," and in the modern development of agency theory.[2] The critique of economic rationality owes much to many other authors whose work is neatly summarized in Richard Thaler's book *Paradoxes and Anomalies of Economic Life* (1992).[3]

Recent interpretations of Aristotelian moral philosophy are used extensively.[4] In particular the concept of "practical rationality" as elucidated by Alasdair MacIntyre in *After Virtue* (1984) and *Whose Justice? Which Rationality?* (1988). This concept also helps place the finance paradigm in an historical context.[5] The synthesis of economic theory and moral philosophy undertaken here reflects, in part, a growing body of literature in the area of business ethics.[6] Finally, the underlying structure of the book's normative thrust is provided by Robert M. Pirsig who, through his evocative "Metaphysics of Quality," provides a pattern by which to weave these heretofore disparate literary threads.

I would also like to acknowledge the help of the editorial staff at Rowman & Littlefield, and the tireless dedication of my student assistant, Erin Yokayama.

Introduction

The paradigm about self-interest leading to a workable and perhaps even optimal social order without any admixture of "benevolence" has now been around so long that it has become intellectually challenging to rediscover the need for morality. To affirm this need has today almost the same surprise value and air of paradox which the Smithian farewell to benevolence had in its own time. Second, and more important, it has become increasingly clear that, in a number of important areas, the economy is in fact likely to perform poorly without a minimum of "benevolence."

— Albert O. Hirschman

Upon listening to the current controversy surrounding the role of ethics in business, financial managers may understandably feel somewhat bemused. On the one hand they will remember their business school training, during which they were continually instructed that the primary objective of the firm is to maximize shareholders' wealth, or as Milton Friedman put it in the title of his oft-quoted *New York Times* article: "The Social Responsibility of Business Is to Increase Its Profits."[1]

But these financial managers may also come across statements from leading business ethicists such as the "primary obligation [of business] is to provide meaningful work for . . . employees," or "if in some instance it turns out that what is ethical leads to a company's demise . . . so be it."[2] Not to mention such proclamations as "provision to meet need is the highest purpose of business; provision to satisfy unreasonable and socially harmful desire . . . perverts the purpose of business," and "it is usually profitable to be honorable, and virtue is more than its own reward."[3]

How, if at all, can these views be reconciled? In the context of financial economics, is shareholder-wealth maximization antithetical to honor and virtue? Are agency problems, such as excessive management remuneration or management's delay in releasing negative financial information, also ethical problems? Assuming that it is relevant, is ethics too nebulous a concept for serious consideration within the financial contracting rubric? In practice, on what basis should decisions be made when an apparent conflict exists between profits and ethics? If corporations should temper their pecuniary aspirations with some ethic, then which of the various moral philosophies is most practical in a financial context?

Business ethics and financial economics both analyze business and thus both address aspects of these and many similar questions. Even the most cursory review of their respective literatures, however, will reveal that they tend to do so from distinctly different perspectives. This difference is often explained in terms of a positive (i.e., descriptive) approach versus a normative (i.e., prescriptive) approach: financial economics attempts to explain what the firm *is*, whereas business ethics attempts to explain what the firm *should be*. But this explanation is lacking. In finance, for example, Merton Miller's invocation of the firm as "an abstract engine that 'uses money today to make money tomorrow'" has both positive and normative elements.[4] It describes what the firm is, but it also describes what—within the finance paradigm—the firm should be: the firm *is* a type of financial engine, and the firm *should be* an engine that makes "money tomorrow."

In essence, finance views the objective of the firm solely in terms of economic efficiency (as the quote from Miller indicates), whereas business ethics extends the objectives of the firm to encompass the moral good, but both disciplines address positive and normative issues. For example, in the case of business ethics theory, normative statements such as "provision to meet need is the highest purpose of business" are in sharp contrast to positive observations such as the finding of "a marked negative association between accountants' position or rank [within large accounting firms] and their level of ethical reasoning."[5]

This positive-normative dichotomy, therefore, does not fully account for the difference between business ethics and financial economics. But there clearly is a difference. Both disciplines are concerned with the same entity, namely the firm, but both disciplines operate in paradigmatically separate universes. Finance essentially takes the values and goals of the agent as given and focuses instead on the contractual structure of the firm. Contrarily, business ethics questions these very values and goals.

But even though the distinction between normative and positive does not adequately account for the difference between business ethics and finance, it can provide some valuable insights. In the context of finance, relatively little distinction is made between normative and positive as regards the concept of the firm itself. The only absolute is the normative dictum that firms should be efficient, but the questions of how firms should be structured in order to maximize efficiency and how they actually *are* structured are recognized as open questions. Michael Jensen and William Meckling, for example, define firms as "legal fictions which serve as a nexus for a set of contracting relations among individuals," but they do not claim that such firms are the normative ideal, nor do they claim that this definition is the definitive positive statement on what the firm actually is.[6] If you compare IBM and Microsoft, for example, both firms fit the above definition of a contractual nexus and both presumably strive for efficiency, but the composition of these firms and the means by which they strive for efficiency are clearly very different. One might convincingly argue that the fact that IBM lost approximately 50 percent of its market value in recent years, and that this market value was temporarily exceeded by that of Microsoft, indicates that the latter is a more efficient contractual nexus than the former. But one could no doubt envisage a still more efficient firm. At the firm level, therefore, finance recognizes the evolutionary nature of both normative and positive concepts.

When one shifts from the structure of the firm to the behavior of individuals within the firm, however, finance's approach becomes considerably more rigid. Here the behavioral prerogatives of the agent are taken as absolute and inviolable. The concept of agents as wealth-maximizing opportunists is finance's *sine qua non*, and any hint of the possibility of other behavioral motivations is summarily dismissed as no more than a "'Nirvana' form of analysis."[7] Thus, when it comes to the behavioral motivations of individuals, finance's conceptual rigidity is absolute.

Turning now to business ethics, the conceptualization is very similar in terms of the firm, but very different in terms of the agent. As regards the firm, business ethicists would generally concur with financial economists that the firm is and should be a contractual nexus, and that the practical specifics of what form this contractual nexus takes, and what form it should take, are indeterminate and evolutionary. Also business ethicists would not necessarily dispute the corporate goal of economic efficiency *per se*: they recognize the firm as an economic mechanism.

Where finance and business ethics diverge, however, is in their respective concepts of the behavior of agents within firms. Business ethics does not accept finance's conceptual rigidity on the questions of what does motivate the agent and what should motivate the agent. On the positive side, business ethics draws on multidisciplinary evidence that agents' behavioral choices and aspirations are malleable, and that the structure of the firm itself can significantly alter behavior.[8] On the normative side, business ethics undertakes the aforementioned "'Nirvana' form of analysis" in earnest. Indeed, the question of what *should* motivate agents provides business ethics' main normative focus.

Finance's conceptual rigidity regarding agents' behavior, therefore, limits its normative focus to the substance-based structure of the firm only, with no consideration given to the value base of the agents. Finance's sole normative quest is to discern the most economically efficient market structure; in the case of the firm, this is the one that will maximize shareholders' material wealth. Contrarily, business ethics spreads its normative net to encompass broader questions regarding the objectives of markets, firms, and individuals. This conceptual difference is reflected in the methodologies of the two disciplines: finance's rigidity regarding behavior has enabled it to achieve a high degree of mathematical rigor in both empirics and theory, whereas the broader normative focus in business ethics has limited mathematical precision to empirical studies only. Indeed, it was this quest for mathematical precision that led the finance paradigm to define rational behavior in such spectacularly narrow terms.

An apologist for the finance paradigm might defend its conceptual rigidity as follows. Although there are undoubtedly motivations other than wealth maximization that influence, and should influence, behavior, the assumptions of the finance paradigm provide a reasonable approximation of agents' behavior over a broad spectrum of business environments. The firm is an economic mechanism and agents act within the firm for fundamentally economic reasons. In addition, the construction of mathematically robust models requires simplifying assumptions. Like perfect-and-frictionless capital markets, wealth maximization is one such simplifying assumption. All disciplines have their conceptual boundaries, and any value-based normative consideration of human behavior simply lies beyond finance's conceptual boundary. Indeed, if finance were to stretch this boundary in an attempt to encompass such questions, mathematical rigor would be lost. Finance would be set adrift in the scientifically unnavigable sea of moral philosophy. Wealth maximization provides a secure anchorage from which a rigorous theory of financial-market behavior can be built. Says Norman Bowie, "Like perfect information and zero transaction costs, psychological egoism [i.e., wealth maximization] is one of the simplifying assumptions needed for the mathematics of equilibrium analysis."[9]

But this defense of the finance paradigm's notion of rationality may be countered as follows. A close scrutiny of the wealth-maximization assumption as invoked in the finance paradigm reveals that its mathematical rigor is in fact a chimera. Consider, for example, the concept of utility-of-wealth that is used frequently in financial contracting models.[10] We may say that this utility increases with increasing wealth, and decreases with increasing risk and effort, but even though the functional relationship may be approximated by a lognormal or similar utility function, this function can never be measured with precision for any one individual or individuals in aggregate.[11] Even wealth maximization, therefore, accommodates a margin of judgment concerning an agent's behavioral prerogatives, which broaches the question of whether other behavioral assumptions might not provide an equally secure conceptual anchorage. Also, the recent history of financial economics has essentially been one of weighing conceptual anchors. Indeed, finance's newer and most informative theories, namely agency, signaling, and reputation theories, arose from the weighing of the perfect-and-frictionless-capital-markets anchor: these theories are built on the recognition of market inefficiencies and have been instrumental in the evolution of the contemporary theory of the firm. Weighing the wealth-maximization anchor, therefore, may simply be the next logical step in the evolution of a theory of what the firm is, and of what the firm should be. Indeed, agency and signaling theory reveal clearly the normative undesirability of wealth maximization. These models inevitably engender equilibria that are inefficient in that wealth is not maximized either for the agents involved or for the economy in aggregate, hence the "finance paradox" in which a strategy of wealth maximization does not maximize wealth. But more on this in chapter 1.

Furthermore, there is increasing evidence that human behavior, even in a financial context, is far more complex and multifaceted than financial theorists have recognized. The behavioral assumptions that form the foundation of the finance paradigm have been criticized on two broad fronts. First, from a descriptive perspective, the empirical validity of finance's simple personal-wealth-maximization assumption has been questioned. Second, arguments have been made to the effect that the descriptive accuracy of economic rationality is inseparable from its prescriptive desirability. Agents change their behavior when confronted with role models or assumptions about how other agents behave. In other words, 'is' inevitably implies 'ought.' A recognition that the descriptive and prescriptive aspects of human rationality are inseparable draws finance inevitably into the domain of moral philosophy: these fascinating questions of how agents *do* behave, and how agents *should* behave, and the extent to which do and should are connected extend our enquiry beyond the boundaries of what has traditionally been regarded as the "finance paradigm." *Financial ethics* is born.

But in general discourse, the term 'financial ethics' often evokes wry smiles and chuckles. "Isn't that an oxymoron?" will often be the sardonic retort. Such cynicism is perhaps not surprising in light of the continual scandals that have rocked both domestic and overseas financial markets in recent years, not to mention the questionable practices of many business organizations and the (handsomely remunerated) executives therein. Indeed, from a pedagogical perspective—with ethics having permeated the disciplines of accounting, marketing, and management—finance survives as the last bastion of a value-free business discipline. Finance has traditionally been regarded as value free because it was seen as dealing with the purely technical aspects of business enterprise: such issues as the optimal mix of debt and equity financing, dividend policy, and the evaluation of alternative investment projects, and more recently the valuation of options, futures, swaps, and other derivative securities. Such questions are essentially technical in nature and would appear to render little scope for ethical evaluation.

But beneath this technical facade financial economics remains, at heart, a *social* science. With the advent of agency theory, the purview of this discipline has been recognized as rightfully and inevitably extending beyond these technical subject areas to encompass the firm as a *human* organization. Until comparatively recently, this social aspect tended to be assumed away by the aforementioned "perfect markets" assumptions. But within the last two decades financial theory has been experiencing—indeed is still experiencing—something of a paradigm shift: a shift away from purely technical finance and toward behavioral finance. By the term 'behavioral finance' I mean an explicit recognition of the importance of human behavior in the financial milieu. As the perfect-and-frictionless-markets-type assumptions are increasingly relaxed, the *contractual* nature of financial interaction is revealed. These contractual models are being built around agents who are unable to perfectly and costlessly enter into contractual relations with other agents. For example, the notion that not all market participants are equally well informed would seem intuitively obvious. Until recently, however, the perfect-and-frictionless-markets assumptions made the gross simplification of invoking omniscient agents. Relaxing this omniscience assumption has enabled finance to recognize the power of information to drive behavior: agents' behavior is to a large extent determined by their conceptions of who knows what when in a given contractual situation. Who-knows-what-when is in turn largely determined by agents' ability to suppress negative information and *signal* positive information. Such signals take many forms: managers of firms with superior earnings prospects, for example, may go to great lengths and some expense to credibly signal this fact to outside investors by committing their firm to a relatively high dividend payout. Thus dividend payment policies, or the timing of earnings announcements, are two examples of signals. But, as will be discussed shortly, recent finance research has identified many more.

General acceptance by financial theorists of the firm as a contractual nexus, therefore, has opened a Pandora's Box of potential contractual problems between principals and agents in the corporate domain whose various claims cannot be explicitly enforced. These agency problems appear to threaten the efficiency with which the corporation can perform its role as a conduit through which real and financial resources are allocated. Agency theory is gaining increasing momentum in financial discourse and represents a dramatic conceptual shift in the discipline of financial economics. From a descriptive perspective, this shift has enabled finance to make significant advances in its ability to model and explain the operations of financial markets. In essence, these theories rest on the conceptual foundation of markets as collections of individual interest groups, each pursuing its own self-interest and each dependent, to a greater or lesser degree, on the beliefs and actions of other groups. This new wave of behavioral financial theory, as opposed to strictly technical finance, places human beliefs and motivations at center stage. Questions of psychology and philosophy, such as, What motivates individuals? and, What should motivate individuals? are rapidly becoming relevant—indeed, are becoming unavoidable—in finance.

Far from an oxymoron, therefore, a congruence of finance and ethics is becoming increasingly clear as an inevitable consequence of financial theory's broadened conceptual stance. Far from an aberration, the concept of financial ethics arises naturally as a means of answering behavioral questions raised by agency theory. Once the ethereal and malleable nature of human rationality is recognized, the descriptive question of what the agent actually does, and the normative question of what the agent should do, become inseparable. Given this recognition, the often-voiced question, Should finance consider ethics? becomes exposed as the real non sequitur. To the extent that it must be premised on some conception of what motivates and constrains human behavior, finance always considers ethics, albeit inadvertently to date. Finance has its own implicit moral philosophy. The meaningful question, therefore, is not *Should* finance consider ethics? but rather, *What type of ethic should* finance consider?

Surprisingly, the ability of finance to effectively answer this question has been greatly facilitated by recent developments—one might even say another paradigm shift—in the oldest academic discipline of all, namely moral philosophy. This development is gaining increasing momentum as a conceptual tool in one branch of moral philosophy, namely business ethics theory, and generally comes under the heading of virtue-ethics theory.

Business ethicists have traditionally taken a situational approach to tackling issues of ethics in financial organizations, what Sherwin Klein has termed the "action-based" approach.[12] This approach, in essence, attempts to develop rules or at least guidelines that will constrain agents' behavior to lie within the boundaries of what is generally regarded as acceptable behavior. These guidelines are drawn from traditional deontological and teleological moral philosophy, from Kantianism and utilitarianism and derivations thereof.[13] They focus on the actions of the agent in a given situation, and on the application of particular rules or guidelines to 'constrain' the agent. The traditional approach to business ethics can be effectively summarized as the ethics of *constraint* or, as Richard Taylor puts it, an ethics of "duty."[14]

Within the last few years, however, a new approach to ethics has garnered an increasing amount of attention from business ethicists. Klein labels this approach "agent-based" or "virtue-based" to distinguish it from the traditional "action-based" approach. Agent-based ethics finds its origin in the virtue-ethics theory of moral philosophy that, in turn, is based on the classical Greek philosophers, in particular Aristotle. Rather than focusing on rules or guidelines to constrain the actions of the agent in given situations, this approach focuses on the agent's motivations. It is, as Taylor notes, an ethics of "aspiration." Virtue ethics, in essence, deals with the agent's pursuit of moral excellence through the exercise of certain virtues such as justice and courage.

At first blush, the virtue-ethics approach might appear too esoteric for application in financial economics: how could a financial manager pursue moral excellence through virtue? On closer scrutiny, however, virtue ethics' focus on the fundamental motivations of the agent dovetails neatly with financial economists' increasing focus on the motivations of agents in financial contracting. It is this holistic motivational focus, transcending contextual specificity, that is the great contribution of virtue-ethics theory. This theory provides an alternative value base upon which to build a morally sensitive theory of financial economics, thereby extending the finance paradigm into the moral universe. Finance becomes a conceptually richer discipline in line with a new epistemology that portrays, in Peter Allen's words, a "unified view of the world which bridges the gap between the physical and the human sciences."[15]

In summary, the three parts of this book—"Within the Finance Paradigm," "Challenging the Finance Paradigm," and "Beyond the Finance Paradigm"—build a sound logical foundation for ethics in financial-economics. I investigate the implications of extending the financial economic concept of substantive rationality along lines suggested by virtue-ethics theory. Such an extension is justified on positive grounds by the growing body of evidence disconfirming the type of material opportunism that currently provides the rationality premise of the finance paradigm. On normative grounds, such an extension is justified both economically and morally. Economically, theories of the firm based on opportunism engender equilibria that are optimal neither for the individual agent nor for the firm in aggregate. Morally, virtue-ethics theory demonstrates the philosophical shortcomings of wealth maximization as a basis for substantive rationality. From this broadened perspective, the extant finance paradigm is exposed as being both narrow and impoverished. It is narrow because it excludes as irrational any behavioral motivation beyond that of personal material gain. It is impoverished because it fails to consider the economic agent as also a moral agent, and the moral dimension of the firm as a community, a dimension emphasized particularly by virtue-ethics theory.

Engendering a paradigm shift in financial economics along lines suggested by virtue ethics is clearly no small undertaking. By focusing attention on the concept of rationality reflected in the finance paradigm, this book provides a start, but only a start. With the exception of its application to debt markets in chapter 8, the task of applying a new 'virtue-enriched' paradigm to the many specific financial-economic contexts remains for future work. Still, as Alasdair MacIntyre wryly observes, "Descartes may have been right about one thing . . . to know how to begin is the most difficult task of all."[16]

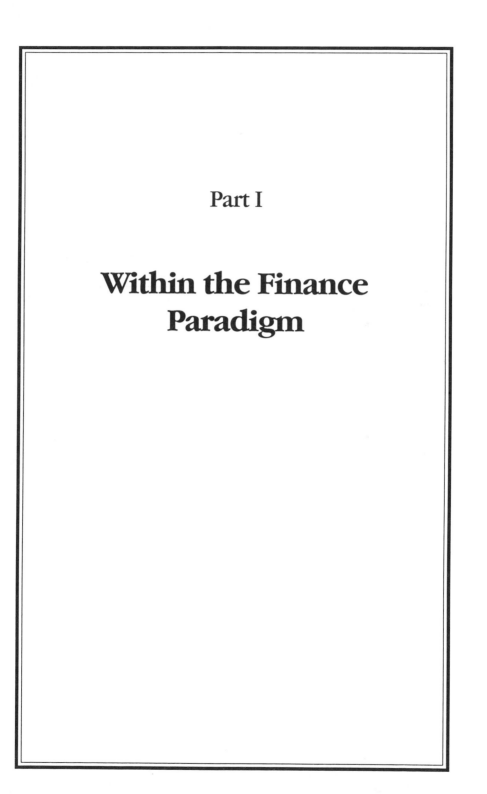

Part I

Within the Finance
Paradigm

1

The Finance Paradox

*What economics, sociobiology, and behavior theory claim to show us
is that people must be slaves to the maximization of self-interest. What
they actually show is that people can be slaves to the maximization of
self-interest. This leaves open for our moral evaluation whether they
should be slaves to the maximization of self-interest.*
— Barry Schwartz

In his *Essay on the Application of Mathematics to the Moral Sciences*, published originally in 1881, F.Y. Edgeworth declares that "the first principle of Economics is that every agent is actuated only by self-interest."[1] Within our century, this "first principle" has been further honed by the discipline of financial economics. Within this discipline 'self-interest' has come to be defined in very narrow, and very specific, terms: "individuals *always* prefer more wealth to less" and act "with, if necessary, guile and deceit."[2] This concept characterizes self-interest as the narrowly individualistic and opportunistic pursuit of material wealth, to the exclusion of all other motivations. I label this behavioral concept the 'finance paradigm.'

Although originally developed by Edgeworth and others as simply a mathematically amenable assumption to facilitate market analysis, this paradigm has evolved in the twentieth century into nothing less than an epistemology.[3] Furthermore, it is an epistemology that is gaining ever greater influence as the implicit philosophical foundation for what is often somewhat ambiguously referred to as Western 'corporate culture.' Indeed, the very idea of the corporation as a culture is a reflection of this influence.

But economic agents have not always been invoked in such conceptually narrow terms. An investigation into the early origins of economic philosophy in the writings of Adam Smith and David Hume reveals, says Stephen Holmes, "the incredible finesse with which Smith and his contemporaries analyzed the human psyche . . . [versus] . . . the pitiful impoverishment that befell us, sometime in the nineteenth century, when Marxism and liberal economics conspired to assert the supremacy of interest and thus to extinguish an older and subtler tradition of moral psychology."[4] These classic economic philosophers envisaged a far richer paradigm of human interaction in the economic sphere. In the case of David Hume: "The epithets sociable, good-natured, humane, merciful, grateful, friendly, generous, beneficent, or their equivalents, are known in all languages, and universally express the highest merit, which human nature is capable of attaining."[5] In the case of Adam Smith:

> All members of human society stand in need of each other's assistance, and are likewise exposed to mutual injuries. Where the necessary assistance is reciprocally afforded from love, from gratitude, from friendship, and esteem, the society flourishes and is happy. All the different members of it are bound together by the agreeable bonds of love and affection, and are, as it were, drawn to one common centre of mutual good offices.[6]

So it appears that, in evolving from the "self-interest" invoked by Smith and Hume, to the "self-interest" of the finance paradigm, something has been lost. We have, in essence, regressed in the last two hundred years from a morally inclusive concept of self-interest to one in which the notion of what Adam Smith called "moral sentiment" has absolutely no "rational" place. By defining the finance paradigm from two perspectives, this chapter illustrates the irreconcilability of moral sentiment and this paradigm's concept of rationality. The first perspective is that of the individual agent, and the second is that of the firm.

The Agent

In the *Odyssey,* Homer's Odysseus says:

> I carved a massive cake of beeswax into bits and rolled them in my hands until they softened. . . . Going forward I carried wax along the line, and laid it thick on their ears. They tied me up, then, plumb amidships, back to the mast, lashed to the mast, and took themselves again to rowing. Soon, as we came smartly within hailing distance, the two Sirens, noting our fast ship off their point, made ready, and they sang. . . . The lovely voices in ardor appealing over the water made me crave to listen, and I tried to say "Untie me!" to the crew, jerking my brows; but they bent steady to the oars.[7]

In his article "The Determinants of Corporate Borrowing," Stewart Myers employs this excerpt from Homer to illustrate the central paradox of financial economics.[8] In finance, the "Sirens' song" is the opportunistic pursuit of personal material gain. The rationality assumption at the heart of the finance paradigm is such that, even though they know that opportunism is self-defeating, agents cannot resist such behavior. Principals enter into contractual relations, therefore, on the assumption that agents will act opportunistically. In Myers's debt-market model, for example, lenders charge a higher interest rate in the expectation that borrowers will underinvest (i.e., will reject profitable projects). Thus, agents pay the price for opportunism even before they act. Opportunism is built into the contract. Agents are never given the benefit of the doubt, no tit-for-tat strategies here. In a repeated contractual situation, financial theory does consider the possibility that an agent acts unopportunistically in some of the repetitions in order to induce the principal to offer future contracts: this is the "reputation effect" to be discussed in chapter 3. But principals assume that agents will renege on their reputation and revert to opportunism as soon as it suits them, thus unopportunistic equilibria based on agents maintaining a reputation are quite fragile.

Opportunism, therefore, is the foundation upon which the finance paradigm's rationality construct is built. Indeed, from the perspective of its behavioral assumptions, the opportunistic pursuit of material wealth *is* the finance paradigm. Like Odysseus, agents within this construct are "lashed to the mast" *ex ante* on the assumption that it is inconceivable that they may resist the Sirens' song of opportunism. But, as Norman Bowie notes, "there is considerable confusion as to whether the profit maximization claim is a universal empirical claim, an approximate empirical claim, a heuristic assumption, or an ethical obligation."[9]

Bowie's intimation that the finance paradigm's concept of rationality is synonymous with "profit maximization" is somewhat of an oversimplification, but only somewhat. Economic rationality is founded on the five axioms of cardinal utility as enumerated in 1947 by von Neumann and Morgenstern, plus one additional axiom. In essence, these five axioms define rationality in terms of an individual's ability to make consistent preference orderings over a broad spectrum of choices: "We wish to find the mathematically complete principles which define 'rational behavior' for the participants in a social economy, and derive from them the general characteristics of that behavior."[10] So, for example, the statement "I like Chevrolets more than Fords and Fords more than Toyotas but Toyotas more than Chevrolets" is not rational.[11] Furthermore, "people are assumed to be able to make these rational choices among thousands of alternatives."[12] Note that these five axioms make no normative statement concerning whether the agent has any specific goal, or what the goal of the agent should be. The axioms simply require that the agent act in a consistent manner in ordering preferences.

The sixth axiom of economic rationality, which is promoted particularly vehemently by financial economists, is that of material acquisitiveness. "Having established the five axioms we add to them the assumption that individuals *always* prefer more wealth to less."[13] The broad acceptance of this sixth axiom is reflected in the behavioral assumptions made by financial economists. Hayne Leland and David Pyle, for example, in their capital structure signaling model, state that "the entrepreneur is presumed to maximize his expected utility of wealth." Kose John and David Nachman directly transfer the traditional objective of the firm to managers when, in their agency model, they assume that management's "overall objective is to . . . invest in non-negative NPV [net present value] projects." Douglas Diamond, in his model of reputation acquisition in debt markets, to be discussed further in chapter 8, defines management's objective as an endeavor to "maximize discounted expected consumption over T periods." Some models assume management is risk averse or effort averse, or both, and therefore maximizes some measure of utility-of-wealth. But this utility is always strictly a positive function of wealth *ad infinitum*. Thus, the sixth axiom holds throughout.[14]

In a broader context, Alasdair MacIntyre isolates three "central features of the modern economic order," namely "individualism . . . acquisitiveness and its elevation of the values of the market to a central social place."[15] Thus, despite its potential ambiguity, the term "wealth maximization" captures succinctly the primary characteristic common to all finance objective functions, namely that they are purely acquisitive in nature, entailing solely the accumulation or consumption, or both, of pecuniary goods. But financial economists go further. Specifically, Michael Jensen and William Meckling argue that one would be indulging in a "'Nirvana' form of analysis" if one were to contemplate management acting in any way save that outlined above.[16] These six axioms are also subsuming any competing notions of rationality.[17] This is made clear by Richard Thaler in his book *Paradoxes and Anomalies of Economic Life*.

> The same basic assumptions about behavior are used in all applications of economic analysis, be it the theory of the firm, financial markets, or consumer choice. The two key assumptions are rationality [the five axioms] and self-interest [the sixth axiom]. People are assumed to want to get as much for themselves as possible, and are assumed to be quite clever in figuring out how best to accomplish this aim.[18]

In addressing the concept of rationality, a useful distinction can be made between *instrumental* rationality and *substantive* rationality. In essence, instrumental rationality concerns how the agent goes about achieving the desired objective, whereas substantive rationality concerns identifying the desired objective itself. For example, Jennifer Moore distinguishes between the two concepts as follows:

> The primary feature of instrumental rationality is that it does not choose ends, but accepts them as given and looks for the best means to achieve them. In instrumental rationality, reason is subordinated to and placed at the service of ends outside itself. In . . . [substantive rationality], in contrast, reason is free ranging. It is not the servant of any end. Rather, it subjects every end to its *own* standards of evaluation and criticism.[19]

Viewing the finance paradigm in terms of this dichotomy between instrumental and substantive rationality reveals that this paradigm's rationality premise has only a partial foundation in logic. The logic of the instrumental part of what the finance paradigm regards as rational behavior finds a sound logical foundation in the five axioms enumerated by von Neumann and Morgenstern. The same cannot be said, however, for finance's substantive rationality premise. This premise is supplied essentially by fiat: by arbitrarily assuming—for reasons of mathematical convenience—that agents are atomistic and opportunistic wealth maximizers. These agents are atomistic in that their decisions are not affected by the impact that these decisions might have on other agents. The agents are 'opportunists' in that they are assumed to take whichever action maximizes their wealth, regardless of prior commitments or agreements; they act, says Noreen, "with, if necessary, guile and deceit."[20] No positive justification is supplied in the finance literature in the form of empirical evidence to support this substantive rationality premise, nor is any normative argument supplied to defend the notion that this is how agents *should* behave. Wealth maximization is just tacitly accepted as the finance paradigm's *sine qua non.*[21]

The Firm

Through the finance paradigm's narrow conceptual lens, the firm is viewed as a purely passive structure—a structure whose efficiency depends upon its ability to mitigate the agency costs engendered by these guileful and deceitful "rational" opportunists. This arbitrary and rigid rationality premise, therefore, not only determines the behavior of individuals in financial markets, but also sculpts the very structure and function of the firm itself.

Within the last decade or so, financial-economic theory has made a significant contribution to economic philosophy. Unfortunately, the broad implications of this contribution have, to date, gone largely unrecognized. This contribution relates both to the theory of the firm and to the theory of what constitutes rational behavior within the firm. Traditionally, the firm has been viewed as an atomistic unit, a single unified decision node or "black box." Theories of this atomistic firm have been conjured in the pristine environment of "perfect and frictionless capital markets" in which agents are omniscient (i.e., there is no informational asymmetry) and there are no transaction costs of any kind.[22] Not surprisingly, models developed in such an environment have exhibited minimal explanatory power in many *actual economic* environments. Kwang Chung and Richard Smith comment, "The firm, in that literature, is an abstraction stripped of such intangible assets as reputation and with no distinction made between the profit objective of investors and the utility maximization objective of agent managers."[23]

More recently, however, financial economists have relaxed perfect-market assumptions to reveal the firm in a more realistic light. In this light the firm emerges, not as an atomistic unit, but "as a nexus for a set of contracting relations among individuals."[24] Michael Jensen and William Meckling go on to make the following observations:

> Viewed in this way, it makes little or no sense to try to distinguish those things which are "inside" the firm from those things that are "outside" of it. There is in a very real sense only a multitude of complex relationships (i.e., contracts) between the legal fiction (the firm) and the owners of labor, material and capital inputs and the consumers of output. . . . In this sense the "behavior" of the firm is like the behavior of the market; i.e., the outcome of a complex equilibrium process.[25]

This "contractual nexus" thus includes the overlapping interests, claims, and objectives of several groups: suppliers and customers, employees and the community, management, shareholders, and bondholders; these could be further subdivided into voting versus nonvoting shareholders or inside versus outside shareholders, secured versus unsecured bondholders, unionized versus nonunionized employees, and so on. Not surprisingly, as the growing body of agency theory to be discussed in the next two chapters demonstrates, these claims and objectives frequently conflict.

The broader philosophical implication of these developments concerns the notion of a 'corporate objective.' If, rather than being an atomistic unit, the firm is in fact an amalgamation of stakeholder groups, then clearly the idea of a corporate objective is something of a misnomer. Management may have one objective, shareholders another, and debtholders yet another, not to mention customers, employees, and suppliers.

One might argue that management represents the pivotal stakeholder group in that it controls the immediate corporate decision making, and acts as agent for other stakeholder groups in the corporate milieu. Thus, the term "corporate objective" is often taken as being synonymous with "management's objective." The corporate contractual fabric is constructed in such a way that management is vested with the fiduciary responsibility of making economic decisions that affect all stakeholder groups. The challenge that all diversely held organizations face is to structure their contractual relations in such a way that one stakeholder is not able to exploit other stakeholders. Eugene Fama and Michael Jensen note the existence of boards of directors as the stakeholder group that adjudicates these conflicts of interest. The board of directors is rarely an autonomous group; there is overlap: some directors are also managers and some are also shareholders, and some are all three. But some directors are neither managers nor shareholders; these are the outside directors. This eclectic board is necessary, in theory at least, in order to control conflicts with sufficient expertise. The inside directors provide expertise on the internal organization of the firm, while the outside directors, who ideally are aligned neither with management nor shareholders, ensure fairness and objectivity. As Fama and Jensen note, "The outside board members act as arbiters in disagreements among internal managers and carry out tasks that involve serious agency problems between internal managers and residual claimants, for example, setting executive compensation or searching for replacements for top managers."[26]

Evidence indicates, however, that the board of directors in practice is often different from—and less unbiased than—the board of directors in theory. For the five hundred largest corporations that comprise the *Fortune 500*, the CEO frequently holds the position of chairman of the board also. Thus, in many cases, we have a situation of what T. Boone Pickens calls the "fox guarding the henhouse." The results of this corporate "incest" are readily predictable. Decisions tend to be made that serve the interests of incumbent managers, rather than all stakeholders.[27] Indeed, in a 1989 *Harvard Business Review* article, Michael Jensen predicts that these conflicts of interest or agency problems may lead to the "eclipse of the public corporation" in which the passivity of outside shareholders is replaced by a more highly leveraged corporate form in which the actions of management are closely monitored and constrained by bondholders. The leveraged buyout (LBO) craze of the 1980s—in which a large and diverse group of shareholders was replaced by a small and homogenous group of bondholders—appeared to augur Jensen's "eclipse." In the 1990s, however, many of these erstwhile LBOs have returned to their pre-1980s structure by issuing public shares to replace debt.

Whether or not the traditional notion of the widely held public corporation is waxing or waning is clearly debatable. What seems certain, however, is that some form of 'corporation' comprising an amalgamation of various interest groups—whatever form these interest groups may take—is going to be the dominant economic and socioeconomic force in world commerce for the foreseeable future. But is the view of these organizations, as supplied by the conceptual lens of the finance paradigm, the only view? If it is not the only view, then is it the most accurate or the most desirable?

In essence, this view is one in which the firm is a machine designed to derive the benefits of divisions of capital and labor while controlling the conflicts arising from irretrievably opportunistic agents. This economic "theory of the firm," sculpted by the finance paradigm, presents itself as a morally neutral positive construct that merely endeavors to define the firm and explain the actions of agents therein. But can a theory that bases itself on such a narrow and rigid concept of rationality be strictly positive and morally neutral, or is it merely another facet of what Richard DeGeorge terms the "myth of amoral business"?[28] If this theory of the firm does have a normative dimension, then is it normatively justifiable? Will any attempt to make it normatively justifiable tend to compromise its descriptive accuracy?

Few would argue that, from the perspective of descriptive accuracy, the conceptual shift away from viewing the firm as a 'black box' and toward the view of the firm as a 'contractual nexus' has been a beneficial one; particularly when one considers the sheer size and complexity of the contemporary corporation. These firms clearly have more in common with the multi-headed Hydra of Greek mythology than with a unit or box. The Hydra analogy seems particularly appropriate when one considers the power and scope of transnational or multinational companies. The rise of these multi-nationals illustrates vividly the degree to which the firm and its habitat, namely the market system, are becoming increasingly global phenomena that not only serve but also direct human activity, not just in the developed world, but in developing countries also. For example, in the case of the latter, according to a UN survey, multinationals currently control "eighty percent of the world's land cultivated for export-oriented crops. . . . Eighty to ninety percent of the trade in tea, coffee, cocoa, cotton, forest products, tobacco, jute, copper, iron ore, and bauxite is controlled in the case of each commodity by the three or six largest transnationals."[29]

Thus the question, What is the objective of the firm? has become as abstruse as the question, What is the objective of the city? Both are increasingly complex human organizations. It is the individuals within who possess the multifarious objectives that characterize these Hydras. Indeed, the analogy between firms and cities is an edifying one. Like the city, the firm is increasingly becoming a social, as well as an economic, phenomenon—hence the increasing usage of the term 'corporate culture.' Whatever ethnic, religious, or other cultural boundaries may have evolved through history, a global corporate culture is increasingly subsuming these traditional divisions with transnational corporations bridging both geographic and cultural boundaries. Indeed, this corporate culture is not merely implicit. Many firms now publish internal codes of acceptable behavior, as do several regulatory bodies; for example, the OECD's "Guidelines for Multinational Enterprise."[30] But despite the contemporary firm's size and complexity, its fundamental *raison d'être* remains the same. As Milton Friedman succinctly puts it: "The social responsibility of business is to increase its profits."[31] This may be constrained by what Friedman calls "ethical custom" but, by definition, the firm would be misconstrued if it were not a *Hydra* concerned primarily with the creation of material wealth.[32]

But a culture, albeit a corporate one, premised solely on the accumulation of material wealth inevitably raises questions of a moral nature. Discussion of these questions has been formalized under the heading of "business ethics." Among both practitioners and academicians, business ethics is probably the most rapidly expanding field of business-related intellectual enquiry.

But, as two heads of the Hydra, business ethics and the finance paradigm clearly comprise—at best—an uncomfortable alliance. Indeed, if ethics is, as Friedman argues, merely some constraint within the wealth-maximizing rubric, then its role in business affairs would appear, at best, peripheral and, at worst, vanishingly trivial. Under these circumstances, for ethics to exist at all within such a strictly material corporate culture the colloquialism "good ethics is good (i.e., profitable) business" *would have to be* believed. If it were not generally believed, then individuals would find ethics an entirely irrational and unintelligible concept, and they would consequently view the practice of ethical behavior as entirely unjustifiable— hence, the daunting conceptual schism that we face in this book between moral "virtue" and the "finance paradigm." In the contemporary social milieu, business must justify morality, which is a far cry from Adam Smith's prioritization in *The Theory of Moral Sentiments* in which the pursuit of the moral *good* justified the pursuit of economic *goods*.[33]

Rather than a leap into the future, therefore, the mission of this book may require a step into the past. What caused the morally rich behavioral paradigm, implicit in Smith's *The Theory of Moral Sentiments* and *The Wealth of Nations*, to become the morally impoverished paradigm reflected in the modern "theory of the firm"? It is interesting that this historical route is also being taken by a new branch of economic philosophy labeled by some as "radical subjectivism": "The essential characteristic of the radical subjectivist position that marks its critical departure from a neoclassical framework is, at the same time, the feature that it shares with the new evolutionary synthesis . . . Its conception of 'a world in which time plays a vital role.'"[34] Similarly, a central tenet of the virtue-based moral philosophy of Alasdair MacIntyre—to be discussed in some detail in part III of this book— is the importance of viewing morality in the historical context of a tradition of belief: "Narrative history of a certain kind turns out to be the basic and essential genre for the characterization of human actions."[35]

As a manifestation of human action, the firm is thus a phenomenon inseparable from its past. Some focus on this "narrative history" may also explain why the behavioral assumptions of the finance paradigm are, via our ever-burgeoning corporate culture, rapidly inheriting the role previously played by the behavioral prerogatives of moral philosophy; namely that of cultural progenitor. But such a focus will clearly take us beyond the finance paradigm and therefore must be postponed for now. Before critiquing the finance paradigm from without, the next two chapters critique it from within. But even here, even as it were on its "home turf," this paradigm is undesirable in that it renders equilibria that are *second best* from the perspective of both the individual agent and the economy in aggregate. Simply put, wealth maximization does not maximize wealth. As Bowie says, "It only pays to lie or cheat when you can free ride off the honesty of others. . . . The conscious pursuit of self-interest by all members of society has the collective result of undermining the interests of all."[36]

2

A Contractual Problem

When people seldom deal with one another, we find that they are somewhat disposed to cheat, because they can gain more by a smart trick than they can lose by the injury which it does their character. . . . Wherever dealings are frequent, a man does not expect to gain so much by any one contract, as by probity and punctuality in the whole, and a prudent dealer, who is sensible of his real interest, would rather choose to lose what he has a right to, than give any ground for suspicion.

— Adam Smith

As chapter 1 made clear, the business environment—as viewed through the lens of the finance paradigm—essentially comprises a complex web of interrelated interest groups or 'stakeholders,' each distinguishable by its unique set of objectives and constraints. This concept of the firm as an amalgamation of interest groups ties in closely with the concept of 'property rights' in economic theory; "different property rights assignments lead to different penalty-reward structures and, hence, decide the choices that are open to decision makers."[1] Indeed, the modern, agency-theory-based theory of the firm finds its origins in this property rights literature.[2] At its most fundamental level, a corporate culture can be viewed as a system of assigning economic rights. As A.A. Alchian states, "The allocation of scarce resources in a society is the assignment of rights to uses of resources."[3]

In contemporary economies, these allocations of property rights are achieved through highly evolved marketplaces such as multinational corporations, global securities markets, and multimedia communications systems. In essence, it is the international linkup of these marketplaces that has rendered contemporary corporate culture truly global. Stakeholder groups may now interact with one another throughout the industrialized world. The thread that links this highly evolved, high-tech conglomeration of marketplaces together is an intricate system of *contractual agreements*. Indeed, since the 1937 pioneering work of Robert Coase on the nature of the firm, corporations have been viewed as mechanisms for minimizing the costs and maximizing the efficiency of these contractual relations.[4] Although contractual agreements between stakeholders take on many forms, a general distinction can be made between *explicit* and *implicit* contracts.

Broadly defined, explicit contracts are those that appear in writing and lend themselves to legal enforcement (albeit at a cost). Examples of such contracts are bondholder covenants, union wage contracts, product warranties, and shareholder voting rights. Conversely, implicit contracts do not readily lend themselves to legal enforcement; they are, as Bradford Cornell and Alan Shapiro put it, "too nebulous and state contingent to reduce to writing at reasonable cost."[5] Examples of implicit contracts are many and varied; the most common include a producer's commitment to product quality, a stockbroker's commitment to execute a client's security transaction at the best available price, or management's commitment to act in the interests of shareholders. In addition, in recent years the international expansion of stakeholder relations has further increased the number of implicit contracts due to the difficulty of explicitly enforcing any type of contract transnationally. J.B. King makes this point clearly: "As a result of our economy's increasing complexity, it is becoming more difficult and expensive to spell out and enforce mutual responsibilities through detailed contracts and administrative hierarchies. . . . Conditions of trust are therefore becoming increasingly crucial to competing—and cooperating—in today's business environment."[6]

King's invocation of "trust" implies that some form of ethic in business could have real economic value. Although uncertainty may exist on the empirical question of whether managers actually act ethically, King implies that no conflicts exist on the normative question of the desirability of ethical behavior. Concerning the conflict of interest between managers and shareholders surrounding the former's consumption of perks, for example, Eric Noreen observes that "the best solution, which is costless, is for the manager to truthfully report his effort and his consumption of perquisites."[7] As chapter 1 clearly illustrated, however, given the conventional objective functions of agents in finance—namely opportunism—such behavior is excluded as irrational. Agents may rationally *act* in a way that honors contracts, for example they may build a reputation. They may not, however, be rationally *motivated* primarily by a desire to honor contracts since this is not a material objective. But for trust to work, agents must be intrinsically trustworthy. They cannot merely act in a trustworthy manner when it suits their material ends. What is required therefore is trust for trust's sake. But clearly from chapter 1, "trust for trust's sake" is irrational within the finance paradigm. Specifically, consider the concept of trust in the rationality enumerated by the six axioms of the finance paradigm. Within this paradigm, an individual who forgoes material gain in order to honor some trust-based agreement would be as irrational as an individual who forgoes material gain because the moon happened to be full: honoring trust would be 'rational' if and only if the individual expected to materially gain by such action. Within the finance paradigm, the act of honoring trust *in and of itself* has absolutely no value.

But, somewhat ironically, by building a theory of the firm on the foundation of this narrow rationality construct, finance has inadvertently strengthened the case for trust having intrinsic worth in business interaction. To see this we must delve inside the financial contracting models of agency theory. In essence, agency theory analyzes situations—ubiquitous in business—in which "one or more persons (the principal[s]) engage another person (the agent) to perform some service on their behalf which involves delegating some decision making authority to the agent."[8] These agency-theory models can be loosely categorized into two types: *adverse selection* and *moral hazard*. The difference between these two categories is essentially a function of the nature and degree of uncertainty inherent in the contractual situation.[9]

Consider adverse selection, where the uncertainty stems from an 'asymmetry of information' that precludes the principal from costlessly identifying the *type* of agent. For example, imagine two firms: "good" and "bad." The good firm has relatively superior future earnings prospects, whereas the bad firm has relatively inferior future earnings prospects. The firms cannot choose whether they are good or bad (formally, the agent's type is exogenously determined). Furthermore, the different earnings prospects of the two firms are not readily apparent from their financial statements or other generally available information. Thus, the contractual environment is one characterized by informational asymmetry: the agents (i.e., the insiders or managers of the firm) know more about their respective firm's prospects than do the principals (i.e., the outside investors). The ability of the principals to make optimal (i.e., wealth-maximizing) investment decisions is a function of their ability to distinguish between the good firm and the bad firm, thus the agency problem stems directly from the informational asymmetry. Since a firm's type is not directly observable, principals attempt to make inferences from signals emitted—either advertently or inadvertently—by the firms.

A successful signal will clearly be one that unambiguously distinguishes the two firms. For example, advertising is generally a weak signal since the bad firm could presumably advertise falsely that it is good: the Ford Motor Company may *advertise* that "Quality Is Job #1," but many consumers are still willing to pay $10,000 more for a European or Japanese import that has signaled its quality in a way that Ford cannot readily imitate, namely through a reputation for reliability.

Agency theorists have identified a fascinating array of corporate signaling devices. For example, in the current context, the good firm may commit itself to a larger dividend payout in order to distinguish itself from the bad firm.[10] The bad firm may be able to mimic this signal temporarily through borrowing funds to pay an equally large dividend, but presumably it cannot do this indefinitely (even IBM, which borrowed funds continually throughout the late 1980s and early 1990s in order to sustain its dividend, was forced eventually to reduce its dividend payout; its stock price dropped by more than 50 percent over this period as investors predicted the impending dividend cut). Alternatively, the good firm might finance its operations through the issuance of very short-term debt, thus committing itself to a large cash outlay in the near future (or to financial scrutiny if it attempts to refinance the debt).[11]

In the case of two private firms that are about to go public through initial public offerings (IPOs) of equity, the "good" firm may offer its shares to investors at a greater discount (i.e., put "cash on the table") because it knows that this loss can be recouped in a future equity issue when the superior earnings prospects of the firm are revealed. In this case, the signal takes the form of the underpricing of initial public offerings.[12]

With the signaling solution to adverse-selection-type agency problems, therefore, the challenge is for the 'good' agent to devise a signal that cannot be mimicked by the 'bad' agent. In addition, this signal must not be so costly that it is uneconomic for even the good agent to emit. If the good agent is able to devise and emit such a signal, then it engenders what agency theorists term a 'separating equilibrium' in which the two agents become distinguishable to principals and thus the informational asymmetry is overcome. If such a signal does not exist, then the informational asymmetry endures and a 'pooling equilibrium' ensues.[13]

Even if a separating equilibrium is achieved, however, there are costs involved. Whether the signal takes the form of a larger dividend, short-term debt, or equity issue underpricing, the good agent bears the cost of emitting the signal. In other words, if there had been no initial informational asymmetry or if the bad agent chose openly to reveal its type, then the bad agent would be no worse off and the good agent would be better off through not having to fund the signal. Formally, the equilibrium is said to be 'second-best' because there is a deadweight or 'dissipative' cost levied on the economy in aggregate (a cost to the good agent not recouped by the bad agent or the principal). Jensen and Meckling label this deadweight cost the "residual loss"; it results directly from the contractual enforcement problem between principal and agent. Thus, agency problems, even if they are overcome, are not zero-sum games. We are not dealing merely with a redistribution of wealth from principal to agent, but rather with an absolute wealth loss to the economy in aggregate.

Turning now to moral-hazard-type agency problems, here the contractual situation is ostensibly a simpler one in which there is only one type of agent. Here there may be no informational asymmetry and the agency problem may simply stem from the principal's inability to control the actions of the agent. Or there may be informational asymmetry in which case the agency problem stems from the principal's inability to observe directly some information that affects the actions or the performance of the agent (e.g., it might be hard for the principal to discern whether the agent was really skillful or trustworthy, or was just lucky). The classic agency problem of this type is managerial perquisite consumption.[14] As a firm moves from private to public ownership, there is a separation of ownership and control. The owners bear the cost of managers' perquisite consumption (e.g., business lunches, corporate jets) but the managers make the decisions on how many perks to consume. Barring effective accountability—in other words, barring a resolution to the agency problem—a 'rational' wealth-maximizing management, which no longer bears the full cost of its perks, may be predisposed to consume perks to an excessive degree: specifically, to a degree that compromises the value of the firm as a whole. Potential shareholders and bondholders, cognizant of management's 'rational' predisposition, will lower the price at which they are willing to buy the firm's equity or debt.

Once again, therefore, the cost of agency is invariably borne by the agent. Hence, the 'finance paradox' that assumes agents are unable to resist the Sirens' song of opportunism, even though they must rationally realize that such a predisposition is self-defeating. In short, a predisposition to opportunistic wealth maximization does not maximize wealth for either the individual opportunist or for the economy in aggregate: it is in essence a 'lose-lose' situation.

But has our discussion so far been strictly fair? Has it been more of a polemic than a balanced evaluation of the finance paradigm? Are there not other feasible means of enforcing contracts and thus overcoming agency problems within the finance paradigm: explicit means such as litigation or collateral, and implicit means such as reputation effects? Clearly, from an economic perspective at least, these other enforcement mechanisms warrant attention before the necessity of a move *beyond* the finance paradigm can be justified.

Contractual Enforcement within the Finance Paradigm

Whether the context is union wage negotiations, the trading of securities, or international currency speculation, some form of contractual relation characterizes practically every business dealing. Although these contracts may differ in detail, they all are built upon a fundamental contractual relation. This fundamental relation is illustrated in figure 2.1.

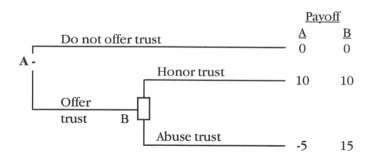

Figure 2.1. Moral Hazard. (From Kreps, D. 1984. "Corporate Culture and Economic Theory." Working Paper, Stanford University.)

Figure 2.1 illustrates a simple game between two players: A and B. Each player represents a stakeholder or group of stakeholders. So, for example, player A might represent a group of shareholders considering an investment in a company whose management is represented by player B. David Kreps summarizes the game's play as follows:

> First A must choose whether or not to trust his opponent. If he (A) elects not to trust B, then both A and B get nothing. If he elects trust, B is made aware of this fact and is given the option either to honor that trust or to abuse it. If A trusts B and she (B) chooses to honor that trust, both get $10. But if A trusts B and she chooses to abuse it, B gets $15 and A loses $5.[15]

Assume that each player's payoff from the game is common knowledge. In other words, there is no informational asymmetry and to the extent that there is an agency problem it would be characterized as one of simple moral hazard. As Kreps explains, the game begins with player A deciding whether or not to trust player B. If he (A) does decide to trust B, then she (B) must decide whether to honor or abuse that trust. Readers familiar with Game Theory will recognize figure 2.1 as a one-sided version of the infamous "Prisoners' Dilemma" game. If we assume that both players are rational *qua* the finance paradigm and thus are primarily motivated to maximize their payoff, then presumably, if called upon to move, B will abuse the trust vested in her by A. Realizing this, A will never offer trust and a contract between these two players will not be entered into. The most *reasonable* outcome for this game, therefore, is for each player to receive a payoff of zero.[16]

Such an outcome is clearly not the most desirable, however, either from the point of view of the two players as individuals or from the point of view of the economy as a whole, in that the maximum total payoff of $20 is not attained (this would be the *first-best* outcome). The unwillingness of player A to trust player B has cost both players $10. But then why should B honor trust when her immediate payoff is maximized by abusing it? And whatever B might actually plan on doing, why should A assume B is going to honor trust when he can see that abusing it yields her the higher payoff?

The three possible outcomes of this game can be generalized as follows. The outcome in which A offers trust and B abuses that trust is one in which implicit contracts are entered into but are not honored. If we envision this game being played more than once, then A will presumably cease to offer trust if it is continually abused; thus, no contracts between stakeholders are entered into and the simple corporate culture represented by this game collapses. Conversely, if B chooses to honor the trust vested in her by A, then stakeholder relations are maintained and corporate culture flourishes, resulting in the maximum total payoff of $20 being attained in each play of the game. In terms of this game, therefore, inducing B to honor trust is the key to sustaining corporate culture.

How can this desirable outcome, based on mutual trust, be reached? It could be reached by invoking any one of three possible contractual enforcement mechanisms:

1. *Explicit Enforcement.* The two players can enter into a legally enforceable contract that forces B to honor trust.

2. *Implicit Enforcement.* Assuming this game is played repeatedly, B may realize that her best interests are served if she honors trust at least some of the time. Thus, given player B has a long-run horizon, enlightened self-interest may induce her to honor trust. This, in essence, is what is meant by a 'reputation effect' as a contractual enforcement mechanism.

3. *Irrational Enforcement.* Player B can choose to act ethically, where acting ethically is defined here as acting with an underlying motivation to honor trust. Note well from our discussion so far that such a choice on the part of player B would be 'irrational' given the finance paradigm's six-axiom-based concept of rationality.

Explicit Enforcement

There are, in essence, two potential caveats to a legally enforceable contract between A and B to 'honor trust,' namely, expense and enforceability. In the case of both these caveats, Oliver Williamson observes that "the assumption, common to both law and economics, [is] that the legal system enforces promises in a knowledgeable, sophisticated and low-cost way. Albeit instructive this convenient assumption is often contradicted by the facts."[17] Indeed, the sheer complexity of reality may preclude explicit contracts. "Presumably one important reason that we do not see explicit, long-run contracts in reality is bounded rationality: individuals simply cannot conceive of all the possible eventualities that may occur."[18] Kreps notes the difference between observability and legal verifiability: even if behavior is observable it may not be legally verifiable. Thus, the absence of informational asymmetry provides no assurance of contractual enforceability.

Even if a contract is legally enforceable, such enforcement may be prohibitively expensive to implement in practice. In figure 2.1, for example, A will invoke legal enforcement only if its cost is less than $10, since this is the payoff that A will receive from a legally enforced contract and he expects to receive nothing in the absence of legal enforcement (he will not offer trust).[19]

Another means by which A might enter into an explicit contract with B is through the use of collateral. Prior to the commencement of each play, for example, B might agree to place collateral with A of at least $5, refundable on condition that B honor trust. But "giving the other party collateral simply switches the reputation problem to the other side of the transaction."[20] Thus, in the case of figure 2.1, the use of collateral would shift the enforcement problem from A to B: B would now have to trust A to return her collateral. If A were known to be more trustworthy than B, then collateral might be a viable enforcement mechanism. If A was a bank, for example, and B a potential borrower, B might willingly place collateral with A.

If neither A nor B regarded each other as particularly trustworthy, a collateral solution might still be feasible if a trustworthy third party (C) exists. If both A and B are willing to trust C, B can place collateral with C who will adjudicate. An example of the use of a third party in this manner can be found in the market for repurchase agreements, where these agreements are collateralized by government securities.

Oliver Williamson suggests a contractual enforcement mechanism along the lines of collateral, namely the use of hostages: "the suggestion that hostages are used to support contemporary exchange is apt to be dismissed as fanciful. I submit, however, that not only are the economic equivalents of hostages widely used to effect credible commitments, but failure to recognize the economic purposes served by hostages has been responsible for repeated policy error."[21] Essentially, Williamson defines an economic hostage as any nondiversifiable asset that has a value dependent upon the contractual agreement. As an example, he cites franchisers' practice of leasing, rather than selling, premises to franchisees. By precluding ownership, the franchiser is able to turn the premises on which the franchisee operates into an economic hostage. By reneging on the franchise agreement, the franchisee not only loses the franchise, but also the premises on which it conducts business.
 In summary, given the shortcomings of legal enforcement, collateral or hostage would seem to present viable alternatives for contractual enforcement, subject to the availability of a trustworthy party that will adjudicate. This prompts the question, how does an individual or institution become trustworthy? An obvious answer would be, by building a reputation for trustworthiness. Thus, as explicit contractual enforcement mechanisms, both collateral and hostage appear to depend upon the efficacy of an *implicit* contractual enforcement mechanism, namely reputation.

Implicit Enforcement

In his 1985 book *Morals by Agreement*, David Gauthier argues that in repeatedly dealing with one another, agents will realize that some form of tacit cooperation is the best strategy for all in the long run (Gauthier's theory assumes that agents believe there is a long run).[22] In his model, therefore, what he calls "morals" emerge naturally through continual interaction among self-interested agents: "Moral restraint . . . is a rational step taken in order to facilitate the emergence of society, an event from which every self-interested individual stands to gain."[23] Thus Gauthier appears to solve the problem of contractual enforcement within the finance paradigm. In a similar vein, on an empirical level, several researchers have found that some form of tacit cooperation emerges in repeated competitive games such as the Prisoners' Dilemma.[24] For example, in laboratory experiments Robert Axelrod finds that a strategy of "tit-for-tat" is very popular, and successful: a player offers to cooperate and continues to cooperate as long as the other player reciprocates, but if the other player reneges then the player who of-

fered cooperation initially copies the reneger and does not offer cooperation in the next round.[25] In essence, a player attempts to build a *reputation*
for cooperating in order to be offered future contracts.

Returning to figure 2.1, if A decides to offer trust to B without recourse
to law, collateral, or hostage, A is entering into an implicit contract with B: A
can be viewed as holding an implicit claim against B. The value of this implicit claim to A will be a function of his probability assessment over B's two
possible moves. If A is certain that, given the opportunity, B will move "honor
trust," A will value the claim at $10. In other words, given A's beliefs, B could
sell this claim for a maximum of $10. Thus, the value of the claim can be
viewed as a function of B's *reputation* for trustworthiness. B's disincentive
to violate her implicit contract with A would be the decline, in future transactions, of the claim value, hence reputation's role as an implicit contractual
enforcement device. Clive Bull defines an implicit contract as follows:

> The whole thrust of the term 'implicit contract' is to suggest that
> although a formal contract may not exist . . . the two sides of the
> trade are nevertheless acting 'as if' one existed, that is, we ex-
> plain their otherwise puzzling behavior by the imposition of an
> extra, unobservable constraint subject to which they maximize.[26]

The viability of Bull's "extra, unobservable constraint" is evidently crucial to the viability of an implicit contract. The above argument clearly implies that a necessary condition for reputation to perform its contractual
function is multiperiods: "in a self-enforcing agreement the only penalty that
can be imposed on the violator is stopping the agreement."[27] But as discussed in chapter 1, the power of reputation to enforce contracts implicitly,
even in a multiperiod setting, cannot be taken for granted. Clearly reputation would appear to provide an economic mechanism for the enforcement
of business contracts *within the finance paradigm.* Indeed, if reputation
will successfully enforce these ubiquitous implicit contracts, then there
seems no need for ethics in business. But how powerful is reputation? In order to enforce contracts in business and thus assuage the misallocative costs
of agency, is reputation enough?

Reputation and Agency Problems

In order to add some intuitive appeal, imagine that figure 2.1 illustrates a
simple game between a customer A (the principal) and a used-car salesman
B (the agent). The customer must decide whether to buy a car from the
salesman, that is, move Offer trust in figure 2.1. If the customer does decide
to buy then the salesman must decide whether to supply the customer with
a quality car (move Honor trust), or with a lemon (move Abuse trust). The
dollar payoffs to each player contingent on his move are given in the payoff
matrix at the end of the game.

This game illustrates George Akerlof's "lemons scenario," in which he explains the large price difference between new and used cars (most new cars lose about half their market value as soon as they are driven off the lot).[28] Akerlof explains this large difference by invoking essentially the game depicted here. New cars are of known quality. The used-car salesman is faced essentially with the moral-hazard-type agency problem of choosing between supplying the high-quality car or the lemon (we assume that the quality of the car is not readily observable). Given that his payoff is maximized by supplying the lemon then presumably, within the finance paradigm at least, he will do so. All used-car buyers, therefore, will expect to receive lemons, hence the large price difference between new and used cars.

Of course, a used-car salesman who is established in a community might wish to build a reputation by not supplying lemons. He will be rewarded for his endeavors by being able to sell his used cars at a premium over less-reputable car salesmen. This price premium will make it worth the salesman's while to maintain his reputation and refrain from selling lemons, unless, of course, he decides to leave the community or enter some other line of work.[29] Under these circumstances, he will 'rationally' cash in his reputation by selling lemons at the higher price.

More generally, figure 2.1 can be viewed as depicting a single repetition of a *supergame*, where a supergame is defined as a series of sequentially played games in which one player endures. In our context, the player that endures is the salesman. Thus, the customers may vary, though we must assume that there is communication among these customers so that the experiences of one can be relayed to others. Assume that there is mutual agreement between the two players that the game depicted in figure 2.1 will be repeated. Now the salesman may choose to supply the high-quality car at least some of the time in order to build a reputation for supplying high-quality cars and thus attract customers to buy in future repetitions. Thus, here we are defining reputation-building behavior as the choice to sacrifice short-run income in the expectation of greater long-run income. Indeed, from a finance viewpoint, we can view an agent's decision of whether or not to build a reputation as essentially one of *capital budgeting*; like choosing whether to invest in a new piece of machinery or build a new factory, or take over another company. Building a reputation entails current expenditure in the expectation of future compensatory gains. Once the agent has commenced building a reputation (e.g., has supplied a high quality car), then the ongoing decision becomes one of abandonment versus continuation. Making figure 2.1 into a supergame, therefore, does not ensure that, in every iteration, the salesman will supply the high-quality car. If the desirable outcome is to have the salesman *always* supply the quality product, then the original contractual enforcement problem still remains.

One might argue that there is nothing 'wrong' with the salesman selling the lemon if this is what consumers expect: consumers are simply buying what they expect and paying the appropriate (low) price for it. There is no deception here, and product warranties could be used as a credible *signal* by those salesmen wishing not to sell lemons. As with the collateral solution mentioned earlier, however, this 'warranty solution' still rests on a premise of trust, since now the customer must trust the salesman to honor the warranty. If trust is not honored then we are once again in the murky waters of litigation. In short, as Akerlof found, in a world of 'rational' wealth-maximizing agents—i.e., in the world of the finance paradigm—it is very hard to see how markets can function, except perhaps in the exchange of 'lemons.'

To give reputation its due, however, it clearly can at least partially work in this simple moral-hazard-type game. Agents' desire to build and maintain their reputations may ameliorate the moral hazard problem. Reputation acts as an implicit contractual enforcement mechanism, inducing the agent to act in compliance with the principal. Thus, as a solution to moral-hazard-type agency problems, reputation can be a viable candidate. But what about a slightly more complex, and more common, contractual situation, namely one of *adverse selection* where informational asymmetry exists?

Figure 2.2 illustrates just such a situation. It depicts a game in which informational asymmetry exists. The consumer knows that there are two *types* of salesman (B and G), the consumer also knows the payoff vectors for each salesman; however the consumer does not know with which salesman she is dealing. Thus, the consumer does not know whether she is at node B or G in figure 2.2. Such information would clearly be of use to the consumer: if she knew she was at node G, and so dealing with salesman G, she could deduce from the payoff matrix that salesman G would always supply the high-quality car. Contrarily, if the consumer knew that she was dealing with salesman B, she would realize that there is a nonzero probability of receiving a lemon.

Figure 2.2 illustrates that, in an adverse-selection-type situation, the fundamental uncertainty stems not from the agent's behavior, but rather from some unobservable characteristic of the agent (type G versus type B in this example). Thus, the contractual problem is more complex than in the case of moral hazard.

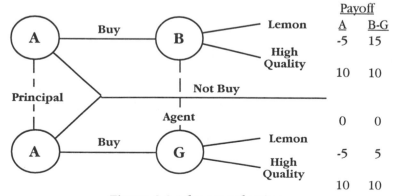

Figure 2.2 Adverse selection.

In the game with salesman G, the equilibrium is clearly Buy, High quality. Thus, if salesman G were the only type of salesman around, there would be no contractual enforcement problem. If this game were only to be played once, then at the end of the game the consumer would know with which type of salesman she had been dealing. Salesman B would supply a lemon (as in figure 2.1) while salesman G would not. In a repeated game, however, the behavior of salesman B becomes less predictable. As in the case of moral hazard, salesman B may choose the reputation-building strategy in at least some of the repetitions. This strategy may confuse the consumer into thinking she is dealing with salesman G who will never supply the lemon. Thus, in the case of adverse selection, a reputation-building strategy will tend to compound the agency problem by enabling one agent to mimic the behavior of another, thus perpetuating the fundamental uncertainty, namely the informational asymmetry. Note, therefore, that the role of reputation in adverse selection may be detrimental in that it tends to confuse the principal. This role for reputation is the opposite to that played in moral-hazard situations where reputation's role as an implicit contractual enforcement mechanism ameliorates the agency problem.

Whether the mists of informational asymmetry will clear in an adverse selection situation depends upon the existence of a signal that will induce a separating equilibrium, as opposed to a pooling equilibrium, as discussed earlier. One might argue that in adverse-selection-type situations, the resolution of the informational asymmetry is not the principal's primary concern. In our example, the principal's primary concern is presumably whether or not she will receive a high-quality car. If either salesman would always supply the high-quality car (i.e., if salesman B always chose to build his reputation), then the customer might not be concerned about her inability to discern the type of salesman with which she was dealing. However, given that there is uncertainty over salesman B's preferred move, a resolution of the informational asymmetry would clearly be of benefit to the customer in making her purchase decision. Thus, the adverse selection problem is still a relevant one in this multiperiod context.

Clearly, therefore, in a multiperiod environment, agents' desire to build and maintain reputations alters the nature of agency problems. When the agency problem stems from unenforceable behavior (i.e., moral hazard), reputation tends to ameliorate the problem by inducing the agent to act in a consistent and compliant manner. In these environments, reputation works as an implicit contractual enforcement mechanism and thus assuages the misallocative costs of agency. When the agency problem stems from informational asymmetry between principal and agent, however, reputation's role is more ambiguous. Reputation tends to perpetuate the agency problem by inducing one agent to mimic the behavior of another. Thus, a principal may be unable to distinguish between two different agents because one has adopted a reputation-building strategy. Thus, for two basic reasons, principals should exercise caution when relying on the agent's reputation to enforce contracts. First, in any agency situation, reputation building may not be the optimal decision for the agent; even if the agent has chosen a reputation-building strategy in the past, this strategy may not necessarily be continued into the future. Second, in a situation characterized by informational asymmetry (i.e., adverse selection), reputation building may deceive principals by enabling one agent to rationally mimic another agent's behavior when in fact these agents possess different characteristics.

In summary, given the infeasibility of explicit enforcement in many contractual situations, the lure of implicit enforcement would appear to be substantial. But "if one appeals to the idea of an implicit contract, one has to say how it is enforced."[30] Within the finance paradigm, the agent's desire to maintain a reputation appears to provide an attractive contractual enforcement mechanism. But how reliable is reputation in this regard? Does it negate any need to consider ethics? Four basic conditions seem necessary for reputation to enforce contracts.

Condition 1: *Compliance with contracts is value enhancing for agents.*
Condition 1 has been met implicitly in the discussion of the previous sections. Clearly, for reputation to be valued, the enforcement of contracts must in some way contribute to the maximization of agents' objective functions.

Condition 2: *Agents are sequentially rational; that is, memory and learning exist.*
Sequential rationality is, in essence, a multiperiod extension of von Neumann and Morgenstern's axioms of choice under uncertainty. A sequentially rational agent has two notable attributes: a multiperiod objective function and a strategy that can be modified in the light of new information. An elegant example of mathematically modeling sequential rationality is supplied by D. Kreps and R. Wilson.[31] They show sequentially rational agents continually updating Bayesian probability estimates of other players' unknown strategies in a study of reputation building in oligopoly markets. In their model, each agent's strategy is dependent upon its beliefs regarding other agents' strategies. These beliefs are continually modified as other agents' behavior is observed. In a contractual environment characterized by sequential rationality, therefore, an agent's strategy is flexible and dependent upon previous experiences, but its fundamental objective is fixed. If we further restrict this fundamental objective to one of pecuniary value maximization, we eliminate the possibility that agents comply with contracts for ethical, moral, or other quasi-rational reasons (i.e., we stay within the finance paradigm). That a full explanation of reputation-building behavior might require extending our traditional concept of rationality is clearly a possibility, and this possibility will be investigated shortly.

Condition 3. *Agents operate in a supergame environment.*
A supergame is a series of contractual situations, that is, subgames like figure 2.1, linked by the participation of a common agent. In the case of reputation building, the common agent who endures throughout the supergame must

be the reputation builder. For example, repetitions of the game depicted in figure 2.1, in which player B endures, would be a suitable supergame. There may be many player As as long as each can observe the previous players' experiences, and thus learn from them. The agent building the reputation (player B in figure 2.1) must also believe that the supergame is either of infinite duration, or that there is some uncertainty over whether or not the supergame is infinite, or that there is some uncertainty over the agent's motivations.[32] These restrictions are necessary to avoid R. Selten's infamous "chain-store paradox": if a supergame is of known finite duration then a simple backward recursion argument reveals that the game collapses into a single-play environment; on the last iteration of the supergame, both players know that the agent will renege, thus the principal will not offer the contract; consequently, the agent will rationally renege on the penultimate iteration, knowing this the principal will not offer the contract on the penultimate repetition; and so on.[33] The game unravels with no reputation effect.

Condition 4. *The behavioral trait upon which contractual enforcement rests (and for which the reputation is built) is observable ex post by the principal, but not costlessly verifiable.*

Condition 4's rationale becomes apparent if extreme scenarios are considered. A firm endeavoring to build a reputation for timely debt-repayment behavior would be unwise to issue twenty-year zero-coupon rate bonds. If it were to do so the firm would clearly not start building its reputation for twenty years since its ability to repay the debt would not be tested until then. Contrarily, if the firm were to issue coupon-paying debt (or short-term zero-coupon debt) its reputation could be built considerably faster. Similar logic has been applied in the context of reputation's ability to distinguish superior mutual-fund performance: "since the amount of time it takes to discern quality of portfolio performance is lengthy in financial markets, reputation is unlikely to have much substantial basis. Inferior performers should survive for a long time, as is consistent with empirical evidence."[34]

At the other extreme, if contracts are costlessly verifiable, then explicit enforcement would be costless and reputation's role as an enforcer of implicit contracts would be trivial. Thus, reputation clearly requires the existence of at least some simple moral-hazard-type market imperfection as is the case, for example, in figure 2.1.

Some Practical Implications

Conditions 3 and 4 above imply that, when valuing an implicit claim, the principal should consider the strategy of the claim seller, that is, the agent. If it appears probable that the agent believes the supergame is near termination (e.g., the agent is soon to retire or shift geographical location), then the principal should exercise caution when purchasing implicit claims valued on the basis of the agent's reputation.

Similarly, if the principal believes that the fundamental tenets of a supergame environment do not apply unambiguously to the claim in question, then caution must again be exercised in valuing that claim. For example, our reputable small-town auto mechanic may have little incentive to maintain his reputation while working on an out-of-state car which he believes is just passing through town (at least this is true within the finance paradigm—we ignore for now the idea that this mechanic may feel some *moral* compunction to service the car well). In this situation, condition 3 is clearly breached; the principal (transient car owner) will be unable to pass on her ex post opinion of the repair work to future principals (i.e., future auto-repair customers).

Condition 4 requires that the behavioral trait for which the agent builds a reputation be observable ex post. Thus, in an environment characterized by informational asymmetry, the principal should be wary of reading too much into the agent's reputational signal. For example, in the Kreps and Wilson (KW) study mentioned earlier a "type B" incumbent-oligopolist (agent) endeavors to deceive potential entrants (principals) into thinking it is "type A" by building a reputation for predatory-pricing practices.[35] Indulging in predatory pricing essentially involves initiating a price war with any firm that attempts to invade the oligopolist's turf. In the KW study, a "type A" oligopolist is one that could maintain these low prices indefinitely and therefore is sure to win in a price war, whereas a "type B" oligopolist does not have the resources to maintain the price war for very long and therefore for type Bs such a strategy can only be successful if the entrant is fooled into believing the type B firm to be a type A. Thus, this is a game of *adverse selection* where the informational asymmetry takes the form of the potential entrants into an oligopoly market being unable to distinguish between different types of incumbent oligopolists, where one type of incumbent has considerably more financial strength than the other.

Whether the incumbent is in fact type A or B is never observable, hence, KW's agency problem is more complex than the one of moral hazard depicted in figure 2.1. As KW note, an entrant that bases its estimation of the incumbent's *type* on the latter's reputation for predatory pricing could be making a costly mistake. The significant distinction here is between an ex post observable trait, namely predatory pricing, and an ex post unobservable one, namely type A versus type B. Note also that the former trait represents a decision by the agent, that is, it is endogenous to the agent's objective function, while the latter trait is beyond the agent's control. Once again, therefore, reputation appears to be more effective in moral-hazard-type situations, as opposed to adverse-selection-type situations where informational asymmetry is present.

From the agent's perspective, a reputation increases the value of implicit claims that it is able to sell. In deciding whether to build or maintain its reputation, the agent must weigh the present value of revenues generated by the reputation-induced implicit claim premiums against both direct costs and opportunity costs of reputation building. An example of a direct cost would be maintaining product quality. The opportunity cost of reputation is the revenue forgone by not adopting a "rip-off" strategy; that is, continuing to sell implicit claims at the reputation-induced premium for as long as possible, while failing to maintain the reputational investment (in, for example, product quality), thus "cashing in" the reputation in a short-term windfall.

As mentioned earlier, therefore, the reputation decision can be viewed as an abandonment-versus-continuation capital-budgeting decision. As with many capital-budgeting decisions, the challenge faced by the reputation builder is to identify and accurately quantify relevant cash flows. An example of how this might be achieved is supplied in John Dobson and Robert Dorsey, "The Finance of Virtue".[36] In our model, the standard cash-flow techniques used in the abandonment-versus-continuation decision of capital budgeting are modified to accommodate the potential reputation costs engendered by an abandonment announcement: this announcement thus represents a negative 'signal' in that it will tarnish the firm's reputation for successfully identifying and completing investment projects. Our model thus provides an explanation for the oft-noted fact that, in reality, firms seem very reluctant to abandon projects, even when they are apparently unprofitable. This 'abandonment delay' may simply be a tangible manifestation of the value that firms place on maintaining their reputations for successfully completing investment projects.[37]

But, from a practical perspective, how powerful a force is reputation in contemporary business environments? Can a manager's desire to build or maintain a reputation be relied upon consistently to enforce business contracts? These questions will be investigated next.

3

Is Reputation Enough?

Good name in man and woman, dear my lord,
Is the immediate jewel of their souls:
Who steals my purse steals trash; 'tis something, nothing;
'Twas mine, 'tis his, and has been slave to thousands;
But he that filches from me my good name
Robs me of that which not enriches him
And makes me poor indeed.

—Shakespeare, *Othello*

Our discussion so far indicates that the general acceptance by financial theorists of the firm as a contractual nexus has opened a Pandora's Box of potential contractual problems between principals and agents in the corporate domain whose various claims cannot be explicitly enforced. These agency problems appear to threaten the efficiency with which the corporation can perform its role as a conduit through which real and financial resources are allocated. But the previous chapter identified a countervailing force that may dissuade stakeholders from breaching implicit contracts; namely, their desire to build and maintain reputations. Given certain economic parameters, reputation may be an effective implicit contractual enforcement mechanism that assuages the misallocative costs of agency while, in addition, providing a valuation mechanism for implicit claims.

In labor markets, for example, B. Holmstrom considers whether implicit-contractual enforcement is possible in wage-mediated auction markets. He suggests that "reputation may have the power to enforce implicit contracts." In a similar context, O.D. Hart hypothesizes that "one thing which may keep a firm to an unwritten wage-employment function is reputation." He goes on to conclude, however, that "while this argument is suggestive, a formal analysis which uses reputation effects to justify implicit contracts has yet to be provided."[1] As suggested in chapter 2, a similar mechanism may be at work in product markets: a producer's desire to maintain the price premium at which its product sells will ensure that the producer maintains product quality; that is, the product will sell at a "quality-assuring price." The future economic rents to be earned from the higher price thus represent "reputational capital" to the producer. The greater the reputation, the greater the incentive to maintain product quality. Thus, an implicit contract for product quality between consumer and producer is enforced by reputation.

In financial markets, Kose John and David Nachman suggest that management's desire to maintain a reputation for superior debt-repayment behavior will induce it to make optimal investment decisions for share- hold- ers.[2] Similarly, research discussed earlier implies that reputation may en- force a contract between the underwriter and purchaser of an initial public offering (IPO), ensuring the latter a normal risk-adjusted rate of return on the IPO investment (more on IPOs later). The idea that individuals will en- deavor to build reputations is further supported in laboratory settings by studies that find subjects choose reputation building over alternative "lemon" and "rip-off" strategies.[3]

Though not exhaustive, the above discussion does give an indication of the degree to which reputation is pervading economic and financial- economic behavioral models. Indeed, the model developed in chapter 2 illustrated the theoretical power of reputation to ameliorate moral-hazard- type agency problems. But is reputation enough *in practice*? In realistic financial environments is the finance paradigm self-enforcing in the sense that the costs of opportunism will be held at bay by a strictly *financial* mechanism, namely reputation? This question is critical because its answer determines whether or not finance needs ethics; more specifically whether financial markets need *trust* as an enforcement mechanism. This chapter, therefore, moves from the theory of reputation acquisition to the practice of reputation acquisition in financial markets. A good place to begin is to define exactly what is meant by a corporate reputation.

Reputation Defined

As a contractual enforcement mechanism in finance, reputation remains largely undefined. Casual empirical observation indicates that economic agents devote significant time and resources to fostering their reputations. Yet even advanced financial-economics texts afford reputation minimal at- tention. This discrepancy is undoubtedly due to the lack of a theory of reputation; which in turn is likely due to reputation's nebulous and ethe- real qualities, and to the traditional theoretical environment of "perfect- and-frictionless" capital markets. In such markets, reputation would have no meaning since it is assumed, clearly unrealistically, that every agent knows everything about every other agent; there are no contractual enforce- ment problems and consequently no need for a contractual enforcement mechanism. To the extent that reputation has value, it is due to the fact that markets are *not* perfect-and-frictionless, and information asymmetries and contractual-enforcement problems do exist.

The omnipresence of reputation in the corporate consciousness is reflected in an annual survey undertaken by *Fortune* magazine. More than eight thousand top executives, outside directors, and financial analysts are polled in an attempt to rank some three hundred of the largest U.S. corporations on the basis of their "reputations." To this end, *Fortune* discerns several "key attributes of reputation," including such diverse attributes as managerial quality, earnings performance, product quality, and environmental responsibility.

One such recent survey resulted in Merck and Co. emerging as "America's most admired corporation." When questioned as to the rewards of reputability, Dr. P. Roy Vagelos, Merck's chairman, replied, "It did great things for the morale of the company and for our recruiting because Merck is not a familiar corporate name."[4] Presumably such morale-related benefits will contribute to an increase in the market capitalization of the company, thus justifying the investment undoubtedly required to attain such widespread recognition. Or perhaps Merck's reputation-building motivation lies outside the mundane rationality of the finance paradigm.

Although *Fortune* does not explicitly define reputation, its use of a questionnaire approach implies that reputation has to do with individuals' *conception* of a corporation, a conception presumably based on observation of the company's past behavior and on the assumption that this behavior will be continued into the future. The *Fortune* study also illustrates the *nebulous* aspect of reputation, in that any firm can have reputations for several attributes.

A reference to reputation building in a specific situation can be found in Harry De Angelo and Linda De Angelo's 1987 study of management buyouts of publicly traded corporations. They offer a reputation-building explanation for Kohlberg, Kravis, Roberts and Co.'s (KKR) behavior during Masco's acquisition of NI Industries. During the acquisition, KKR, a buyout specialist who controlled two-thirds of NI's stock, "agreed to receive $20 per share, while simultaneously negotiating a price of $22 per share for the shares held by the public."[5] The authors conclude: "The long-term confidence of the public, who will undoubtedly be offered the opportunity to buy shares in future K.K.R. stock sales, was apparently more important to K.K.R. than the opportunity to earn a greater return on one particular transaction."[6] This example illustrates the *dissipative* nature of reputation: albeit costly in the short run, KKR's actions are designed to maximize long-run wealth.

A similar example, on a divisional level, is provided by Pan Am Inc. In the late 1980s, Pan Am began to face serious problems in meeting its sizeable debt obligations. Paradoxically, in an attempt to alleviate these liquidity problems and streamline the company, Pan Am sold off its *profitable* divisions while retaining its unprofitable division. It sold the Pan Am building in New York, the Intercontinental Hotel chain, and its Pacific air routes, all of which were profitable enterprises. It retained the unprofitable transatlantic air routes because these have traditionally been Pan Am's business core. Pan

Am's strategy, therefore, was an attempt to minimize reputation costs by continuing the business that, in the eyes of investors and other stakeholders, identified the company.

A similar strategy has been followed by Rolls Royce PLC. It also attempted to minimize reputation damage by retaining an unprofitable flagship division (automobiles) while diverting profits from another division (jet engines). Unlike Pan Am, the strategy appears to have worked for Rolls Royce: Rolls Royce Automobiles is once again becoming a profitable enterprise and the firm's reputation for quality remains intact.

Bradford Cornell and Alan Shapiro help illustrate the *contractual* nature of reputation in their study of implicit claims. As mentioned earlier, they define an implicit claim as "too nebulous and state contingent to reduce to writing at reasonable cost," and note the abundance of such claims in the corporate environment. Cornell and Shapiro elucidate their discussion with an account of IBM's decision to discontinue its PC jr. product line. They point out that "the price at which IBM sold the PC jr. included both the price of the hardware and the prices of the implicit claims for future support, software, product enhancements, and the like." Thus, on selling a PC jr., IBM entered into an implicit contract with the purchaser. If IBM were to simply scrap the PC jr. line outright, it would be seen to be reneging on this implicit contract and would, consequently, lose its reputation for post-sales product support. That IBM valued this reputation is reflected in its decision to provide parts, service, and full support to its PC jr. purchasers for five years after its decision to scrap the PC jr. IBM estimated, therefore, that the current costs of maintaining its reputation would be outweighed by its ability to sell future products at a price premium over its less reputable competitors. An example of a less-reputable competitor was Exxon Office Systems. As Cornell and Shapiro note, "when Exxon's Office Systems division performed poorly, Exxon chose to eliminate the entire division and provided minimal support for customers and other stakeholders of that division." Thus, Exxon did not view a reputation in office products as worth maintaining if it lay outside its future mainline of business.[7]

In balance sheet terms, a firm's reputation at any time can be viewed as both an asset and a liability. On the asset side is the increased value of the implicit claims sold by the firm now and in the future. On the liability side is the present value of honoring these claims in the future. For example, consider a durable-good producer that has built a reputation for superior post-sales service. The present value of the price premiums that the firm receives on sales of its product as a result of the reputation would be an asset, while the present value of the cost of providing superior after-sales service in the future would be the liability. Thus, our discussion so far has identified four key characteristics of a corporate reputation.

1) A firm can have several reputations for different attributes, not to mention the reputations of individuals within the firm that may be distinct from the overall firm reputation.

2) A firm builds a reputation by demonstrating a consistent mode of behavior to its stakeholders (e.g., customers, creditors, shareholders, etc.)

3) The building or maintaining of a reputation can require net expenditures in the short run, presumably in the expectation of net revenues in the long run. Thus, the decision whether to build or maintain a reputation at any time can essentially be viewed as a capital-budgeting decision.

4) A firm's reputation can act as an implicit contractual enforcement mechanism: An agent's long-term desire to maintain its reputation may induce it to act in the interest of the principal in the short term.

These four characteristics, in turn, prompt the following definition of a corporate reputation: A reputation is a behavioral trait. A firm builds a reputation by demonstrating a consistent mode of behavior through a series of contractual situations. Once built, a reputation increases the value of implicit claims sold by the firm to stakeholders. Thus, a firm's desire to earn future profits by maintaining its reputation may act as an implicit contractual enforcement mechanism.

For example, a firm with a reputation for creditworthiness will be able to sell its subordinated debt at a premium compared to less-reputable firms. This premium represents the value of an implicit claim. By paying the premium, creditors buy an implicit claim that the reputable firm will make timely interest and principal payments (assuming that, in the event of default, these creditors would be unable to recoup their losses from the residual assets of the firm, thus making their claim explicit). Mortgage bondholders, on the other hand, need not be as concerned with the firm's reputation for creditworthiness because their claim is explicit: in any outcome they recoup their investment.

Our discussion so far indicates that reputation is a real economic force in financial markets. But how strong a force is it? And is it ubiquitous throughout business? In order to address these questions further, I turn now to a closer look at two specific financial markets. Both markets are characterized by informational asymmetry and should therefore be fertile ground for the existence of reputation effects. The first market includes the contractual relations between firms and the banks from which they borrow funds. In this market, the power of reputation is such that, rather than continually shopping around for the cheapest banking services, firms may limit their relations to the same small number of banks with which they have built a reputation. The firm, in essence, builds a reputation over time for trustworthiness in its dealings with these banks. Albeit costly in the short run, this reputation leads to long-run value maximization.

The second market comprises the financial context that has attracted more attention than any other among agency theorists. It is the market for *initial public offerings* (IPOs). In this case, the reputation of the underwriter may be used by IPO investors as a certification device for determining *ex ante* (i.e., prior to issuance) the quality of the IPO shares. But let us turn first to the case of banking relations.

When "Shopping Around" May Not Pay

In their banking relations, firms face a basic choice. They may continually shop around for the cheapest source of financial services, or they may choose to continually deal with the same cadre of banks. The term 'shopping around' is used here to imply that the firm actively seeks alternative banking services with a view to switching if cheaper services are available. Thus, shopping around implies more than merely monitoring alternative banking services. A firm that is shopping around is undertaking a short-term-oriented strategy of dealing with whichever bank is cheapest at any point in time. A clear illustration of this choice can be found in the initial public offering (IPO) market, to be discussed in more detail shortly. Firms wishing to go public can do so through either a negotiated-bid or competitive-bid process. In a competitive-bid process, the firm essentially shops around for underwriting services. It solicits bids from any interested underwriters then chooses to go with whichever bank bids highest. In a negotiated-bid process, the firm chooses an underwriter "up front" (the lead underwriter) and negotiates an offer price with this bank *only*.

A priori one might expect all firms going public to do so through a competitive-bid process. This method would seem most likely to yield the firm the highest possible offer price since it solicits bids from all banks. Paradoxically, it is not the method chosen by most firms. Most IPOs are handled via the negotiated-bid process. In addition, most firms that go public issue additional shares within two years of the IPO and they invariably stick with the original underwriter for these secondary offerings.[8] Why do firms choose to build relations with a single bank or group of banks, rather than shopping around for the most advantageous banking services? It is conceivable that the same small cadre of banks will consistently offer the least expensive banking services. If this were the case, then a firm that is actively shopping around would behave no differently to one that is endeavoring to build a reputation; both would stick with the same small cadre of banks, albeit for different reasons. The implicit assumption here, therefore, is that the same small cadre of banks will not *always* offer the cheapest array of banking services. Presumably, competition among banks and changing externalities will see to this.

By continually dealing with the same relatively small cadre of banks, a firm can build a *reputation* for trustworthiness. Albeit costly in the short run, building a reputation for trustworthiness may lead a firm to long-term value maximization. Acquiring a reputation will be costly in the short run for two reasons. First, it will necessitate dealing with the same contractual partner—a bank in the current context—continually over time, thus precluding a short-run strategy of shopping around for the least expensive banking services. Second, it will necessitate the firm's acting in a trustworthy manner throughout these continual contractual relations. Opportunistic behavior that maximizes short-run value would tarnish the firm's reputation for trustworthiness.

Returning to our original game tree depicted in figure 2.1, in the current context player A can be viewed as the bank and player B as a firm that is a potential customer of the bank. If the bank offers a favorable credit arrangement to the firm, it can be viewed as offering trust. An implicit contract has been formed between the bank and the firm predicated on the firm's honoring the credit agreement. The firm (player B) must then decide whether to honor the contract (i.e., honor trust) or breach it (i.e., abuse trust). Abusing trust could take several forms. The more obvious forms would be failure to make timely loan repayments or, in extreme cases, outright loan default. Also, continually dealing with new customers results in higher monitoring costs for the bank. Shopping around for banking services may, in and of itself, represent an abuse of trust since many services are offered by a bank on the assumption of continuing service. This assumption is not always implicit. A stipulation that the firm retain some form of contractual relation with the bank for a prespecified period of time may be *explicitly* written into the contract. In this case, shopping around is explicitly prohibited and reputation effects are not relevant.

Honoring trust would simply imply that the firm acts in good faith with the bank, by not, for example, shopping around or exploiting any informational asymmetry that may preclude the bank from accurately monitoring the activities and condition of the firm.

How the firm acts in this contractual situation depends fundamentally on whether the firm believes that the banking relation is going to be repeated: more precisely, it depends on the firm's conception of the nature of the repetitions. Clearly, if the firm believes that the relation is to occur only once (the firm faces imminent liquidation, for example), it will optimally— within the finance paradigm—abuse trust. In this case there is no long run.

A more realistic scenario is one in which the firm does not expect imminent liquidation and therefore believes that the relation will be repeated. How the firm acts depends upon how the firm views player A, namely the bank. If the firm views player A as merely one of a very large pool of banks that do not communicate with one another, then the firm may still abuse trust because in each repetition of the game it can shop around for another bank. Given the payoffs in figure 2.1, the initial investment necessary to start building a reputation is $5, which is the difference between player B's payoff from honoring versus abusing trust. In this scenario, the firm will clearly not view the $5 investment as worthwhile since it can consistently earn $15 by shopping around for a different bank in each repetition of the game.

What if the firm does not believe that it is dealing with a large number of isolated banks? Reputation building becomes a rational strategy if either the firm views player A as one of a *finite* number of banks, or if the firm believes

that the banks communicate with one another regarding the firm's past behavior through, for example, credit history data sources. Note that the bank
loses $5 each time it offers trust and the trust is abused. A rational bank,
therefore, will not offer trust to a firm that is known to have abused trust in
the past. Realizing this, the firm will rationally honor trust in the current play
of the game in order to ensure that trust is offered in future repetitions. An
investment in reputation building of $5 in the current play of the game will
lead directly to a payoff of $10 in the next play when trust is once again of-
fered. Contrarily, an opportunistic strategy of abusing trust in the current
play will lead to a payoff of zero in the next play when trust is not offered. In
just two plays of the game, therefore, a reputation-building strategy leads to
a net cash inflow of $5.

   This analysis is clearly somewhat of an oversimplification. For example,
it may be rational for a bank to continually offer trust even if the trust is honored only some of the time. For example, banks continue to issue credit
cards to students even though many students will default. Also, if both players believe that they know exactly how many times the game is to be played,
and if each player knows that the other knows this, then player A will *never*
rationally offer trust because of the "chain-store-paradox" logic discussed in
chapter 2.[9] Despite these caveats, however, the above analysis does demonstrate that reputation building is a rational strategy for a firm to pursue over
a broad set of reasonable assumptions. More precisely, the following conclusion can be drawn: In any given contractual relation with a bank, the firm's
optimal strategy is to build a reputation for trustworthiness if the firm believes that (1) it will be dealing with *any* bank in future time periods, and (2)
each individual bank has access to information concerning the firm's behavior in past dealings with other banks.

   In many realistic business environments, therefore, the short-run benefits to be gleaned from opportunistically shopping around for banking services may be outweighed by the long-run payoff from building a reputation
for trustworthiness with some small cadre of banks. The fact that we often
observe long-term relations between firms and their respective banks indicates that reputation functions effectively in this economic environment.

Initial Public Offerings

   Private firms raise capital in public equity markets through initial public
offerings (IPOs). The market for IPOs is one replete with agency problems.
There are essentially four players: the firm going public, the bank underwriting the issue, inside investors in the IPO (e.g., managers of the firm going
public, and the underwriter itself), and outside investors. Between these
groups there are several layers of informational asymmetry and many conflicts of interest. The actual earning potential of the firm may only be known
by the firm's managers; the firm's managers must rely on the underwriter to

market the IPO at the best possible price; outside investors must, in turn, rely on the underwriter to exercise due diligence in its evaluation of the firm's prospects. In any given IPO, the ability of one group to exploit its informational advantage over other groups forces these contractual partners into an uncomfortable alliance. There is clearly a need for a contractual enforcement mechanism here, and, in this context, reputation appears to fulfill that role.

As discussed earlier, IPOs generally reach investors through negotiated, firm commitment, offerings in which the firm deals with a single lead underwriter that determines the IPO price and other characteristics of the issue. In recent years, for example, 87 percent of the proceeds from IPOs in the United States have been raised in this manner.[10] In a firm commitment offering the bank purchases the shares from the firm and then attempts to profit by offering the shares to the public at a higher price.

A salient feature of IPO markets is that they are not free; that is, prices are not set merely by supply and demand for the issue. As Randolph Beatty and Jay Ritter note, "once the issuing firm and its managing underwriter set an offering price, any excess demand for the issue creates a situation of quantity rationing, rather than further adjustment of the offering price. The majority of initial public offerings are subject to this quantity rationing."[11] As evidence of this rationing, Beatty and Ritter note that the personal records of a major IPO investor revealed that he was often allocated less than 5 percent of the requested shares. Thus, substantial rationing of IPO issues appears to be the norm rather than the exception.

Several studies have found that, on average, these IPOs are offered to the public at prices significantly below their equilibrium market values. For example, for the approximately five thousand firms that went public during 1960 through 1982 in the United States, the average issue was trading at a price 18.8 percent above its offering price shortly after being placed on the market. In contemporary markets, 'shortly after' generally means within the first day of public trading.

The question of why banks "underprice" IPOs rather than merely equating supply with demand has attracted considerable attention in the finance literature. Four basic reasons have been proposed.

1. Most firms that go public issue additional shares within a year or two. The initial underpricing represents a sweetener that is designed to encourage investors to purchase additional shares in the firm at a later date. The healthier the firm, the more it is able to underprice the initial offering in the expectation of a profitable additional issue. The underpricing therefore represents a type of "signal" of firm quality.

2. There is evidence of a link between the level of IPO underpricing and the bank's perception of its legal liability: "underpricing serves as an efficient form of protection against legal liabilities and the associated dam-

ages to the reputations of the investment bankers and the issuers."[12] During periods when the legal environment is more conducive to successful lawsuits by investors in poorly performing IPOs, the level of IPO underpricing is significantly greater. Banks underprice IPOs, therefore, in an attempt to both minimize the probability of future legal retribution, and to minimize the cost of such retribution should it occur.

3. The underpricing may simply be a compensation to investors for the high degree of uncertainty inherent in IPOs.

4. The most popular explanation for IPO underpricing is Kevin Rock's "winner's curse" argument. Rock assumes that a minority of investors are privy to information that is not available to the majority of IPO investors concerning an IPO's true value. Thus, the IPO portfolio of outside investors tends to contain more shares in poorly performing issues as the insiders "snap up" all the most promising IPOs. This results in the classic "winner's curse" phenomenon in which average uninformed investors are able to earn only a normal risk-adjusted rate of return on their IPO portfolios. Thus, Rock posits that underpricing is necessary in order to yield the average uninformed IPO investor a normal rate of return; an investor's return is commensurate with his or her informational investment and there is no opportunity for consistent above-normal returns in IPO markets.[13]

Although Rock's implication that IPO markets are efficient is intuitively appealing, it prompts the following question. What dissuades banks from exploiting their assumed informational advantage and overpricing IPOs, that is, what mechanism enforces the underpricing equilibrium? Several studies have addressed this question and find evidence of some form of 'reputation effect' as the enforcement mechanism.

Rather than forming a single homogeneous group, underwriters are differentiable by their reputations for a commitment and ability to underwrite issues of a certain risk class. The "big name" underwriters such as Morgan Stanley and Salomon Brothers will agree to act as lead underwriter only for issues of known quality. Highly speculative issues are thus passed on to less-reputable fringe underwriters that "typically lack the experience and the capabilities to conduct thorough due-diligence investigations."[14] The reputable underwriters are rewarded for their diligence and expertise by being able to issue IPOs at relatively higher prices than less-reputable banks. This price premium thus represents reputational capital for the reputable banks and, in turn, dissuades the reputable banks from exploiting their informational advantage and overpricing an issue.

The reputable banks are therefore characterized by their tendency to underwrite less-risky IPOs, and thus to underprice issues relatively less than other banks. Consequently, their clientele tends to encompass a greater proportion of institutional investors who wish to avoid particularly speculative IPOs.[15]

At the other end of the spectrum the fringe underwriters tend to underwrite more risky IPOs, which are consequently underpriced to a relatively greater extent. An IPO investor, therefore, can use the reputation of an IPO underwriter as a signal of the riskiness of the IPO.[16] In IPO markets, therefore, reputation effectively plays the role of reducing uncertainty by being a signal for uncertainty.

So Is Reputation Enough?

It is time to weigh this evidence of the power of reputation in financial markets. Is reputation enough for the successful enforcement of implicit contracts in business? If it is, then we have no economic need to challenge or move beyond the finance paradigm. The ill effects of opportunism will be successfully reined in by agents' desire to build and maintain their reputations. There will be little or no need for ethics, or more precisely an intrinsic commitment to honor trust, as a constraint on behavior.

Despite the promise of reputation in the two environments just discussed, there is much evidence that reputation is not enough. Consider, for example, the frequent scandals that appear in the financial press. These scandals are numerous and invariably involve some breach of trust between contractual partners. For example, E. F. Hutton and Co. was the nation's second largest brokerage house. Through a widespread advertising campaign, Hutton had endeavored to build an image of reliability and respectability. Yet the company pleaded guilty to some two thousand counts of mail and wire fraud. Hutton's executives were "managing the float" to an illegal extent.

Where was the concern among some of Salomon Brothers' senior executives concerning their reputations and the reputation of the firm in the recent Treasury-bond bid-rigging scandal (more on this scandal in part II)? In the case of Salomon, it is also interesting to note how rapidly the firm bounced back after the scandal: although its stock price fell initially, within three years Salomon's stock was trading at record highs. The long-term cost to Salomon resulting from its tarnished reputation, therefore, appears to have been negligible.

One only needs to read the financial press or to flip through a business ethics casebook to find many similar scenarios. In all of these cases implicit contracts were not adequately enforced by the desire of agents to preserve either their own reputations or the reputation of their firm. In short, reputation was clearly *not enough*. In addition, as I show in part II, the power of reputation to enforce contracts has become *weaker* in recent years.

It appears, therefore, that a financial milieu conceived entirely within the finance paradigm is not self-enforcing. Contractual relations between opportunists are not self-enforcing. Even if markets could survive by relying solely on the explicit "stick" of litigation and the implicit "carrot" of reputation, these markets would be extremely inefficient with large-scale resource misallocation.

But can some form of *moral sentiment*, albeit socially desirable, ever be economically 'rational'? In the current context, can morally based motivations—such as a desire to honor trust—be embraced by the finance paradigm?

Several economic arguments have been made for the desirability of trustworthy agents.[17] For example, Eric Noreen recognizes the value of religion or ethical rules as contractual enforcement mechanisms. But these strictures lie beyond finance's "six axioms" and therefore adherence to them is hard to "rationalize." Thus, Noreen concludes that "[b]ehavioral norms (or ethical rules) are clearly a most fragile enforcement mechanism": opportunistic agents have no rational *a priori* reason to abide by them.[18] It may be generally recognized that all agents would benefit from cooperation but, as Noreen observes, any finite cadre of agents who choose to adopt this cooperative strategy, in the midst of a majority of opportunists, are clearly placing themselves in a very precarious position. In other words, to label the equilibria engendered by the finance paradigm as "second-best" implies that there is some feasible "first-best" alternative. But the implied first-best alternative, in which all agents trust one another, surely is logically insupportable since "defection" in such an environment is sooner or later the most profitable strategy (game theorists call this "sooner-or-later" point the *endgame* where defection becomes the dominant strategy). Michael Jensen and William Meckling, in their seminal article on the *Theory of the Firm*, come to a similar conclusion:

> Finding that agency costs are non-zero (i.e., that there are costs associated with the separation of ownership and control in the corporation) and concluding therefrom that the agency relationship is non-optimal, wasteful or inefficient is equivalent in every sense to comparing a world in which iron ore is a scarce commodity (and therefore costly) to a world in which it is freely available at zero resource cost, and concluding that the first world is "non-optimal"—a perfect example of . . . [a] "Nirvana" form of analysis.[19]

But is the notion of a cooperative equilibrium so far fetched that it warrants such dismissive treatment? Robert Frank thinks not. He undertakes just such a "'Nirvana' form of analysis." In his 1988 book *Passions within Reason,* Frank attempts to overcome the dilemma of opportunism while staying essentially within the finance paradigm's rationality construct. Through his "commitment model," Frank argues that acting in one's material self-interest need not be antithetical to acting ethically:

> The commitment model is a tentative first step in the construction of a theory of unopportunistic behavior. It challenges the self-interest model's portrayal of human nature in its own terms by accepting the fundamental premise that material incentives ultimately govern behavior. Its point of departure is the observation that persons *directly* motivated to pursue self-interest are often for that very reason doomed to fail. They fail because they are unable to solve commitment problems.[20]

Frank claims that inherently trustworthy agents will inadvertently betray their predisposition through emotional signals, namely facial expressions and body language. Conversely, the shifty eyes and other uncontrollable emotional signals of opportunists will reveal their underlying motives to the principal. Thus, to paraphrase the title of Frank's book, our uncontrollable "passions" betray our "reason."

Frank's commitment model is an innovative attempt to combine economics and ethics so as to avoid the "Sirens' song" of opportunism. However, the model has two basic flaws. First, emotional signals presumably require face-to-face interaction if they are to enforce contracts. Indeed, in supporting the reliability of emotional signals, Frank refers to one-on-one laboratory sessions of thirty minutes' duration in which interviewers determined the honesty of interviewees. In the contemporary business environment, however, any contractual enforcement mechanism requiring this degree of intimacy has serious limitations. Computerization of stakeholder interactions has dramatically reduced the frequency with which individuals deal with each other on a face-to-face basis.

The second flaw in Frank's model is more fundamental. Frank invokes ethics as something beyond rationality. Agents do not choose to become ethical through some logical thought process. Frank merely argues that an agent who is *a priori* ethical may be no worse off materially than an opportunistic agent. Frank remains within the aforementioned sixth axiom: unlimited material gain defines completely the agent's objective function. Ethics is merely a means to an end, and the end is material. His commitment model thus casts ethics in a role that is both trivial and fragile. It is fragile because the justification of ethics in a material universe rests on the validity of non-mimickable emotional signals. It is trivial, because ethics functions only as a tool for the accumulation of personal wealth.

What in essence is needed in order to counter Jensen and Meckling's 'Nirvana' form of analysis" argument, therefore, is some rationalization of trustworthy behavior as an objective *in and of itself*. Even though trustworthy agents may suffer economically, they may consistently offer trust if such behavior has intrinsic value. Thomas Jones and Dennis Quinn argue that such agents may in fact *not* suffer economically. In an argument similar to that made by Frank, they suggest that "the number of opportunities expands for the person who is intrinsically honest."[21] Thus, an intrinsically honest agent may reap economic rewards sufficient to make this an economically optimal strategy. But to make this argument, both Frank, and Jones and Quinn, have to fall back on either emotional signals or reputation. They fail to address the following critical question. What rational mechanism would induce an agent to be "intrinsically honest" in the face of Prisoners' Dilemma–type scenarios such as that depicted in figure 2.1; that is, in the face of real economic costs? Given the tenuous effectiveness of emotional signals or reputation, economic rationality clearly cannot answer this question: the dominant strategy for an economically rational agent is opportunism. In order to rationalize intrinsic honesty, our focus must shift from the material payoffs accruing to the agent to the agent's fundamental concept of rationality itself. We must, in essence, move beyond economic rationality toward a broadened rationality construct that, albeit a Nirvana to some, is no less real.

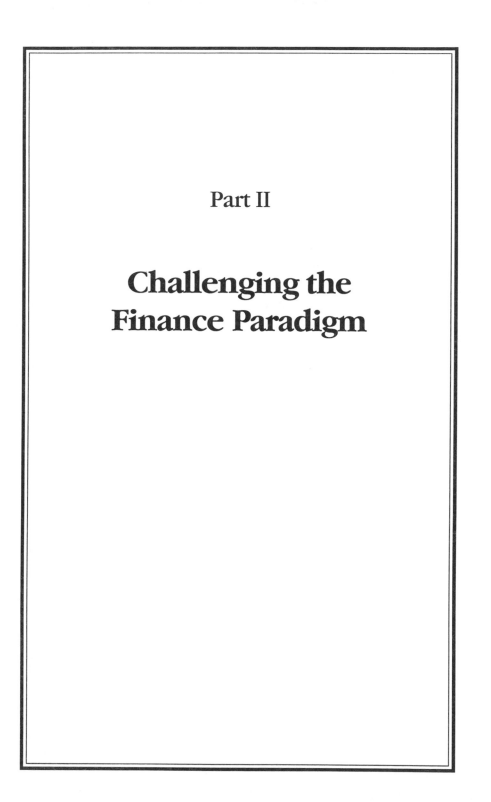

Part II

Challenging the
Finance Paradigm

4

Toward Reconciling Ethics and Finance

The fact is that boards of directors or corporation executives are often faced with situations in which they quite humanly and simply consider that such and such is the decent thing to do and ought to be done. . . . They apply the potential profits or public relations tests later on, a sort of left-handed justification in this curious free-market world where an obvious moral or decent or humane action has to be apologized for on the ground that, conceivably, you may somehow make money by it.

—David S. Ruder

The previous three chapters defined the firm within the finance paradigm as a complex network of contractual relations between various interest groups. Within this network agents pursue their self-interest, which is defined strictly in terms of individualistic, and opportunistic, wealth maximization. In order to function, the financial milieu must be able to reliably enforce this myriad of contractual relations. Many of these contracts are implicit, and therefore some means of implicit contractual enforcement is crucial.

The only means of implicit contractual enforcement that lies strictly within the finance paradigm is reputation. Specifically, given certain conditions, agents will honor implicit contractual arrangements in order to maintain reputations that will enable them to participate in future contractual arrangements. The problem with reputation is that it requires the existence of a certain environment. If this environment does not prevail, then agents will not value their reputations, and opportunism will hold sway, resulting in, at a minimum, inefficiencies (Jensen and Meckling's "residual loss") or, at worst, a total collapse of financial markets.[1] As an implicit contractual enforcement mechanism, therefore, reputation is quite fragile.[2] Indeed, part I of this book concludes that reputation, as the sole means of contractual enforcement, is not enough. Quite simply, financial markets cannot function well, and may not be able to function at all, without another means of contractual enforcement. This one lies beyond the finance paradigm: it is *trust*.

Trust, and ethics generally, lies beyond the finance paradigm because for trust to work it must have intrinsic value to agents: agents must honor trust for trust's sake, not for the sake of some anticipated future material gain. If only the latter applies, then trust becomes as fragile as reputation.

But, as was made clear earlier, a "rational" agent within the finance paradigm is strictly one who pursues material objectives only. In essence, therefore, the challenge we face is that of rationalizing trust, or fairness, or any
moral concept as an objective *in itself*. In the following chapters, I take up
this challenge.

Justifying Ethics in Business

Perhaps, by assuming that the only reasonable motivation for human behavior is personal wealth maximization, the financial paradigm has sanctioned
and promoted such behavior within the financial community. Although
many practitioners and theorists realize the need for ethics in finance, the financial paradigm's conceptual rigidity has led them to view ethics only within this light. This has resulted in a fatal dilution of ethical precepts. Ethics is
forced into the subservient and ambiguous role of merely supporting some
fundamental materialistic objective.

But is there really a natural schism between ethics and business, or will
business tend naturally toward some form of moral self-enforcement? The
argument has indeed been made that financial markets do in fact have some
implicit moral 'control mechanism' that sanctions unethical behavior. An excellent example of this argument is Clifford Smith's analysis of the investment banking firm of Salomon Brothers in the wake of its Treasury-bond
bid-rigging scandal.[3]

Treasury bonds are initially issued through an auction market. Smith
summarizes the process as follows:

> When auctioning Treasury bonds, the U.S. Treasury awards them
> first to the highest bidder at its quoted price, then moves to the
> next highest bidder. This process continues until the issue is ex-
> hausted. If the Treasury receives more than one bid at the price
> that exhausts the issue, it allocates the remaining bonds in pro-
> portion to the size of the bid. Treasury auction rules limit the
> amount of an issue sold to a single bidder to 35% of the issue.[4]

In an endeavor to circumvent this 35 percent rule and to, in effect, cor-
ner the market for a given bond issue, Salomon's bond-trading desk submit-
ted bids under the names of some of its customers without the customers'
prior authorization, thereby making one large bid under the auspices of several smaller bids. When these clandestine activities became known to the
public, Salomon found itself embroiled in a classic Wall Street scandal.

Smith tallies the economic costs incurred by Salomon as a result of the
Treasury-bond bidding scandal. Smith attributes these costs to Salomon's
tarnished *reputation for trustworthiness* within the financial community.
He notes that a reputation for trustworthiness in investment banking has
economic value. This value stems from the reduced uncertainty involved in

dealing with an agent who has demonstrated a consistent mode of behavior in the past. Salomon's unscrupulous T-bond bidding activities represented a breach of trust between it and its stakeholders. This breach of trust increased the market's perception of the risk involved in doing business with Salomon. This, in turn, lowered the market's valuation of Salomon's reputation, as reflected in a lowered stock price and reduced underwriting revenues. Thus, the recent history of Salomon can be summarized in three stages:

1. Over the years, by demonstrating a consistent mode of dependable behavior, Salomon had built a reputation for trustworthiness and expertise in its investment banking activities. This reputation had real economic value as reflected in a higher stock price and underwriting revenues.

2. Some employees of Salomon chose to free ride on this reputation. They in essence exploited lax enforcement of rules governing Treasury-bond auctions.

3. The subsequent revelation of these individuals' activities caused outsiders to revalue Salomon's reputation for trustworthiness. This revaluation was reflected in Salomon's lowered stock price and underwriting revenues.

Note that the scenario described here is strictly economic. But in the title of his article, in addition to the word 'economics,' Smith uses the word 'ethics.' He goes on to imply that financial markets *punished* Salomon for its *unethical* behavior, and that this punishment took the form of the economic costs incurred by Salomon as a result of the scandal. Smith implies, therefore, that financial markets are not merely an economic mechanism, but also a moral one. But is this the most plausible explanation for the market's reaction? Is it not far more plausible to explain all these events in strictly economic terms as above, without recourse to moral philosophy? In moral philosophy the concept of reputation is far more complex than merely that of a dollar value placed on behavioral consistency. Clearly financial markets and the individuals that comprise them *value* reputation in an economic sense, hence Salomon's postscandal stock-price decline. But Smith fails to realize that this says nothing about whether or not these individuals value reputation in a *moral* sense. In order to address this question, we must look beyond the actions of individuals. We must, instead, focus on the underlying motivation for the observed action. In the wake of the scandal, when individual market participants sold Salomon's stock or chose not to avail themselves of Salomon's investment banking services, was their *motivation* economic? If the answer to this question is yes, then these actions have nothing to do with ethics. We may observe financial markets valuing a reputation for trustworthiness, just as they value dividend consistency and timely debt repayment, but what they are valuing is the reduced uncertainty engendered by the observed action. Indeed, even if they did want to value ethics, investors would be very naive to do this on the basis of an agent's observed action. Clearly, as was demonstrated in part I of this book, an agent who acts in a trustworthy manner could be doing so for economic, not ethical, reasons.

Enter Warren Buffett

Interestingly, this ambiguity concerning the ethical-versus-economic concept of reputation was highlighted in the wake of the scandal by Warren Buffett in a statement made shortly after his appointment as the interim chairman of Salomon Brothers. While testifying before the House Telecommunications and Finance Subcommittee, he gave the following warning: to paraphrase, "If I hear of an employee losing the company money I'll be understanding. However, if I hear of any employee losing Salomon one shred of reputation I'll be ruthless!"[5]

This powerful and concise message garnered kudos from the financial community. The popularity of Buffett's declaration presumably stems from a belief, both on and off Wall Street, that abuse of financial regulations—either in letter or in spirit—has become far too prevalent in recent years. By elevating reputation above profits, therefore, Buffett is seen as resurrecting the heretofore downtrodden banner of honesty and integrity among financial practitioners. But how, exactly, is Buffett defining reputation here? Is this economic reputation *qua* the finance paradigm, or some deeper reputation concept?

The various motivations for acquiring a reputation provide a good example of the financial paradigm's conceptual rigidity. Buffett's statement can be used to demonstrate why this paradigm affords no place for ethics. Consider the statement's meaning within the finance paradigm. The concept of "reputation" was clearly defined in this context in chapter 3.

> A reputation is a behavioral trait. A firm builds a reputation by demonstrating a consistent mode of behavior through a series of contractual situations. Once built, a reputation increases the value of implicit claims sold by the firm to stakeholders. Thus, a firm's desire to earn future profits by maintaining its reputation may act as an implicit contractual enforcement mechanism.[6]

Thus, firms build and maintain reputations in order to garner future profits. Reputation is defined in purely materialistic terms. Finance's underlying precept remains intact, namely that the objective of all activity within the firm should be directed at maximizing firm value. Reputation building is solely another means to this end.

Applying this precise definition of reputation to Buffett's statement renders its logic circular: tarnishing the firm's reputation or losing the firm money become synonymous. One way to possibly salvage some meaning from the statement is to assume that tarnishing Salomon's reputation would lose the firm a very large amount of money, perhaps through the loss of significant future profits and a dramatic stock price decline. Given this interpretation, Buffett is merely stating that if employees lose a modest amount of money, he will be understanding, whereas if they lose a large amount of money, by tarnishing the firm's reputation, he will be ruthless.

This interpretation, however, is clearly a distortion of the statement's original intent. It is certainly not how the statement was interpreted by the financial community. The distortion stems from finance's narrow definition of reputation. But the underlying behavioral assumptions of finance force it to define reputation in this way. As was established in part I, finance is premised on the assumption that the underlying objective of all economic agents is the accumulation of personal wealth. Thus, although agents may act in an ethical manner (they may be trustworthy, for example), they may not be motivated to act in a trustworthy manner. The only reason for trustworthiness is that it may increase personal wealth. The motivation is always personal material gain. One possible reason, therefore, for an apparent lack of ethical conduct among financial practitioners is engendered by financial theorists. The finance paradigm's assumption that motivations other than personal wealth maximization are irrational may send a dangerous message to the financial community.

Clearly Buffett was attempting to send a different message. He was looking beyond the narrow economic definition of reputation. His intent was to invoke some moral standard that goes above and beyond the profit motive. In order to clarify this intent, his statement could be usefully rephrased as follows: "If I hear of an employee tarnishing Salomon's reputation through ineptitude or bad luck I'll be understanding. However, if I hear of any employee losing Salomon one shred of its reputation through unethical behavior I'll be ruthless!" For example, Buffett would be only moderately upset with an employee who, through lack of experience and expertise, misprices an initial public offering. Salomon has a reputation for accurately pricing IPOs, and this agent's error will undoubtedly tarnish Salomon's reputation in this regard. But the problem here stems from the agent's ability, not her motivation. The agent is inept but, assuming that she was attempting to price the issue accurately, she is not unethical.

Contrarily, Buffett would be *very* upset with an employee who knowingly overpriced an IPO in order to enrich Salomon at the expense of outside (less well-informed) investors. The problem with this employee is clearly not that he is inept. Nor does the problem lie in the employee's allegiance to the company (i.e., an agency problem): if the employee believed that such action would significantly increase underwriting revenues and that any reputation costs—should the activity be discovered—were likely to be outweighed by these increased revenues, then his actions and motivation are consistent with shareholder wealth maximization. The problem with this individual is purely and simply that he is unethical. The fact that he is willing to deceive in pursuit of profit betrays a predisposition to circumvent generally accepted ethical standards. More fundamentally, this employee may be characterized as one whose primary motivation is material gain rather than some 'higher' form of excellence. But what is meant here by excellence? Surely a certain amount of deception is just an inevitable and accepted facet of doing business? Anyway, is this morally inclusive "excellence" a reasonable objective to have in a business environment?

Before addressing these questions by defining excellence, some clarification of the argument so far may be useful. One might reasonably ask, from a practical standpoint, why does the agent's motivation matter? The above analysis may be of interest to moral philosophers, but surely—from a practical perspective—all that really matters is whether or not the employee acts in a trustworthy manner. As long as the employee upholds the firm's reputation for trustworthiness, then this question of whether her motivation is primarily economic or moral is purely *academic* (i.e., irrelevant).

I would counter this argument as follows. From a practical perspective, the agent's underlying motivation matters because an agent who is not motivated to act ethically will sooner or later act unethically. An agent whose primary motivation is material gain will only act in a trustworthy manner for as long as she believes that such action is in her material best interests. She will readily sacrifice her reputation and the firm's reputation when she believes that such action is economically optimal. Game theorists label this point the "endgame," at which time the agent adopts a "rip-off strategy" (i.e., cashing in one's reputation for an immediate payoff). Thus, a reputation for trustworthiness built for economic reasons can be a very fragile edifice.

But, returning to Buffett's statement, our analysis presents an interesting paradox. His statement essentially places ethics above profits. He does not mind about employees losing the firm some money so much as he minds if they are unethical. But even the most casual reflection indicates that there are situations in which unethical behavior is economically optimal (in game theory, for example, rip-off strategies and the like are often the optimal strategies in competitive games). Buffett's declaration, therefore, is not necessarily in the interests of shareholder wealth maximization. As agent to shareholders, Buffett is presuming that shareholders *en masse* also wish to place ethics above profits. A noble presumption but clearly contrary to the assumptions of financial-economic theory. This brings our discussion full circle by addressing the original question of whether Salomon's stock-price decline in the wake of the T-bond bidding scandal was the result of moral outrage or economic adjustment. What was the primary motivation of shareholders in selling Salomon's stock?

Most market practitioners would undoubtedly agree that the primary motivation behind this or any stock-price adjustment is economic rather than ethical. But this fact does not make market participants unethical. Financial markets are economic mechanisms. It would be highly disruptive and ineffectually arbitrary for shareholders *en masse* to act as some moral police force. Ethics is too complex to identify and too personal to be punished and rewarded in a marketplace, particularly in light of the fact that the majority of today's shareholders—certainly the majority of Salomon's shareholders—are themselves institutions with economic obligations to their respective stakeholders. Enticing agents to act ethically through economic rewards and punishments will only encourage superficially ethical acts, not ethical motivations. Ethics, like charity, begins at home. Specifically, it begins with a process of educating individuals about ethics and the moral ideal. But what form exactly should this education take? How, for example, can the logical and sophisticated minds of senior executives in an investment bank—handling billions of dollars on a daily basis—be convinced of the absolute superiority and desirability of ethical motivations over and above all others?

The 'Confidence School': A False Justification for Ethics

Many listeners understood Buffett's intent in using the concept of reputation. Reputation was not meant to be defined in a manner consistent with finance theory, but rather in broader terms. Reputability was envisaged as possessing some intrinsic quality, beyond mundane materialism. But in a world where material gain is the measure of all things, what role can reputation possibly play except that of a vehicle for material gain? The Confidence School represents an attempt to answer this question within the confines of finance. It attempts to justify and promote ethics as a necessary constraint on the ultimate objective of wealth maximization. But, albeit popular in current discourse, it is a corruption of the ethical ideal.

As the name implies, the Confidence School argues that 'scandals' within the financial community—like that recently perpetrated by some employees of Salomon Inc.—erode confidence in financial markets. Over time, a loss of confidence could result in fewer market participants, which would lower the efficiency of financial markets as a vehicle for allocating risk and generating wealth.[7] Thus, ethical behavior is desirable because it maintains confidence.

This 'confidence' justification for ethics, therefore, views ethical behavior as a type of lubricant in the financial machine: actions are unethical if they inhibit economic efficiency. A simple dialectic can illustrate this argument's logical ambiguity. Assume that the questioner is an employee of Salomon Inc. and the respondent is a business ethicist of the Confidence School:

Q. As an employee of Salomon Inc. my job is to maximize the value of the company. Given that I believe that I can make more money for the company in a given situation by acting in a manner that is generally regarded as unethical (being dishonest, for example), why should I act ethically?

Specifically, I am cognizant of the fact that the firm's reputation has economic value, and that unethical behavior may tarnish this reputation. However, I believe that the economic benefits of my behavior will outweigh the possible economic costs to the firm. Thus, my unethical action is entirely consistent with financial theory.

A.   It is entirely possible that your unethical actions may increase firm value, even net of reputation costs. However, the likely revelation of your unethical conduct, at some future time, will lead to a loss of confidence in financial markets.

Q.   Given my fiduciary responsibility to Salomon Inc.'s shareholders, why should I put the objective of maintaining financial-market confidence above that of maximizing firm value?

A.   Salomon Inc. is part of the financial marketplace; a very significant part. If you damage financial markets you will therefore be damaging Salomon Inc.'s future earning potential.

Q.   But you already conceded that my actions may increase firm value. You are merely implying that I must add another variable to my decision; namely, the possibility that my unethical action will lower firm value through some loss of confidence in the financial system as a whole. What if I believe that my action, albeit dishonest, will maximize firm value, net of reputation costs to Salomon and 'loss-of-confidence' costs to the system as a whole?

A.   Then, by my definition of ethics, your action is ethical.

Q.   So dishonesty or deception, if it does not lead to a significant loss of confidence in the financial system, is ethical?

A.   Correct.

This simple example illustrates the tenuous nature of ethics in the Confidence School. If ethics is merely a constraint in the wealth-maximization rubric, then an individual may easily rationalize unethical behavior given some low probability estimate of information disclosure or public concern. As Sherwin Klein observes, this Confidence-School justification for ethics has led to a moral schizophrenia in the financial community: "Corporate people, then, function according to a double standard—amorally as an official of an organization and morally as a private person."[8] Given this logic, therefore, in governing business behavior 'ethics'—together with legal and economic factors—becomes just one of many constraints.

Toward a True Justification of Ethics: Traditional Approaches

Any failure to find an adequate justification for ethics has certainly not been through lack of trying. If the growth industry of business-ethics consulting is any guide, the idea that corporate behavior should be ethically motivated, as well as financially motivated, is becoming increasingly popular and increasingly voiced. For example, the Harvard Business School recently received a thirty million dollar grant to fund a new program in ethics and leadership, and many other business schools are implementing similar programs.

This increasing popularity is probably due in part to the recent scandals on Wall Street and in the trading pits of Chicago, and also due to a general conception that over the past few decades individuals have become increasingly motivated to maximize personal wealth without regard to religious or other moral strictures. Recent financial scandals include the Bank of Credit and Commerce International's (BCCI) money laundering and financing of organized crime; the excessive lending practices of U.S. savings and loans, fueled by unrestricted federal deposit insurance; insider trading scandals involving prominent individuals (Ivan Boesky, Dennis Levine, and Michael Milken) and institutions (Drexel Burnham Lambert); and Salomon Inc.'s manipulation of the Treasury-note auction market. There are many others. In the context of securities trading, for example, the Securities and Exchange Commission (SEC) estimates that it successfully identifies only a small fraction of all insider trading activity.

In addition, recent financial scandals are by no means limited to the United States. Global derivatives markets have been shaken by the ability of individual 'rogue' traders to conceal huge financial losses. In Singapore, for example, Nicholas Leeson managed to conceal losses from his superiors which, when revealed, were large enough to bankrupt the firm for which he traded, namely Barings Bank, one of the largest and oldest investment banks in Europe.

Similarly in Japan, which in the 1980s temporarily overtook the United States as the largest financial market in the world in terms of the total value of securities traded, has had its fair share of scandals. Sumitomo Bank, one of Japan's largest, has recently been connected with financing organized crime and nepotism among its senior executives. Industrial Bank of Japan (IBJ), Fuji Bank, and Tokai Bank all appear to have been involved in excessive real estate speculation and the related forgery of deposit verification documents. In 1993, a major scandal rocked the Japanese securities industry involving the paying of compensation to large investors who had lost money in an equity market downturn. These compensation payments were made by brokerage houses in order to retain large customers. For example, the big-four brokerages, Daiwa, Nikko, Nomura and Yamaichi, paid 128.3 billion yen in compensation to large clients in 231 incidents. "Even after the Ministry of Finance specifically directed the firms not to compensate their clients, from April 1990 to March 1991, another 43.5 billion yen was paid out in 78 separate incidents."[9] Another recent scandal in Japan's securities markets concerns Nomura and Nikko, the two largest brokerage houses. Both have been identified as having links to organized crime. Specifically, says Norimichi Okai, "in October 1989 Nomura . . . 'loaned' Mr. Susumu Ishii, the don of Tokyo's most powerful criminal organization—the Inagawa-Kai—16 billion yen, and Nikko 'loaned' him 20 billion yen."[10]

The recent apparent resurgence of interest in business ethics both in the United States and abroad, precipitated no doubt in part by this litany of scandals, has two interesting implications. First, it implies that some form of ethical code is important in business dealings. Second, it implies a general perception that whatever ethical code may have existed in the past is no longer being adhered to. Is our business environment indeed becoming less ethical?

Financial scandals in the United States are often blamed on cultural or regulatory factors. In the case of the former, a tradition in the United States of individualism and wealth as the ultimate measure of success is often cited as the cause of financial scandals. Also, United States insider-trading laws—the most stringent in the world—are blamed for driving insider-trading activity underground unnecessarily. Japan, for example, has minimal insider-trading regulations.

If financial scandals were limited to the United States, then these cultural and regulatory arguments might be vindicated. But as the Japanese and European examples clearly illustrate, the 'scandalization' of financial markets has not been limited to the United States. Other markets have experienced similar phenomena. It appears, therefore, that one needs to look beneath the surface of Western individualism and materialism when attempting to account for these egregious activities. Consider the following three factors:

1. Dehumanization of Financial Markets. As discussed earlier, the existence of imperfect markets is a necessary condition for reputations to have value. But if substantial asymmetries of information exist between stakeholder groups, the relative value of building a reputation will be diminished because opportunistic behavior will not be exposed. As a necessary condition for reputation effects, the efficient flow of information is even more critical in contemporary corporate culture where individual stakeholders rarely, if ever, meet repeatedly on a face-to-face basis. It is essential, therefore, that the information gleaned from the experiences of one stakeholder be made generally available. Alas, informational asymmetries are so pervasive in our financial markets that the necessary 'track record' of individuals and institutions is often not generally available.

Specifically, computerization of stakeholder interactions has dramatically reduced the frequency with which individual stakeholders deal with each other on a face-to-face basis. In addition, the increasing size of our corporate culture means that any individual is less likely to deal more than once with any other individual. Returning to figure 2.1 in chapter 2, player B is more likely to act ethically (i.e., honor trust) in her dealings with player A if she believes that the likelihood of future dealings with A is high. Thus, the impersonalization of corporate culture has increased the incentives for individual stakeholders to breach any generally accepted moral code. This dehumanizing trend supplies the central weakness in Frank's passions-within-reason argument, discussed in chapter 3, and it is also the source of reputation's impotence as a sufficient contractual enforcement mechanism in contemporary markets.

2. A Short-Term Consciousness. Building a reputation generally entails immediate sacrifice in the expectation of future compensatory gains. It is clearly inconsistent, therefore, with behavior designed solely to attain short-term goals. U.S. corporate culture, however, appears to be increasingly motivated toward such myopia.

For example, the continual threat of takeover is forcing corporate managements to adopt short-term defensive strategies such as leveraged buyouts (LBOs). These strategies encumber firms with burdensome debt loads that require immediate and continual cash flows to service. Similarly, the rapid growth of financial futures and options has given contemporary securities markets what some observers call a 'casino' atmosphere, where short-term program-trading strategies, such as portfolio insurance and index arbitrage, may create volatility and uncertainty in markets originally designed as a means by which corporations could raise capital for the pursuit of long-term goals.

In addition, the increasing secularization of society in general tends to shorten goal horizons. For example, the Protestant work ethic has traditionally espoused hard work combined with an ascetic lifestyle in order to attain a long-term goal of building wealth for future generations. Indeed, it was this work 'ethic' that fueled the Industrial Revolution in eighteenth-century Europe: steam engines, built to power factory machinery in the late eighteenth century, still run smoothly today. These machines were built by individuals with both a long-term horizon and a commitment to quality in mind. Their construction contrasts sharply with contemporary designed-obsolescence manufacturing techniques.

Another implication of this growing substitution of a 'corporate' culture for one based on religious belief is the disappearance of any meaningful *faith-based* moral stricture. This point is made eloquently by Donald T. Campbell.

> Rewarding and punishing reincarnations and afterlives promise individuals a net hedonic gain optimized over a longer period than their own immediate lives. . . . Belief in an afterlife was fundamental in protecting the production of protective goods

> against the erosion of individually optimizing free riding. . . . [If]
> in the past market mechanisms . . . have worked well, it is be-
> cause of the helpful residue of such awed indoctrination and
> moral restraint.[11]

Thus, the general adherence to some arbitrary moral stricture, whether based on religious tradition or otherwise, appears to be no longer a valid assumption in contemporary stakeholder relations. This point is echoed in a 1988 book by Amitai Etzioni, who attempts to imbue rationalistic contemporary economic theory with a "moral dimension." He argues that the more stakeholders operate purely on the basis of economic self-interest, "the more the ability to sustain a market economy is undermined."

3. Diminished Sense of Individual Responsibility. The regulatory environment in which business operates is being increasingly relied upon to explicitly enforce stakeholder contracts, thus diminishing the perceived importance of a moral code's role in this regard. Stakeholders are relying on government agencies, such as the Securities and Exchange Commission (SEC) and the Environmental Protection Agency (EPA), to regulate generally accepted ethical norms. As a result, stakeholders feel a diminished responsibility to make ethical choices for themselves: "If it's legal, then it's ethical" is a temptingly simple ethos by which agents may judge their behavior. Undoubtedly, government regulations are designed to enforce generally accepted ethical procedures. Such a simple ethos, however, assumes that government agencies are able to adequately regulate all areas of business behavior and foresee all possible moral contingencies. Given the multiplicity and ephemeral nature of many implicit contracts in business, this is clearly an unreasonable assumption, particularly when one considers the high degree of informational asymmetry that is generally present.

This generally increasing reliance on explicit contractual enforcement via government fiat has been paralleled by an increasing reliance on the legal system to enforce contracts. For example, Earl Fry characterizes the United States as suffering from a "Litigious Affliction." He argues that "too many people and corporations are resolving their differences in the adversarial-structured legal system."[12] Stakeholders are endeavoring to substitute the explicit legal system for an implicit business ethic.

As discussed in chapter 2, however, there are two fundamental caveats to a corporate culture founded primarily on the rule of law, namely cost and enforceability. A litigious business environment is expensive in a direct sense with legal fees and lost work time; however, it is also expensive in an indirect way. As Fry observes, "U.S. schools are currently graduating 10 lawyers for each engineer, whereas Japanese schools are graduating 10 engineers for each lawyer."[13] Thus, an ever-expanding legal system exerts both a financial and a human drain on an economy's resources.

In addition to cost, there is the problem of enforceability. For example, recent evidence has demonstrated that the mere existence of laws prohibiting insider trading will not prevent insiders from trading illegally. With no moral code, illegal trading activities are undertaken whenever the probability of getting caught seems remote. If the threat of legal action is the sole restraint on opportunistic behavior, then this threat must be perceived as imminent. Monitoring costs therefore become significant, not to mention the distasteful specter of a Big-Brother-type infringement into what many regard as a constitutional right to privacy. Consequently, for reasons of both expense and enforceability, a business environment characterized by an abundance of civil lawsuits would seem to be a poor substitute for one based on voluntary adherence to a moral code.

One might question our discussion so far by noting that ethical 'scandals' are by no means unique to contemporary corporate culture. Economic history provides many examples of unethical behavior between stakeholders. The South-Sea Bubble, an incident in the early eighteenth century in which unscrupulous brokers sold shares in a fictitious company to unsuspecting investors, provides an early example of contractual failure between stakeholders in a diversely held company. More recently, one of the primary factors contributing to the stock market crash of 1929 was the unethically excessive use of margin lending by brokerage houses. Unethical behavior, therefore, is clearly not unique to present-day financial markets.

There is, however, a discernible difference between past and present views on ethical violations in business. Even though many instances of unethical behavior have occurred throughout business history, there has also been a general consensus on the need for some form of moral code governing business dealings. But, in contemporary markets, there appears to be no general consensus on this point. In addition, even among advocates of some form of moral code, there is widespread disagreement as to what form this code should take (Milton Friedman's "the social responsibility of business is to increase its profits" versus Norman Bowie's "the primary objective . . . is to provide meaningful work for employees").[14]

The current debate surrounding business ethics, therefore, is not simply whether stakeholders should act ethically or be 'value' neutral, but rather whether a universal moral code exists by which stakeholders can judge their actions. If morality is strictly relative, then who is to say what is ethical versus unethical? If there is no generally accepted moral code governing stakeholder behavior, then an 'ethic' of trust or honesty—as an implicit contractual enforcement mechanism—becomes impotent. Returning to our game tree of figure 2.1, player B cannot be expected to sacrifice immediate personal gain in order to honor trust if there exists no general consensus that honoring trust is the right thing to do. Of course, even if there is such a general consensus, the $5 premium that player B can earn by abusing trust may prove too great a temptation. Indeed, one could argue that contemporary corporate culture still has some residual moral code. The difference now is that fewer stakeholders abide by it in preference to immediate personal gain. The objective of material gain has become the overriding objective, and the 'best solution' becomes measurable solely in material terms.

Part I of this book concluded that, if agents acted ethically in the sense that contracts can be reliably enforced with trust, first-best outcomes could be obtained in financial contracting (i.e., there would be no deadweight residual loss). As Noreen observes in the case of moral hazard, "The best solution, which is costless, is for the manager to truthfully report his effort and his consumption of perquisites."[15] But is this always the best solution? And, more fundamentally, what exactly is meant by the "best solution"?

In attempting to answer this question, business-ethics theory has tended to focus on what are commonly called the Enlightenment ethical theories.[16] These theories have been labeled by Sherwin Klein as "action-based" because they focus on the actions of agents in contractual situations. These theories can be categorized into two types: deontological and teleological. The latter encompasses ethical theories based on consequences, for example, utilitarianism; while the former encompasses ethical theories based on universally applicable rules of conduct or 'duties,' for example, Kantianism.[17]

Our game tree depicted in figure 2.1 affords a simple illustration of the implications of these theories in the context of financial contracting. To summarize from the discussion of the game in chapter 2, the outcome in which A offers trust and B abuses that trust is one in which implicit contracts are entered into but are not honored. If we envision this game being played more than once, then A will presumably cease to offer trust if it is continually abused; thus, no contracts between stakeholders are entered into and the simple corporate culture represented by this game collapses. Conversely, if B chooses to honor the trust vested in her by A, then stakeholder relations are maintained and corporate culture flourishes, resulting in the maximum total payoff of $20 being attained. How can this desirable outcome be reached? If the game is to be repeated an infinite number of times, or if there exists uncertainty among the players concerning the number of iterations, then the reputation solution discussed above might work some of the time. Or some form of explicit legal enforcement may be feasible, albeit costly.

So far the implicit assumption has been made—as always in finance—that the agent (player B) is a wealth maximizer (what ethicists term a 'psychological egoist'). But what if the agent adheres to some other 'ethic'? Will this lead to a more desirable outcome?

Consider first a teleological agent. What if A believes B to be a utilitarian? Now B's objective is to maximize *overall* payoff. So B will honor trust. But what if the $15 payoff to B for abusing trust were instead $26? Now the utilitarian B will presumably abuse trust since this results in the maximum overall payoff of $21. If the *ultimate objective*, therefore, is to invoke trustworthy agents, then utilitarianism would seem to be an unreliable guide.

Consider a deontological agent. What if A believes B to be a Kantian? In essence, a Kantian endeavors to apply the "Categorical Imperative" by taking only those actions that the agent would wish to become universally applicable, irrespective of consequences. Presumably, honoring trust is such an action, and therefore a Kantian B will always move "honor trust" regardless of the expected payoff. But if the ultimate objective is to maximize the overall value of the economy—as appears to be the implicit assumption within the finance paradigm—then a Kantian agent may be something of an economic liability: even if her payoff from abusing trust is $1,000,000 the Kantian B will still honor trust, netting $10.

A less-extreme example would be a rule-utilitarian agent. A rule-utilitarian combines teleological and deontological theories by endeavoring to maximize overall payoff while tempering this endeavor with some cognizance of deontological rules of conduct. A rule utilitarian, therefore, will be reluctant to abuse trust. As the payoff from abusing trust becomes increasingly large, however, the rule utilitarian may feel that the substantial payoff resulting from the abuse of trust justifies such abuse. The behavioral choice distills to an unresolvable impasse, namely that of pricing trust.

Our game tree depicts the simplest of contractual situations, and our discussion of Kantianism and utilitarianism has likewise been very simplistic. The ambiguities multiply, however, when more complex contracts are invoked. Consider a signaling game in which, by concealing the truth, the inferior agent can mimic its superior. Would not this pooling equilibrium be the best solution from the inferior agent's perspective? And might it not be possible to justify the agent's dishonesty on utilitarian and rule-utilitarian grounds? This once again broaches the question, what is meant by the "best solution"?

A considerable amount of attention has been given to this question by philosophers and social scientists, and a plethora of socially optimal objective functions have been proposed. Finance's preoccupation with psychological egoism (i.e. personal wealth maximization) negates the question, but as noted earlier the underlying implication in finance is essentially utilitarian. The implicit assumption seems to be that maximum aggregate wealth is the best solution, which in the models of finance is generally no broader than maximizing the value of a single firm. Finance does not invoke utilitarian individuals directly because such motivation is deemed unrealistic; what O.D. Hart terms "bounded rationality: individuals simply cannot conceive of all the eventualities that may occur."[18]

But what if this utilitarian "best solution" is attained by means of dishonesty, as in the above pooling equilibrium? Should the utilitarian objective be constrained by a stipulation that all agents are honest; that is, some form of rule utilitarianism? Is honesty always the best solution, regardless of the economic cost? If honesty is actually to be inserted as a nonabsolute constraint in an objective function, then it must be financially measurable. But is honesty or trustworthiness quantifiable? Even if honesty could be quantified, there is no universal agreement on the ultimate desirability of honesty in all situations. Even deontological ethical theories, which do not concern themselves with consequences and therefore need not necessarily quantify moral attributes, fail to supply universally applicable rules of conduct.[19]

Clearly the ultimate desirability of any of these ethical theories depends fundamentally upon the desired ultimate objective. If a single ultimate objective were universally accepted and logically proven, then the corresponding ethical theory could merely be inserted into the finance rubric. Finance would thus fulfill its normative obligation. The central problem is that post-Enlightenment moral philosophy has failed to distill a clear ultimate objective. Any agent attempting to apply post-Enlightenment ethical theory is thus set adrift in an unnavigable sea of ambiguity between the two pedagogical extremes of Kantianism and utilitarianism:

> The existence of these divisions makes one wonder why [post-Enlightenment] theory is viewed as helpful in any way. On the surface, it would seem that the opposite would be true: that a familiarity with theoretical debates would only complicate students' approaches to concrete cases. . . . It would seem that the presence of fundamental disagreement at the theoretical level would tend to reinforce the impression . . . that ethics is ultimately "subjective."[20]

An additional complication in finance is that some individuals are invariably constrained by a fiduciary responsibility to other individuals. To the extent that a fiduciary duty can be construed as an ethical obligation, a manager may be ethically justified in deceiving bondholders if such behavior increases the wealth of stockholders. Given the post-Enlightenment view of ethics, therefore, the morality of agency problems is unclear. Agency problems concerning the interaction of debtholders and management could be viewed in a moral light different from agency problems between management and shareholders. Two examples of the former type of agency problem discussed earlier are *underinvestment* (Myers) and *risk-shifting* (Jensen and Meckling).[21] In both cases managers undertake deceptive behavior that is designed to expropriate wealth from unwitting debtholders. But surely one could argue that managers are morally obligated to attempt such behavior in order to honor their fiduciary duty to shareholders. Far from being unethical, therefore, the existence of these agency problems can be construed as evidence of managers fulfilling their moral obligations.

The same defense cannot be made for agency problems between management and shareholders. When managers act deceptively by consuming excessive amounts of perquisites, to the detriment of firm value, they are also breaching their fiduciary duty to shareholders. Any moral defense of such behavior, therefore, would be extremely tenuous. But to the extent that such behavior is expected and is priced by shareholders, a utilitarian-type defense is no doubt possible. Indeed, the fact that such a defense could conceivably be made further illustrates the ambiguity of post-Enlightenment moral philosophy. This school provides no clear direction for the accommodation of ethics in finance.

'Futile' is not too strong a word, therefore, with which to label any attempt to imbue the mathematical objective functions of the finance paradigm with some 'ethic' derived from traditional Enlightenment approaches. In short, the conceptual logic from which the six axioms of the finance paradigm are drawn is simply irreconcilable with post-Enlightenment moral philosophy. This chapter's brief and simplistic foray into what I have chosen to call 'traditional' ethical theory thus appears to have left us back at square one or more precisely, back at the end of part I of this book. We are once again faced with the ubiquitous "Prisoners' Dilemma" impasse illustrated in figure 2.1. We can identify no 'rational' reason for the agent to sacrifice material gain in the interests of honoring trust.

This chapter's critique of deontological and teleological ethical theory has clearly been superficial. Even if these theories cannot provide a single unified ethical principle, they do provide useful general guidelines. But I am not alone in criticizing this traditional approach to ethical theory. Other philosophers have provided far more detailed and logically coherent critiques of this approach, and the work of these authors will be summarized in chapter 7 when I move beyond the finance paradigm. Indeed, if moral philosophy comprised the traditional or post-Enlightenment school only, then the absence of ethics in finance may be justifiable on the grounds that ethical behavior simply cannot be *rationalized*. But moral philosophy has spawned another school that views ethics in a quite different light. This is the *virtue-ethics* school and it makes no attempt to quantify ethics, or even rationalize ethics, in an economic context. Ironically, however, it may provide the key to accommodating ethics in finance. It is thus to virtue-ethics theory that I turn in part III, where a quite different rationality concept—one that lies well beyond the finance paradigm—is invoked. But first, the stage must be set by taking a closer look at some of the practical and international implications of morally challenging the finance paradigm.

5

Ethics in Financial Practice

And what is good, Phaedrus,
And what is not good —
Need we ask anyone to tell us these things?

— Plato

Given the many complexities and ambiguities of ethical theory, highlighted in the previous chapter, does it really make sense for financial practitioners to look beyond straightforward codes of conduct? When it comes to exercising moral judgment, might practitioners do better simply to rely on these codes plus their common sense, rather than delving into moral philosophy? To paraphrase Plato, do managers really need to ask anyone to tell them these things? Moreover, from a practical perspective, given their fiduciary obligations to shareholders, are financial managers really at liberty to exercise their personal moral judgment? In other words, are managers free moral agents? Shouldn't ethically charged decisions of a significant nature be referred to the owners of the firm, the shareholders, if not to all stakeholders, thus leaving managers free to perform their proper function as *economic* agents? More fundamentally, is it really feasible to evaluate financial decisions, most of which are technical in nature, from an ethical perspective? These practical and pragmatic questions relating to ethics in finance will be addressed in this chapter.

Consider the following scenario. An oil company plans to build a petrochemical plant. Management is considering two possible locations, one in California, the other in China. Current antipollution laws in California will add considerably to the costs of building and running the plant. Conversely, the lack of similar regulations in China means that the plant can be built relatively cheaply and waste can simply be flushed into the nearby river. As a direct result of these different regulatory environments, the project team's estimates indicate that firm value will be maximized if the plant is built in China. These cost estimates assume that, given location in China, the new plant will be equipped with merely the minimal toxic-waste-handling facilities, in compliance with nascent Chinese corporate law.

Although the decision seems clear in economic terms, the project manager is uncomfortable. She feels that there is something wrong with locating in China in order to economically exploit lax antipollution regulations. She is unable to justify her concern on economic grounds. For example, China's political environment appears to be stable, and there is no indication that environmental pressure groups will berate her company if it pollutes outside the United States and Europe. So the probability of future economic costs, engendered by consumer boycotts or other environmental-group actions, is negligible. She also is cognizant of her fiduciary responsibility to shareholders and other stakeholders within the corporation; her job is to maximize firm value. Her moral dilemma appears to leave her with three fundamental choices:

1. She can suppress her personal moral apprehensions, honor her fiduciary responsibilities, and locate the plant in China.

2. She can choose not to locate the plant in China, thereby failing to maximize firm value, and so possibly breaching her fiduciary responsibility to shareholders.

3. She can shift the perceived moral dilemma from herself to shareholders by conducting a referendum. Let shareholders vote on whether or not to locate the plant in China in order to exploit (in an economic sense) the lax environmental regulations.

Of the three alternatives, the third might appear to be optimal from the project manager's point of view. A referendum enables her to maintain her moral integrity while not breaching her fiduciary responsibility to shareholders. A referendum could be justified on philosophical grounds as follows: it recognizes the diversity of moral sentiments among individuals. The corporation becomes a democracy in which the moral majority of residual claimants holds sway. In reality, this notion of corporate-moral democracy is gaining popularity. Moral issues are appearing more frequently as topics for debate and ballot during American corporations' annual general meetings (AGMs). The Investor Responsibility Research Center (IRRC) in Washington, D.C., for example, identified 175 large corporations that faced "social responsibility resolutions" at their 1989 AGMs. The 'referendum solution' would certainly seem desirable in the sense that it shifts moral responsibility away from managers. In effect, it accomplishes the desired separation of ethics and finance. This solution, however, has serious drawbacks.

First, referendums are expensive and time-consuming procedures and therefore would only be a feasible remedy for major moral dilemmas, such as the decision faced by many firms a few years ago of whether or not to divest themselves of subsidiaries in South Africa. Interestingly, the three corporations that chose to make this decision via referendum—Kellogg, Union Carbide, and Variety Corporations—ended up *not* divesting. This can perhaps be explained with reference to the second problem with referendums.

This problem is caused by the complexity of the contemporary financial milieu. What part I of this book made clear is that financial markets are networks of contractual relations. The majority of the shares of the largest corporations are not held by individuals, but by institutions. For example, on the New York Stock Exchange, some 80 percent of all outstanding shares are held by institutions, the largest single group being pension funds: these funds own more than 50 percent of all shares outstanding. The money managers who run these institutions are not free moral agents because they have fiduciary responsibilities to their members, subscribers, policyholders, and others. Given the referendum logic, therefore, if an institutional investor were to provide ethical guidance for a corporation, it would have to conduct its own referendum in order to determine the moral consensus of its claimants. Thus, in the case of, for example, the California Public Employees Retirement Fund (which has some $60 billion invested, primarily in equity), a meaningful referendum on the location of this petrochemical plant would involve several million public employees in California.

Another major problem is that of information disclosure. Corporations cannot be reasonably expected to release the type of sensitive information necessary for shareholders to make adequately informed ethical decisions. If released, such information might dramatically reduce the firm's competitiveness, and might expose the firm to greater potential legal liability.

In summary, as a democratic means of alleviating managers, ethical obligations, the referendum solution has serious drawbacks. Agents within the firm must face up to the fact that, when it comes to day-to-day decision making, there is no way to simply pass the 'moral buck' on to shareholders, directors, or any other group. In the final analysis, finance and ethics are not entirely separable. Managers have to take moral responsibility for financial decisions: in many cases, the moral buck must start and end with them.

How should financial managers approach ethics in their day-to-day operations? Traditional approaches have generally involved developing some corporate credo or a list of rules of conduct, usually founded on some simple interpretation of Kantianism or utilitarianism, or a combination of the two. But how successful have these traditional approaches been?

Corporate Codes

Within the firm in practice, the most popular means of introducing ethics is through a corporate credo or code of conduct. Just how effective these codes are, and the motivations of the managers who introduce them, has been the source of much debate. In a recent study, for example, the content of 160 corporate codes of conduct are analyzed in relation to the firm's business environment.[1] The authors find that "managers choose code content so as to reduce the expected cost of adverse legal or regulatory action." They go on to conclude that "our findings are consistent with code adoptions and development as good *business* decisions." This study lends support, therefore, to the finance-paradigm concept of managerial behavior lying within the bounds of material objectives: not 'ethics for ethics sake,' but rather 'ethics for profits' sake.'

As regards the likely effectiveness of corporate credos, managers are extolled to "relentlessly emphasize that codes are merely guidelines, that rules have exceptions, and that the essence of ethics is independent thinking and question."[2] Also, "it is the responsibility of those who construct codes of ethics to ensure acceptance of the covenant of the code. It is not enough to make up a set of rules, laws or codes and expect everyone to follow blindly."[3]

Clearly, what a code should provide is a framework of values by which managers can make ethically charged decisions. One of the most widely acclaimed credos is that of Johnson & Johnson, Inc. (J&J). The credo begins with the following statement: "We believe our first responsibility is to the doctors, nurses and patients, to mothers and fathers and all others who use our products and services." The credo proceeds to enumerate responsibilities to employees, and the community at large, and only toward the end of the credo are stockholders mentioned as deserving "a fair return." No specific moral guidelines are given for individual financial, marketing, or other decisions. But what is enumerated is a value system predicated on the classical virtues of honesty, integrity, courage, justice, and respect for human life and dignity over and above the need to return stockholders their "fair return." The existence of this credo at J&J is credited with enabling it to react quickly, decisively, and ethically to the crisis concerning cyanide-contaminated Tylenol capsules: "The firm's recall of the Tylenol capsules was a result of the culture in place at Johnson & Johnson."[4] Procter and Gamble (P&G) reacted similarly to the Rely tampon crisis. At the first sign of health problems, it immediately, without hesitation, demarketed a product that had taken twenty years to develop at a cost of $74 million. As Edward G. Harness, chairman of the board of P&G, commented, "profitability and growth go hand in hand with fair treatment of employees, of customers, of consumers, and of the community."[5] Such behavior lies in sharp contrast to Union Carbide's (UC) dithering in the wake of the Bhopal tragedy. As John Ladd points out, UC lacked a corporate ethos with which to make complex decisions that involved both financial and ethical aspects. He concludes that UC's behavior "reflected a perfectly commonplace and 'normal' preoccupation with matters of self-interest and of self-advancement to the exclusion of any consideration of the wider implications of their actions or non-actions and of their absence of concern for the safety and the welfare of others."[6]

Although a corporate code of ethics may provide a manager with a valuable framework for ethical decision making, it is not in and of itself sufficient to ensure ethical conduct: "Ethics codes cannot simply be handed out to employees who are then expected to follow the standards. Training programs are essential to introduce the employees to the code."[7] This point is made clearly by Dennis Gioia who draws on his personal experience as vehicle recall coordinator for Ford Motor Company. Gioia participated directly in the decision to keep the Ford Pinto on the road in the face of mounting evidence concerning the faulty fuel tank design, which eventually resulted in over five hundred burn deaths in rear-end collisions. While analyzing his experience at Ford, Gioia concludes that "codes of ethics . . . are too often cast at a level of generality that cannot be associated with any specific script," where a "script" is some generally accepted decision procedure within the firm.[8] Gioia suggests that management must be exposed to "learning or training that concentrates on exposure to information or models that explicitly display a focus on ethical considerations."[9] One approach designed to provide managers with this practical exposure to the resolution of ethical dilemmas within the firm is the Critical Incident Technique.[10]

This technique contains two central features: (1) the idea that ethical behavior has intrinsic value to the agent, and (2) the general acceptance of the need to identify role models or "exemplary performers" (both these features are characteristic also of virtue-ethics theory). It is from observation of how these individuals handle ethically charged decisions that other members of the organization learn practical ethics. Peter Dean emphasizes the practical nature of the Critical Incident Technique (CIT), originally developed by the United States Air Force during World War II: "In its simplest form, the technique involves bringing together professionals familiar enough with the job area under study to be able to share 'real life' examples of both effective and ineffective job performance, or in this case ethical and unethical decisions."[11]

Through a series of workshops, the experiences of these professionals are relayed to other employees in order to demonstrate the effective *application* of a corporate code of ethics. Once a code of ethics is established, the behavior of experienced and exemplary individuals is then tapped in order to perfect the delicate balance between the pursuit of material objectives, and the pursuit of moral objectives, that tends to appear in day-to-day managerial decisions. As regards the content of the code, Dean identifies eight tenets: (1) exercise of due care, (2) confidentiality, (3) fidelity to special responsibilities, (4) avoidance of the appearance of a conflict of interest, (5) willing compliance with the law, (6) acting in good faith in negotiations, (7) respect for human well-being, and (8) respect for the liberty and constitutional rights of others.[12]

He emphasizes, however, that the mere adherence to these tenets is insufficient. "The Critical Incident Technique facilitates the identification of those behaviors that distinguish really outstanding accomplishments, from those that achieve minimum standards only. . . . Further, if outstanding decisions are labeled as such, they are more likely to be emulated."[13] Thus, once again, ethics is cast as an objective rather than a constraint. The *moral minimalism* of traditional approaches to ethics, in which some ethical rule was merely one more constraint to be circumvented in the pursuit of material gain, is clearly inconsistent with the CIT. The implementation of the CIT generally begins with a focus on senior-level employees: "a corporation's top management sets the ethical tone for its employees."[14] Similarly, in an extensive study of ten major corporations undertaken by the Business Roundtable, the conclusion was reached that "with regard to corporate ethics, no point emerges more clearly than the crucial role of top management."[15] These senior employees thus become the "exemplary performers" to whom Dean refers. Once established, the CIT's moral import filters down the corporate hierarchy to impact, not only financial decisions, but all aspects of corporate activity.

The case of Cummins Engine, Inc., an international designer and manufacturer of diesel engines and accessories, provides an example of a firm with a strong corporate ethos that was fostered through procedures consistent with the CIT: "top management, from the founding of the company, committed the firm to ethical business practices, support for the local community, and respect for all stakeholders whose lives or interests are affected by company action."[16] The actual steps involved in the initiation and perpetuation of such a value system within the firm was outlined in some detail by Michael Rion, corporate responsibility director for Cummins Engine. Rion's division organized regular three-day workshops for groups of eighteen to twenty-four middle-level and upper-level managers. Attendance at these workshops was entirely voluntary, but Rion notes that the sessions are always oversubscribed, reflecting a keen interest among managers concerning ethical issues. Rion enumerates three learning goals. These progress logically from a broad recognition of the value of ethics, to specific application of ethical precepts in financial decisions:

1.   To increase recognition of ethical dimensions in management decisions.

2.   To acquire concepts and methods for analysis of ethical issues.

3.   To strengthen the capacity for practical resolution of ethical issues.[17]

These goals were addressed sequentially in three sessions. The first session focused upon recognition. Through discussion of the importance of implicit contracts based on trust (similar to our discussion above), managers are led to a recognition of the role of ethics in business. Managers analyze their own personal motivations in relation to those of the corporation in accordance with Sherwin Klein's suggestion that "corporate people . . . function according to a double standard—amorally as an official of an organization and morally as a private person."[18] Through open discussion they are brought to realize that such schizophrenia is inappropriate: ethics permeates both personal and professional life.

The second session narrows the focus by applying the broad conclusions of the first session to the "ordering and analysis" of individual business decisions. Managers are made aware of the fact that there are no simple solutions to ethically charged decisions. In addition, they realize that practically *every* decision they make has an ethical dimension. For example, decisions such as receivables-collection policy or project abandonment versus continuation, which might at first appear entirely economic, do in fact entail some moral deliberation inasmuch as they entail honesty, or fairness. Indeed, it is certain moral "virtues" that provide the foundation from which managers order and analyze business decisions. Rion lists these virtues explicitly:

> Promise-keeping
> Truth-telling
> Reparation (compensating for previous wrongful acts)
> Gratitude
> Justice
> Beneficence (doing good, preventing or removing evil)
> Nonmaleficence (refraining from doing evil)
> Morally virtuous self-development[19]

The third and final session focuses on morally enlightened business judgment. Managers are faced with a series of realistic scenarios in which they must exercise sound moral judgment in accordance with the conclusions drawn in the previous two sessions. Classic moral dilemmas such as whistle-blowing and information disclosure are thus addressed in a realistic setting. Managers realize that in many situations profits and ethics need not conflict: although opportunism may increase returns in the short run, morally restrained behavior will lead to greater long-run profitability through the acquisition of 'Buffett-type' reputational capital.

In summary, it is hard to imagine a more thorough attempt to bring ethics within the financial activity of a firm than that undertaken by Cummins. But, as Rion admits while evaluating the success of his approach, "Cummins does not meet its goals with perfect accuracy and the problems of sustaining and implementing ethical management arise regularly."[20] Thus, even this attempt to combine moral and financial paradigms met with, at best, partial success. And, of course, actually measuring how successful these programs are is very difficult since what really needs to be evaluated are the underlying motives, while only the resulting action is observable. A single financial action could conceal a variety of possible motivations for that action. Thus, managers may be seen as complying with the *letter* of a corporate credo through their actions, while their latent motivations reveal that they are by no means complying with the *spirit* of the credo; their motivations may be strictly unethical, and unobservable. A good example of this dichotomy between actions and motivations in the context of financial practice is supplied by the continuation-versus-abandonment decision of capital budgeting.

Test Case: Ethics in Capital Budgeting

The continuation-versus-abandonment decision of capital budgeting is an archetypal 'finance' decision and is amenable as a test case because it entails the agent (project manager) choosing between two mutually exclusive and exhaustive alternatives, namely whether to terminate an investment project immediately, or to continue the project until the next evaluation. Although only two courses of action are observable, there may be many possible *motivations* underlying a given action. Research in this area has supplied five possible motivations for the manager's choice between continuation versus abandonment.

1. *The NPV Rule.* The Net Present Value (NPV) rule of financial theory supposedly gives management a clear and decisive criterion for choosing between abandonment versus continuation of capital projects. The rule can be summarized as follows: "sunk costs should be ignored and . . . projects should be terminated when the expected present value of cash flows, given that the project is terminated today, is greater than the expected present value of cash flows given that the project is continued for at least one additional period."[21]

Agents who abide by the NPV rule are endeavoring to maximize firm value, and thus are honoring their fiduciary duty to stakeholders. If the firm is taken as the relevant universe, then firm-value maximization is consistent with utilitarianism.[22] Given that no deception or unfairness is involved, such a motivation seems readily universalizable viv-à-vis Kant. An agent who abides by the NPV rule under these circumstances, therefore, will be acting ethically. But note that the motivation is strictly economic, strictly within the finance paradigm.

2. *An Agency Problem.* Managers' concern for their personal reputations may induce them to delay project abandonment at the expense of firm value.[23] A manager might choose to continue a negative-NPV project in an attempt to, at least temporarily, preserve her reputation for successfully completing capital investments. She would thus be acting in accordance with the tenets of narrowly defined economic self-interest (i.e., she would be acting within the finance paradigm), but she would not be acting in the interests of firm-value maximization.

From the perspective of ethics, an agent who acts opportunistically is not motivated by a desire to maximize firm value, and is therefore acting unethically from a utilitarian perspective. Given that opportunism may be deceptive, depending upon whether stakeholders expect the agent to act opportunistically, and that such behavior invariably incurs agency costs, it is not a behavioral principle that is readily universalizable viv-à-vis Kant.

3. *Signaling.* Some researchers have argued that the NPV rule itself, given in (1) above, is misspecified.[24] It fails to account for the real costs associated with tarnishing *the firm's* reputation: a reputation for successfully identifying and completing profitable projects. Assuming informational asymmetry, these costs are incurred by the announcement of a project abandonment. Such an announcement, at the time dictated by the NPV rule, represents a significantly negative signal. Thus, a project abandonment may be more costly than the NPV rule implies. Firm value may in fact be maximized, therefore, by continuing with a project that, according to the NPV rule, should be abandoned immediately. The length of the abandonment delay would be a function of the degree of informational asymmetry, and the amount of reputational capital at stake as dictated by the perceived importance of the project. A *reputation-adjusted* NPV rule (RANPV) may therefore be the appropriate, firm-value maximizing, decision criterion.

The ethics of signaling is somewhat complex. Once again, the *motivation* of the agent is the determining factor. Continuing the negative-NPV project in order to avoid the reputation costs associated with an abandonment announcement does appear to involve deception. By not abandoning the project, the manager is depriving the market of information concerning the project's poor performance. But is it deception for the greater good? Because they believe the NPV rule to be misspecified, insiders are suppressing information concerning the fact that the project has a negative NPV. But, in doing this, are insiders merely protecting outsiders from themselves? The project is currently losing the firm money, but a negative signal in the form of an abandonment announcement will lose the firm even more money. Is the deception thus excusable on the grounds that it is in the interest of firm-value maximization?

More specifically, is the continuation of this project really deceptive? The answer to this question depends upon the expectations of stakeholders. If stakeholders believe and desire that managers abide by the NPV rule, then the agent's choice to continue a negative-NPV project is deceptive. But if stakeholders believe and desire that managers choose whichever action maximizes firm value, then the agent's continuation choice is clearly not deceptive: it is consistent with stakeholders' expectations and wishes.[25]

Alternatively, by delaying the abandonment announcement, are insiders merely buying time for current shareholders to liquidate their holdings at the expense of future shareholders?[26] In this case the abandonment delay represents an agency cost borne by future stakeholders, namely those with a stake in the firm when the true worth of the project is revealed.

The apparently deceptive nature of the action could make it unethical from a Kantian perspective. The fact that the deception is perhaps in the interests of firm-value maximization, however, may render the action ethical *qua* utilitarianism. Clearly, the fact that financial management involves deception does not, in and of itself, render it unethical. In order to determine the ethicality of the action, the motives behind the deception must be evaluated. An agency problem betrays unethical behavior because the underlying motive is invariably opportunistic. A "deceptive" signal betrays nothing concerning the underlying motivation for the signal. If management believes the NPV rule to be misspecified and thus continues the negative-NPV project in order to maximize firm value viv-à-vis the RANPV, then the motivation is ethical in the sense that the ultimate objective is firm-value maximization.

4. *Psychology.* Individuals are generally reluctant to admit defeat, and thus management's "regret aversion" may lead it to delay the termination of unprofitable projects.[27] Managers pursue a *psychic* payoff rather than a personal or corporate *economic* payoff. An agent may therefore continue an unprofitable project in the hope, rather than any realistic expectation, that the project will become profitable in the future. Because it involves self deception and serves no greater good, the continuation of an unprofitable project for egocentric reasons is unethical: as Iris Murdoch sagaciously observes, "in the moral life, the enemy is the . . . ego."[28]

In summary, what this capital-budgeting test case illustrates is that even the most apparently 'cut-and-dried' type of financial decision may conceal a variety of motivations. All of these motivations have some ethical implications, and the implications are not always readily discernible. Consider, for example, deception. Generally, deception is unethical, as in the case of agency problems caused by opportunism, but a possible exception might be a deceptive signal, such as continuing an apparently unprofitable project, that management chooses to emit with shareholders' interests in mind, as was the case with the RANPV. Even the most coldly technical of financial decisions, therefore, such as the continuation-versus-abandonment decision, may contain a variety of ethical implications.

Of course, in addition to the above motivations, the agent may continue or abandon the project on purely *ethical* grounds. For example, an unprofitable project may be continued because the agent believes that its immediate abandonment will cause severe distress to certain stakeholders; for example, delaying the closure of a factory in order to give employees time to search for alternative employment. Conversely, a profitable project may be abandoned because the agent believes that the nature of the project itself is unethical; for example, the building of the aforementioned petrochemical plant in China.

How should the manager choose when the profitability of the project and the ethicality of the project appear to conflict? In a competitive environment, can a firm that makes the moral choice survive? Interestingly, in reality such a conflict may not occur as frequently as one might expect. Several studies find a positive correlation between a firm's moral worth and its economic worth.[29] John Swanda, for example, notes that "the value of the firm's moral character . . . can result in a market value of the firm that is greater than the firm's net assets." He conjectures that "even in the short run one can argue that the firm with an excellent ethical reputation can have a special economic advantage." Swanda characterizes corporate virtue as both an asset and a source of income, as a stock and a flow.[30] He concludes:

> While morality as a resource cannot be considered in the same context as tangible assets or goods, it can be considered, however, as a highly valuable but volatile asset, one which reflects the perception of the community. . . . In this sense, it will use outflows of resources to establish *stocks* of morality in order to encourage various publics to hold the firm in trust.[31]

A perceived conflict between profits and ethics may be illusory, therefore, because the method used to evaluate the profitability of the project fails to value the project's moral worth. Thus, the NPV rule may be misspecified, not only because of its failure to consider reputation costs as suggested above by the RANPV, but also because of its failure to consider costs and benefits associated with stakeholders' perception of the *ethicality* of the project. Once these costs and benefits are included in the financial evaluation, profits and ethics may converge. Of course, for this convergence to take place, stakeholders must be aware of the moral ramifications of the project. But in view of the informational asymmetry frequently present in these environments, and the clear temptation for managers to actively suppress the dissemination of just this type of information, stakeholders may frequently be unaware and therefore unable to accurately *price* the firm's moral worth. Despite these interesting observations, therefore, it seems very unlikely that merely a concern for the financial bottom line will be a sufficient moral restraint on corporate activities, although the observations of Swanda and others clearly lend support to the implementation and active enforcement of corporate disclosure laws. At best, however, these laws will reveal only actions, not motivations.

This financial kind of justification for ethics in business brings us back to the earlier critique of the Confidence School. If managers' motivation for being ethical is that they believe it will 'pay' financially, then presumably they will be unethical if and when it, too, 'pays': clearly a very tenuous justification for ethics given the high degree of informational asymmetry that characterizes financial markets. The idea that 'good ethics' in the rigid rule-based form generally enumerated in corporate credos, is always 'good business' can be a dangerously misleading maxim in a competitive market environment (witness Cummins's recent financial difficulties—maybe these have something to do with its aggressive ethics program). To always be honest, for example, is probably a prescription for financial disaster in informationally imperfect markets where the *signaling* implications of many corporate acts are so crucial. As discussed earlier, deception for the greater good may actually be the truly moral motivation, but more on this in part III.

In summary, for ethics to work in financial practice requires in essence a *micro* focus, a focus not merely on the individual agent, but actually on the underlying *motivations* of the agent. Much as they might like to, managers cannot simply pass on the moral buck to other stakeholders through referendums, or a reliance on market forces to 'price' morality. Although corporate credos and the like undoubtedly provide some moral guidance, their general reliance on traditional approaches to ethics makes them an ambiguous guide in some environments. Should managers abide by them because 'good ethics is good business'? What if the apparently ethical choice is not good business? Traditional credos, which generally provide merely a list of constraints, fail to address the crucial question of how to *rationalize* ethics as a motivation that supersedes profit. Even more sophisticated credos such as J&J's, and even when implemented through sophisticated techniques such as the CIT, require some sound philosophical foundation. This foundation should demonstrate unequivocally the absolute superiority of 'moral excellence' over 'material gain' as the motivation for all human endeavor. For managers to rationally act ethically, ethics must be rational. Ethics in financial practice, therefore, like ethics in financial theory, requires a sound logical foundation, a foundation that has been lacking in the traditional approaches to moral philosophy. Just such a foundation will be supplied in part III.

But first some international implications of ethics in the finance paradigm will be briefly discussed. These implications provide further support for the approach taken later.

6

Some International Implications

We are witnessing the creation of a purer form of capitalism, practiced globally by managers who are more distant, more economically driven—in essence more coldly rational in their decisions, having shed the old affiliations with people and place. Vanishing . . . are the paternalistic corporate heads who used to feel a sense of responsibility for their local community. Emerging in their place is the new global manager, driven by the irrefutable logic of global capitalism to seek higher profits, enhanced market leadership, and improved stock price.

—Robert Reich

One of the most significant financial developments of this century has undoubtedly been the virtually complete globalization of business commerce. Traditional national, religious, and political boundaries are weakening in the wake of this internationalization of Western 'corporate culture.' With international securities markets and sophisticated transportation and communication systems linking all industrialized countries, the world is rapidly becoming a single financial market. The extent of these international money flows is reflected in the phenomenal growth in currency trading: as of mid-1993, the average volume of currency-trading activity (adjusted for double counting) is approaching a staggering $1 trillion per *day*. Perhaps the most dramatic illustration of the degree to which financial markets are now interconnected was the stock-market crash of October 19, 1987 (alias 'Black Monday'): on this day, all major securities markets experienced a one-day decline in value of 20 percent or more almost simultaneously: in essence, the London, New York, Tokyo, and other major equity markets acted as one market.[1]

The globalization of financial markets is being mirrored by a similar process in product markets. Robert Reich supplies a typical example: "Mazda's newest sportscar, the MX-5 Miata, was designed in California, financed from Tokyo and New York, its prototype was created in Worthing, England, and it was assembled in Michigan and Mexico using advanced electronics components invented in New Jersey and fabricated in Japan."[2] Today most large firms operate transnationally, that is, their operations extend across one or more national boundaries. Indeed, during the postwar expansion of Western economies, the transnational corporation (TNC) has risen to a role of dominance. Today the largest one hundred corporations in the world are all TNCs. The annual earnings of any one of these companies exceeds the annual GNP of many developing nations, for whom international trade generally represents more than 50 percent of GDP.[3] As mentioned earlier, TNCs control "80 percent of the world's land cultivated for export-oriented crops. . . . Eighty to ninety percent of the trade in tea, coffee, cocoa, cotton, forest products, tobacco, jute, copper, iron-ore, and bauxite is controlled in the case of each commodity by the three or six largest transnationals."[4]

In the case of U.S.-based TNCs, these companies increased overseas capital spending by 24 percent in 1988, and by a further 13 percent in 1989. American firms now employ 11 percent of the industrial workforce of Northern Ireland manufacturing a broad range of products from cigarettes to software. Singapore's largest private employer is General Electric, while AT&T, RCA, and Texas Instruments are three of Taiwan's largest exporters. Texas Instruments is currently constructing a new $250 million semiconductor fabrication plant in Taiwan, and AT&T plans to build a similar facility in Spain. In their book *Managing across Borders*, Christopher Bartlett and Sumantra Ghoshal account for this dramatic growth in TNCs as follows: "technological, social, and economic developments over the last two decades have combined to create a unified world marketplace in which companies must capture global-scale economies to remain competitive."[5]

But when a U.S. corporation expands its business beyond the domestic economy, it is no longer protected by a comprehensive and familiar regulatory environment. Indeed, few would argue that U.S. commerce is the beneficiary of the most sophisticated regulatory environment in the world. More important, this environment is designed generally to foster commercial activity rather than to inhibit or exploit it.[6] As J.C. Francis notes, in the case of financial markets, "no foreign markets are as efficient as the large, deep, and resilient securities markets in the United States."[7]

The additional risks associated with international diversification are generally categorized into one of four types: political risk, foreign exchange risk, reduced liquidity or marketability risk, and inferior information risk. Clearly these categories are not mutually exclusive, and all international transactions will likely be exposed, in varying degree, to all four types of risk. In general, therefore, a firm expanding outside the U.S. regulatory web is faced with the risks involved in enforcing transnational business contracts. The issue of contractual enforcement, therefore, whether through implicit or explicit means, is particularly pertinent in contemporary global markets.

Part I of this book identified two fundamental mechanisms by which business contracts may be enforced: explicit enforcement via some legal mechanism, or implicit enforcement via the firm's or agent's desire to maintain a reputation. Under scrutiny, both of these mechanisms appeared to have serious weaknesses—hence the role for ethics as a contractual enforcement mechanism. In this chapter, a recognition of the increasing extent to which business relations extend across national borders reveals that the role of law or reputation as *effective* contractual enforcement mechanisms becomes even more questionable. The weaknesses of these mechanisms, which were identified earlier in a domestic setting, are extenuated as business becomes more international. In a global marketplace, therefore, the need for ethics in business interaction becomes even more pressing.

Outside the United States, the lack of a cohesive global regulatory body and the dramatic difference in economic power between nations combine to make the probability of explicit enforcement through law much lower than in domestic transactions. Consequently, in international dealings, corporations are forced to rely heavily on *implicit* contractual enforcement mechanisms. In chapter 3, information availability was identified as critical to the effectiveness of reputation as an implicit contractual enforcement mechanism. But in an international context the complexities of implicit enforcement multiply: business interaction becomes even more impersonal, and the degree of informational asymmetry—given minimal corporate disclosure laws in many countries—increases commensurably. These points are made clearly by Thomas Donaldson in his book *The Ethics of International Business*. Donaldson argues that, given the impersonality of most international transactions, the chances of any type of implicit cooperation along the lines of a reputation effect—or like that suggested by David Gauthier's *Morals by Agreement* in which enlightened self-interest leads to cooperation—become much lower: "[Gauthier's] attempt to generate international ethics from the concept of refined self-interest fails in the end . . . A major problem for Gauthier's theory in application to international contexts is that an individ- ual nation is not so impotent as an individual person. In international contexts the fruits of interaction are less certain."[8] The remainder of this chapter examines this argument in a financial context by investigating the potential for explicit and implicit enforcement of international business relations within the finance paradigm.

Explicit Enforcement in International Markets: Power Corrupts

To build a smokeless factory when no competitors are incurring the cost is individual firm suicide.

— J. Thomas Gilmore

The incentives for an expanding company to become a TNC are several. A company that is unable to grow further in its domestic market, either due to market saturation or antitrust regulation, may reap further economies of scale and scope through not only exporting its product but also producing it abroad. Similarly, a company may wish to diversify its political and economic risk by spreading its operations across national boundaries. A major trend in corporate expansion has been from the developed world (such as Europe and the United States) to the developing world. The primary incentives for TNCs to expand into developing countries are the availability of lower-cost

labor and the opportunity to exploit natural resources that have been depleted at home. More recently, an additional reason has been the lack of an
extensive and intrusive regulatory environment in many developing countries, particularly in the context of environmental regulation. It is no coinci-
dence that the most polluted cities in the world are in developing
countries.[9]

In light of their market power, which is particularly prevalent in developing countries, TNCs are attracting increasing attention from environmental-
ists and ethicists. Within the last two or three years, questions concerning the
ethicality of various business practices, particularly those affecting the natural environment, have garnered increasing public attention. As regards controlling the activities of TNCs *explicitly,* the most extensive global regulatory
body is the General Agreement on Tariffs and Trade (GATT), which recently
metamorphosed into the World Trade Organization (WTO)—different name
but same basic function. Today, GATT (in view of its greater familiarity, I will
use the acronym GATT rather than WTO) adjudicates over approximately 90
percent of world trade among nearly one hundred countries. The history of
GATT, therefore, is the history of the most ambitious attempt, to date, to implement a global explicit contractual enforcement mechanism. But how successful has GATT been in this regard?

A Brief History of GATT

The reconstruction immediately following the end of the Second World War
marked a watershed in international economic cooperation. Both the International Monetary Fund (IMF) and GATT were initiated in an attempt to co-
ordinate and foster economic growth throughout the world. Both
organizations were founded on the same philosophy, that of *laissez-faire*
capitalism as developed by Smith, Ricardo, Marshall, and other classical
economists.[10]

In the case of GATT, this philosophy rested firmly on the theories of
comparative and absolute advantage, originally enumerated by Ricardo. In
essence, these theories postulated that, given one central assumption, two
countries could benefit from trade even if one country was more efficient at
producing all goods. The central assumption was that the relative efficiency
of production between the two countries was not constant across goods,
thus implying that no single country had complete economic power over
other countries. Thus, the inefficient country would specialize in producing
the good in which it was relatively less inefficient, and *all* countries would
benefit from trade.

GATT also arose from a desire to escape the mercantilist protectionism
that had characterized international trade in the years between the two
world wars. International trade was recognized as a noncooperative Prisoners' Dilemma–type game in which the optimum solution could be reached

only through some form of cooperation between players, the primary players being the corporations and governments of developed nations. In order to dismantle the cobweb of tariff barriers and achieve free trade, GATT was founded on three basic principles:

1. *Nondiscrimination.* A country is prohibited from levying different tariffs on the same good imported from different countries.
2. *Reciprocity.* Reductions in tariffs should be balanced between countries.
3. *Impartial adjudication of trade disputes.* This occurs through machinery developed and controlled by GATT.

For the first three decades of its existence, GATT appeared to serve the international community of developed nations well. Trade barriers worldwide were reduced during these years and membership in GATT grew from twenty-three countries at its inception in 1947 to almost one hundred countries today. The membership of GATT, therefore, has expanded from essentially a "club" for developed nations into an organization spanning all stages of the development life cycle.

The active history of GATT is characterized by intermittent rounds of trade negotiations. The most recent round began on 20 September 1986, at the seaside resort of Punta del Este, in Uruguay. This Uruguay round, however, took on characteristics very different from earlier rounds and led many observers to seriously question the future viability of GATT. As Arthur Dunkel, the current director-general of GATT, recently observed, "[the Uruguay round is] as bedeviled by accusations, self-righteousness, mutual misunderstandings and inability to distinguish special-interest pleading from the public good as seems possible."[11] The Uruguay round, therefore, through disagreement and disarray and may portend the demise of GATT itself.

Clearly, this demise, was not the result of any global philosophical shift. As the collapse of communism in eastern Europe recently demonstrated, the classical economists' construct of free-market capitalism is as attractive as ever. Although economists have always debated the merits of free trade versus protectionism (as indeed economists are known to do on most subjects), the latter has not gained ground on the former since the inception of GATT. The causes of GATT's demise clearly lie outside the realm of ideology. They lie, rather, in the mundane realm of political economy, and are twofold.

First, the scope of the Uruguay round was far more ambitious than previously attempted by GATT. This, in part, is simply a reflection of the increasing complexity of international trade, and also of the expanding role of transnational corporations (TNCs). For example, GATT is attempting to reach international consensus on intellectual and biotechnological property rights, and is attempting to expand its agenda beyond trade in tangibles to trade in intangibles such as technology, investment, and financial services (i.e., banking).

The second reason for the demise of GATT, and most important in the current context, centers on the expanding membership of GATT. A world trade organization should certainly represent all participants in world trade. But, as discussed above, GATT has only recently achieved this by swelling its membership ranks to include a significant representation of developing nations. Ironically, this achievement may prove to be the driving force behind GATT's disintegration. By making themselves heard within GATT, developing countries are beginning to expose past policies, and current proposals, as being morally unjustifiable. The economics of free trade is becoming entwined with the ethics of fair trade as the tradition of GATT—as a tool for rich nations—is exposed.

As discussed earlier, TNCs' postwar expansion has become increasingly focused on the exploitation of developing countries' natural and human resources. As natural resources become depleted or protected in the developed world, TNCs are looking increasingly to the developing countries to supply raw materials. As environmental regulation and labor costs increase in the developed countries, the developing world becomes increasingly attractive to TNCs for the location of labor-intensive production, or that entailing pollutant by-products.

At the behest of TNC pressure groups, GATT has facilitated this exploitation. As Steven Shrybman notes: "The General Agreement on Tariffs and Trade is committed to liberalizing trade through lifting import and export controls and removing non-tariff barriers. The result is that international and national measures intended to protect the environment are being undermined—or abandoned—in the pursuit of growth.[12]

Initially, GATT's free-trade ideology dovetailed with the interests of developed nations' TNCs, so the strong hand that the latter had in shaping GATT policy was cloaked in ideology. With the entry of developing nations, however, this cloak no longer hides the blatant bipartisanship of GATT and the TNCs. This link has been further exposed recently by the increasing interest among developed nations for protectionism. As *The Economist* magazine notes, "While America was unchallenged as an economic power, it sought open international markets for its exports; when its economic strength, at least in relative terms, started to shrink, it was less keen."[13] Thus, GATT is now under pressure to compromise the philosophical principle that justifies its very existence, namely the promotion of free trade.

In summary, rather than being an unbiased adjudicator in the world trade arena, GATT has been exposed as little more than an avenue for TNCs to pursue their economic exploitation of the developing world. As M.K. Peng notes in his critique entitled "The Uruguay Round and The Third World," "there are double standards in the industrial world's approach [to GATT]; liberalization if it suits us, protectionism too if that suits us—*the real underlying principle is pure self-interest.*"[14] To illustrate his argument, Peng takes the example of the world cigarette industry. This industry is dominated by six TNCs, four American and two British. Asian markets have traditionally protected themselves from the import of foreign-made cigarettes. This was, in part, a legacy of China's disastrous experience with imports of British opium in the nineteenth century: Britain's military pressure on China to import opium resulted in a national addiction throughout China.

Asian countries' fears, in the context of the import of foreign cigarettes, appear to have been justified. As Peng notes, "in Japan, South Korea and Taiwan, heartening declines in the rate of cigarette consumption were reversed or halted when U.S. pressure forced open their cigarette markets to imports."[15] Cigarette sales in Taiwan, for example, grew by 4.3 percent in 1987, the first year of unrestricted foreign cigarette sales. These trends are due, in large part, to the massive advertising budgets available to tobacco TNCs.

Thailand is currently battling to retain its recent nationwide ban on cigarette advertising. R. J. Reynolds and Philip Morris have asked the U.S. government to impose trade sanctions through GATT against Thailand unless the advertising ban is lifted and Thailand is opened to foreign cigarette imports. Such attempts by TNCs to distort GATT's free-trade ideology in the interest of commercial exploitation is further tarnishing GATT's image, particularly among developing countries.

Even the concept of free trade itself has become tarnished in reference to the agenda pursued by GATT:

> Freedom of investment—freedom to expatriate profits, to manipulate local politics, to pay workers slave wages, to block social programs, to spoil the environment unhindered by regulation—has been the true meaning of the word "free" in "free market." It involves stealing away national sovereignty, repressing labour organizing and political parties, destroying self-sufficiency in food and basic goods (and imposing food and basic goods import dependency), keeping wages and the standard of living low, and broadening the gap between rich and poor.[16]

The distinction is increasingly being made between free trade and *fair* trade. The latter invokes the *infant industry* arguments under which the fledgling industries of developing countries are protected from the market power of the TNC. Indeed, as global environmental issues become pressing, the whole logic of eternal expansion and progress through trade is being questioned. These antiprogress arguments are echoed by E. Goldsmith:

> The need is not to increase the freedom of commercial concerns but, on the contrary, to bring those concerns back under control—to limit the size of markets, rather than expand them; to give local people control over their resources, not to hand them

over to the transnationals. Such goals are the antithesis of the
proposals being put forward within GATT.[17]

To the extent that GATT has acted merely as a tool for TNCs' exploitation of the developing world, its existence is clearly unjustifiable both from
an ethical and an economic standpoint. What is also clear, however, is the
need for some form of international communication on matters of trade. If
the Prisoners' Dilemma alluded to earlier is to be avoided, some form of
transnational cooperation is necessary. The problem then becomes one of
what form this cooperation should take.

The deadlock surrounding the recent round of GATT negotiations has
made one fact clear; namely, that the interests of developing nations tend to
diverge considerably in matters of trade regulation from those of developed
countries. In general, developing nations wish to protect their infant industries and natural resources from the market power of TNCs, while developed
nations—under pressure from their TNCs' affluent political lobbies—wish to
dismantle such protection in order to exploit developing countries' human
and natural resources. Any single organization that attempts to represent
and reconcile these diametrically opposed viewpoints is likely to face frustra-
tion and eventual failure.

The free-trade ideology undoubtedly has its validity. But so does the ideology of infant-industry protection in the context of developing nations. Any
organization that purports to serve global trading interests, therefore, cannot be built on a single economic ideology. Nor can its policies be dictated
by its most affluent contingency. GATT exhibited both these shortcomings.

The history of GATT, therefore, illustrates vividly the difficulty of implementing some form of explicit enforcement mechanism in transnational
business. Given the wide discrepancy in market power between international trading partners, any such organization naturally becomes controlled
by the most powerful lobby; in this case the TNCs. Rather than Gauthier's
"Morals by Agreement," international commerce seems to be more a case of
a Hobbesian "state of nature" characterized by a war of "all against all" in
which the interests of the powerful self-interested few hold sway.

Implicit Enforcement

Our discussion of GATT and "fair trade versus free trade" illustrates clearly
that in an international context the complexities of ethics in finance multiply.
Business interaction becomes even more impersonal and power-imbalanced,
and the degree of informational asymmetry—given minimal corporate disclosure laws in many countries—increases commensurably. Table 6.1 illustrates
that corporate disclosure laws and shareholder-voting-rights laws are less extensive outside the United States. The numbers in the table are percentages
relative to the United States, where the United States equals 100 percent.

Thus, for example, Canada/disclosure of 80 percent implies that Canadian corporations disclose to their shareholders 20 percent less information than do U. S. corporations.

Table 6.1. Corporate Information Disclosure

	Disclosure	Voting Procedures	Resolution Notification	Shareholder Rights	Average
Canada	80	70	80	90	80
Britain	80	70	60	80	73
Australia	70	70	60	60	65
Germany	40	40	40	70	48
France	60	40	50	40	48
Japan	40	50	40	60	48
Italy	50	50	30	30	40
Holland	70	40	30	30	40
Switzerland	30	10	10	20	18

Note: Scores are calculated relative to the United States, which equals 100.
Source: IRRC, from *The Economist*, 29 April 1989, p. 76.

This lack of information flow raises questions about the viability of *reputation* as an *implicit* contractual enforcement mechanism in international markets. Consider the case of Merck Inc. In the discussion of reputation in chapter 3, Merck was identified by *Fortune* magazine as "America's Most Admired Corporation." There is evidence, however, that Merck's desire to maintain its reputation does not constrain its *offshore* operations: specifically its sizeable operations in Ireland.

Approximately one-quarter of the waste produced by pharmaceutical companies is classified in the United States as 'hazardous.' Such plants operating in the United States, therefore, are forced by law to go to considerable expense to treat and dispose of their waste substances. Several American pharmaceutical companies are operating production plants in Ireland. Ireland currently produces fifty-eight thousand tons of hazardous waste each year and, according to Department of the Environment figures, from 1986 to 1988 between four thousand and five thousand tons 'disappeared.' Kieran Keohane observes that "poor record keeping may account for some of it but the bulk is likely to have found its way into drains or to have been illegally dumped."[18] Apparently, at this time, the maximum penalty in Ireland for the illegal disposal of toxic wastes was a trifling $1,500.

Merck began production of chemicals at its Irish facility in 1976. At this time the local residents were assured that "Merck would operate a clean plant without detriment to the local environment."[19] As Keohane observes, two years later several local farmers lodged complaints that they and their families were suffering from respiratory problems, and that the mortality and stillbirth rate among their livestock had increased inexplicably since the Merck plant began operations.

These farmers accused Merck of emitting dangerously high levels of various toxins. Although Merck's lawyers vehemently denied the allegations, the company was eventually found guilty by the Irish Supreme Court in July 1988. By this time over two hundred head of neighboring farmers' cattle had died from toxic poisoning. The court heard evidence that dangerously high levels of hydrogen chloride and hydrochloric acid were present in the atmosphere for a radius of several miles from the plant. Keohane believes it highly unlikely that the company itself was unaware of the existence of these toxins in the atmosphere. He cites the firm's willful emission of these chemicals for almost ten years after complaints were initially lodged as a signal of a clear lack of concern at Merck regarding the impact of such behavior on its reputation. It seems very unlikely that Merck would have behaved this way in the United States, its home turf, where reputational capital would clearly be at stake. Such examples can readily be found elsewhere, in other toxic industries. Koy Thomson and Nigel Dudley, for example, tell a similar story in the context of United States petroleum TNCs.

Significant oil reserves have been discovered in the Amazon basin. Several TNCs are currently exploiting these reserves. Occidental Petroleum Corporation, for example, recently reached an agreement with the Government of Peru to "increase its production from rain forest areas by 20,000 barrels a day. . . . Texaco has acquired rights in four areas of Colombian rain forest."[20]

These developments have damaged, and presumably will continue to unnecessarily damage, rain forest ecology in two primary ways. First, the oil companies routinely spill oil from ships, drill holes, and build pipelines. "In the Oriente region of Ecuador, there have been at least 30 major oil spills . . . with an estimated loss of 16 million gallons of petroleum."[21] Given greater care and attention on the part of the oil companies, these spills could clearly be avoided or at least ameliorated. Given the minimal environmental regulation in these regions and the lack of press and public scrutiny, however, the oil companies have little economic incentive to do so. Second, oil field development in Amazonia has been accomplished by the oil companies constructing access roads into the rain forest interior. These roads have facilitated the colonization of many square miles of heretofore virgin rain forest. This colonization by settlers leads to slash-and-burn clearance of vast tracts of rain forest that otherwise would be inaccessible to these indigent farmers. When the oil companies leave, the settlers stay; thus such damage is irreversible. In many cases the construction of these roads is unessential. Labor and materials could be airlifted or transported by water.

But the oil companies have little economic incentive to seek more ecologically sensitive alternatives. Once again this behavior abroad contrasts dramatically with the behavior of these corporate behemoths within the

United States and Europe. For example, the oil drilling undertaken by firms off the California coast is subjected—by the firms themselves—to very careful screening for even the slightest environmental damage. As with Merck, these oil companies' concern for their reputations does not appear to enforce implicit contracts with residents and other stakeholders involved in offshore operations. This is no doubt due to a certain parochialism on the part of U.S. stakeholders, and to a general lack of information disclosure and flow between domestic and international operations. This anecdotal evidence supports Donaldson's critique of Gauthier in an international context: the broad power discrepancy between nations renders the likelihood of any natural emergence of morals by agreement seem vanishingly small. If morality is to function as a contractual enforcement mechanism transnationally, it will clearly not arise naturally as a *reputation-effect-type* mechanism.

Toward a Universal Ethic

In an international context, given the shortcomings of explicit and implicit enforcement mechanisms, the need for *ethics* as an enforcement mechanism would seem paramount. What was true for domestic business transacting, as discussed in earlier chapters, seems *doubly* true for transnational contracting, particularly in the case of TNCs operating in developing countries.

But applying traditional ethical precepts in an international context adds new challenges. The traditional theories of justice and human rights upon which practically all post-Enlightenment ethical theories are based exhibit, many would argue, a distinct Western flavor. What we in the West call bribery may be morally wrong (not to mention illegal) here, but is it wrong in eastern Asia where business has been conducted for centuries with a tradition of "gift giving" to cement contractual relations? Western ethics tends to be rule or code based, whereas the Confucian tradition prevalent in much of Asia is much more subjective, being concerned with relationships and harmony.

Albeit fascinating, these issues of cultural and moral relativism are clearly complex and cannot be adequately addressed here. Suffice it to say that the shortcomings of post-Enlightenment ethical theory, discussed in chapter 4, are magnified when these models are applied across national and cultural borders. This chapter has made clear the need for international ethics as a means of implicit contractual enforcement in business. But what is needed is a more universal ethic than that supplied by Kant, Mill, Rawls, and other post-Enlightenment theorists—an ethic with less Western bias, based less on rules and rights.

There is just such an ethic, and it was enumerated over two thousand years ago by a philosopher whose cultural milieu straddled the origins of both Eastern and Western tradition.[22] The philosopher was Aristotle, and the remainder of this book is devoted to applying recent interpretations of his philosophy to the context of financial ethics. This will involve an assault on the very core of the finance paradigm, that is, its concept of rationality. By re-defining rational behavior, we will now move beyond the finance paradigm.

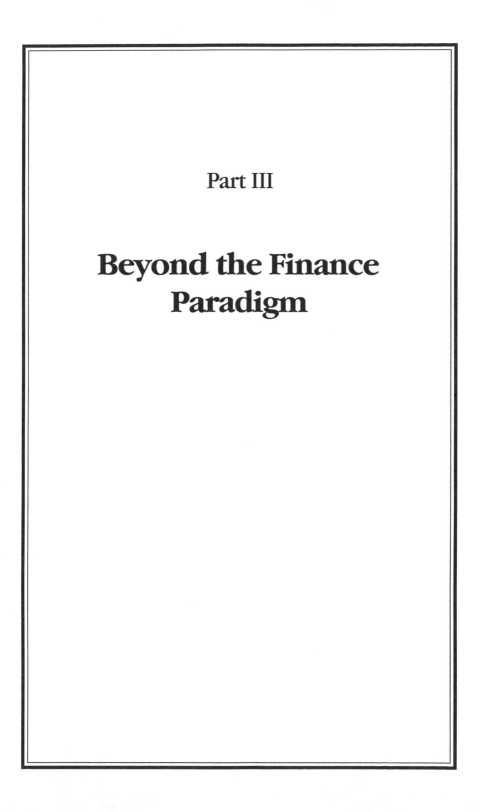

Part III

Beyond the Finance Paradigm

7

Which Rationality?

It can be argued that the presence of what are in a slightly old-fashioned terminology called virtues in fact plays a significant role in the operation of the economic system. . . . The process of exchange requires or at least is greatly facilitated by the presence of several of these virtues (not only truth, but also trust, loyalty, and justice) in future dealings.

— Kenneth Arrow

In his widely acclaimed book *The Structure of Scientific Revolutions,* Thomas Kuhn describes the evolution of the sciences as "a succession of tradition-bound periods punctuated by non-cumulative breaks"; he labels these breaks *paradigm shifts.*[1] Kuhn recognizes that the evolution of knowledge is not uniform over time; it tends rather to go in fits and starts. There may be long periods in which nothing more is achieved than merely fine-tuning of extant conceptual rubrics. Then suddenly, as if it were out of the blue, a radical new idea appears that recasts and redirects the entire discipline—a paradigm shift.

Within the last two decades, both financial economics and business ethics have experienced paradigm shifts. The ramifications of these shifts are yet to be determined, but the evolutionary direction of both disciplines has been, and is being, radically altered by the introduction of these new ideas. As academic disciplines, financial economics and business ethics are rarely viewed as having much, if anything, in common. What will be revealed in this chapter, however, is that these two apparently unrelated paradigm shifts in fact share certain tenets. The shift under way in business ethics, which finds its roots in moral philosophy, has a great deal of light to shed on recent developments in financial economics. So what are these shifts and how are they related?

Finance began to experience its paradigm shift when it formally recognized, in the guise of agency theory, the conflicts inherent in the separation of ownership and control. These conflicts stem from the uneven distribution of information between principal and agent, and in the inability of principals to costlessly monitor and control the actions of agents. As discussed in part I, prior to these developments, finance was firmly anchored by the rigid assumptions of perfect-and-frictionless capital markets. These assumptions were originally adopted for reasons of mathematical expedience, but have been subsequently relaxed in an attempt to have theory more closely mirror reality. Methodologically, this trend is reflected in the growing use of game theory in preference to other less behaviorally oriented mathematical techniques. As Eric Rasmusen notes, "During the 1980s, game theory has become dramatically more important to mainstream economics. Indeed, it seems to be swallowing up microeconomics."[2] This paradigm shift is further evidenced by the increasing willingness among financial theorists to draw on other disciplines, such as psychology, when explaining *a priori* anomalous behavior in financial contracting.[3] *In toto*, these trends reflect a broadened and more humanistic conceptual stance. Rather than an aberration, therefore, this book's critique of the finance paradigm may be viewed as a logical consequence of the discipline's recent conceptual shift.

In essence, therefore, the advent of agency theory has led finance away from a conception of itself as strictly a descriptive and technical discipline. Agency theory, as the name implies, focuses on the 'agent,' a human being. Thus, finance is increasingly recognizing itself as a 'social' science in which human behavior and motivation are central. The milieu in which these agents operate, namely the firm, is no longer viewed as a black box but rather as a "contractual nexus"; hence the importance of contractual enforcement mechanisms. In essence, therefore, the paradigm shift in finance is a "humanizing" one, away from the technical and toward the behavioral.

This behavioral shift has forced financial economists to model human interaction, hence the increasing use of game theory as a methodology in theoretical finance. As discussed earlier, the finance paradigm conjures human behavior with reference to a very narrow and rigid rationality construct. But what the history of moral philosophy makes clear is that the concept of rationality can be defined in several different ways. The Aristotelian concept of "practical rationality," for example, includes the pursuit of moral excellence as integral to the very notion of rationality itself. D.S. Hutchinson summarizes the Aristotelian approach to rationality thus: "We can discover what the standards are for human conduct by discovering what it is reasonable to do."[4] Similarly, Alasdair MacIntyre, in his seminal work on virtue ethics, challenges the very core of the finance paradigm's concept of rationality as "natural" by arguing that there is no absolute rationality; "rationality itself, whether theoretical or practical, is a concept with a history: indeed, since there are a diversity of traditions of enquiry, with histories, there are . . . rationalities rather than rationality."[5] That which is deemed rational, according to MacIntyre, is entirely dependent upon cultural tradition.

> It is an illusion to suppose that there is some neutral standing ground, some locus for rationality as such, which can afford rational resources sufficient for enquiry independent of all traditions. Those who have maintained otherwise either have covertly been adopting the standpoint of a tradition and deceiving themselves

and perhaps others into supposing that theirs was just such a neutral standing ground or else have simply been in error.[6]

But a recognition of the relativistic nature of rationality need not necessarily invalidate the finance paradigm's narrow rationality rubric. Specifically, the paradigm can emerge unscathed if two conditions *both* hold true. First, the rationality premise of the finance paradigm must mathematically reflect or at least approximate observed behavior. Second, this rationality premise must make no normative claim on behavior; that is, there is no implicit normative agenda within the finance paradigm, and "is" is not taken by anyone as implying "ought."

A defense requires that both these conditions hold because if the second does not hold then the first may hold simply by inference: if finance *does* possess a normative agenda and so *does* influence behavior it will sculpt behavior rather than simply reflect independently motivated behavior. But the evidence to be reviewed in this chapter implies that neither condition holds: finance's rationality is unjustified on both normative and positive grounds. For example, Amartya Sen makes the following comment:

> While this view of economics is quite widely held [i.e., the view of rationality as atomistic and opportunistic wealth maximization] . . . there is nevertheless something quite extraordinary in the fact that economics has in fact evolved in this way, characterizing human motivation in such spectacularly narrow terms. One reason why this is extraordinary is that economics is supposed to be concerned with real people. It is hard to believe that real people could be completely unaffected by the reach of the self-examination induced by the Socratic question, 'How should one live?'[7]

Similarly, C. R. Plott notes that "the weakest forms of the classical preference hypothesis [i.e., wealth maximization] are systematically at odds with the facts."[8] H. A. Simon suggests that "we stop debating whether a theory of substantive rationality and the assumptions of utility maximization provide a sufficient base for explaining and predicting economic behavior. The evidence is overwhelming that they do not."[9] Several studies have observed that conceptions of *fairness* often eclipse opportunism in sculpting behavior of agents in economic situations. Laboratory experiments indicate that strategies based on fair distribution, or tit-for-tat, tend to be more popular—and often more successful—than outright opportunism.[10] In his book *The Winner's Curse: Paradoxes and Anomalies of Economic Life*, Richard Thaler has amassed a disquieting array of behavioral "anomalies" and concludes that "assumptions aside, the theory [of opportunism] is vulnerable just on the quality of the predictions." He notes:

> We can start to see the development of the new, improved
> version of economic theory. The new theory will retain the idea
> that agents try to do the best they can, but these individuals will
> also have the human strengths of kindness and cooperation,
> together with the limited human abilities to store and process
> information.[11]

Similarly, in concluding his book *On Ethics and Economics*, Sen makes a plea for this "new theory": "The wide use of the extremely narrow assumption of self-interested behavior has, I have tried to argue, seriously limited the scope of predictive economics, and made it difficult to pursue a number of important economic relationships that operate through behavioral versatility."[12]

In addition to the question of its descriptive accuracy, the finance paradigm can be challenged also in terms of its prescriptive desirability. As was established in part I, a normative evaluation of the finance paradigm, even from a strictly economic perspective, indicates that it is suboptimal in the sense that it levies a welfare cost on the economy (what Jensen and Meckling term the "residual loss"). The economic cost of agency is thus not merely a distributive cost. This is *not* a zero-sum game. Agency equilibria are inevitably second best: there is a deadweight loss. Furthermore, in equilibrium, this loss is borne by the irretrievably opportunistic agent (the Sirens' song again). Thus wealth maximization is ultimately self-defeating. Wealth is maximized neither for the individual agent, nor for the economy in aggregate.

Turning to a moral evaluation of the finance paradigm, several empirical studies find evidence that 'is' does indeed imply 'ought.' In an experiment involving 267 Prisoners' Dilemma–type games (similar to figure 2.1 in chapter 2), economics students defected 60 percent of the time, while noneconomists defected only 30 percent of the time. Also, when compared to students in different disciplines, economics students were found to be less honest in hypothetical situations, and both economics students *and professors* were found to be less likely to donate to charity.[13] "People change their behavior when confronted with assumptions about how other people behave," observes Norman Bowie.[14] In *Challenging the Egoistic Paradigm*, he concludes that "looking out for oneself is a natural, powerful motive that needs little, if any, social reinforcement. . . . Altruistic motives, even if they too are natural, are not as powerful: they need to be socially reinforced and nurtured."[15] In a broader context, the susceptibility and suggestibility of human behavior was made very clear in the famous laboratory experiments conducted by Stanley Milgram:

> Ordinary people, simply doing their jobs, and without any partic-
> ular hostility on their part, can become agents in a terrible de-
> structive process. . . . Even when the destructive effects of their
> work become patently clear, and they are asked to carry out ac-

tions incompatible with fundamental standards of morality, relatively few people have the resources needed to resist authority.[16]

From his experience as a professor of business ethics, Bowie supplies anecdotal evidence that exposure to the finance paradigm and related rubrics modifies behavior: "They [business school students] believe that they will have to be unethical to keep their jobs. They believe that everyone else will put their [own] interests first." But he goes on to note that "the evidence here is not merely anecdotal."[17] Two other researchers find solid empirical evidence that, compared to the aggregate student body, "economics graduate students are more inclined to behave in a self-interested fashion."[18] Similarly, Gregory Dees argues that the value systems of business theory influence those of business practice. He observes that "how concepts are introduced in an academic setting can have a significant influence on their use later on." While commenting on the value system underlying business theory, Ronald Duska notes that "as it gets accepted as a legitimating reason for certain behavior in our form of life, it becomes subtly self-fulfilling."[19]

Thus, the finance paradigm presents itself as morally neutral, but fails to recognize that its narrow and rigid invocation of self-interest has *moral* implications. Alasdair MacIntyre makes a similar point:

> Managers themselves and most writers about management conceive of themselves as morally neutral characters whose skills enable them to devise the most efficient means of achieving whatever end is proposed. Whether a given manager is effective or not is in the dominant view a quite different question from that of the morality of the ends which his effectiveness serves or fails to serve. Nonetheless there are strong grounds for rejecting the claim that effectiveness is a morally neutral value.[20]

Models developed within the finance paradigm, therefore, do not merely endeavor to explain observed phenomena. To a significant degree they *create* those phenomena. When, in their seminal article, Jensen and Meckling propose that managers' thirst for perquisites at the expense of firm value is as inevitable as "a world in which iron ore is a scarce commodity," they make a value judgment.[21] Specifically, they accept increased perquisite consumption by managers who no longer bear the full cost of that consumption as the inevitable and therefore by inference the "right" mode of behavior. They make a value judgment concerning the behavioral prerogatives of management. They do not attempt merely to describe reality, but to (however inadvertently) *shape* it. More generally, when finance adopts as its premise that "the objective of the firm is to maximize shareholder wealth," it implies that this is the 'right' objective. It indoctrinates its audience with a certain moral philosophy.

By assuming away other motivations and thus elevating wealth maximization to the status of a necessary law of nature, finance may be sanctioning behavior that society at large regards as immoral. In the corporate milieu, by *assuming* unbridled self-interest, finance *promotes* unbridled self-interest. Even if empirical evidence were to overwhelmingly support wealth maximization as the dominant motivation among contemporary economic agents (which it does not), finance's normative dimension would still obligate it morally to consider alternatives.

An Ethic of Ideals

The second paradigm shift alluded to earlier is one under way in business ethics theory. This shift can be viewed also as a "humanizing" one. Indeed, in comparing the old and new approaches to business ethics, Sherwin Klein labels the new approach "agent-based" because of its focus on the individual agent, rather than on the contractual situation. He labels the old or "traditional" approach "action-based."[22] This traditional approach was that outlined in chapter 4, and the shortcomings of the approach were outlined there also: in essence it assumed some neutral standing ground, some absolute rationality, from which general rights and principles could be derived and applied.

The *new* approach recognizes that there is no neutral standing ground, that ethics essentially entails context-specific judgment calls. Rather than focusing on rules and principles, therefore, the new approach focuses on the aspirations and ideals of the agent. This new approach is founded on *virtue-ethics* theory.

To highlight the difference between the virtue-based approach to ethics versus the traditional approach, consider the general questions posed by business ethics: How should I, as a business professional, approach ethical issues? When faced with an ethically charged decision, how do I identify ethical alternatives and choose appropriate actions?

The traditional answer to these questions would have the individual step out of the specific situation and make a decision on the basis of some universal deontological or teleological principle. The individual adopts some "neutral standing ground" from which to judge the situation. As Jack Sammons puts it, "we must stand apart from our professional roles in personal moral judgment of them."[23]

A financial accountant, for example, may be able to enhance her company's reported results of operations by crafting a sale-leaseback arrangement whereby some of the company's assets are sold, a gain is recorded, all the appropriate accounting pronouncements are adhered to, and the company still has use of its assets. The intent of the transaction was never to rid the company of unwanted assets, but rather to record a gain and thus possibly avoid breaching debt-covenant agreements or circumvent regulatory requirements.

To conclude that this example of "creative accounting" is unethical, traditional approaches of examining the accountant's actions would have her step out of her accounting role and don the hat of a Kantian (e.g., "does this action violate the rights of users of the financial statements to fairly presented financial information?) or of a utilitarian (e.g., "does this action maximize the welfare of *all* stakeholders?"). So, in essence, the accountant would view the ethical evaluation of her decision as fundamentally separate from the economic merits of the decision; two different and incommensurable rationality criteria are being used.

In this traditional approach, therefore, a professional—whether accountant or otherwise—adopts a type of moral schizophrenia in which being a good professional in the sense of being an *effective* accountant becomes separable from being a good professional in the sense of being an *ethical* accountant. Thus, given this approach, an accountant could be a "good" accountant, in the sense of being very efficient and effective, yet at the same time not be a "good" accountant, in the sense of being ethical. Similarly, statements such as "You 'ought' to be an ethical accountant!" become problematic. Clearly, given the aforementioned separation of ethics and efficiency, such a command of "ought" cannot be premised on the idea that being an ethical accountant will in some way engender greater efficiency. If one were to challenge this command with the question, "Why 'ought' I to be an ethical accountant?," the traditional approach to professional ethics would have trouble providing a simple answer beyond "You ought to be an ethical accountant because being ethical is what accountants ought to be," which clearly does not really answer the original question.

Indeed, a new and growing school of moral philosophy argues that this is the central flaw of the traditional approach to ethics: it fails to answer the fundamental question, "Why should I be ethical?" In essence, the traditional approach uses a language that is rooted in religious dogma—with concepts of duty, obligation, absolute right and wrong—but does not premise its philosophy on religion: clearly, from within a religious perspective answering the question, "Why ought I to be ethical?" is simple: "I ought to be ethical because that is God's will." But from a secular perspective, within the traditional approach, such an answer is not appropriate.

The traditional approach to business ethics, therefore, encompassing Kantianism, utilitarianism, and variations thereof, fails to provide logical grounds for ethics in business.

Within the last decade, however, a new philosophical approach to ethics has been gaining popularity. This approach is based on Aristotelian moral philosophy and generally comes under the heading of *virtue-ethics theory*. Virtue ethics focuses on the character and motivations of the agent, and on the agent's ability to pursue excellence through virtuous acts. In essence, Aristotle viewed a virtue as some desirable character trait, such as courage, that lies between two extremes, such as rashness and cowardice: hence the

Aristotelian concept of the "mean," and of moderation in all things—a very different concept from that of ethics as adherence to a set of rules, which is so common in contemporary corporate codes of conduct. Before discussing further the application of virtue ethics to finance, a brief summary of this new approach will help those readers not already familiar with the theory.

Virtue Ethics: An Overview

Virtue-ethics theory can be thought of as exhibiting four basic attributes. First is a strong emphasis on the importance of certain generally accepted *virtues* of character such as honesty, perseverance, consistency, and fairness. Second, a strong emphasis is placed on the existence of an active *community* that nurtures these virtues. Third, virtue-ethics theory makes clear that in the moral life one cannot rely merely on rules or guidelines. In addition, an ability to exercise *sound moral judgment* is requisite. Finally, the successful identification and emulation of moral *exemplars* or role models is essential for the dissemination of morality within the aforementioned nurturing community.

The remainder of this section will view virtue-ethics theory from these four perspectives: the role of the virtues, the role of community, the role of moral judgment, and the role of exemplars.

Role of the Virtues

An essential feature of rationality within virtue ethics is that, rather than focusing on the material goals of the agent, it focuses on the character and motivations of the agent, and on the agent's ability to pursue a certain very particular type of excellence. A characteristic of this excellence is that its pursuit necessitates adherence to certain virtues or traits of character. These virtues entail the exercise of sound judgment. As Julia Annas observes, "Virtue lies in the reasons for which one acts rather than in the type of action one performs."[25] In the context of business, Kenneth Goodpaster lists five key virtues: (1) *Prudence*—neither too short-term nor too long-term in time horizon; (2) *Temperance*—neither too narrowly materialistic (want-driven) nor too broadly dispassionate (idea-driven); (3) *Courage*—neither reckless nor too risk-averse; (4) *Justice*—neither too anarchic regarding law nor too compliant; (5) *Loyalty*—neither too shareholder-driven (private sector thinking) nor too driven by other stakeholders (public sector thinking).[26]

Clearly, to achieve excellence through the exercise of these virtues of character requires a sense of moderation. Managers who are said to be "weathering the storm" or "sticking to their guns" may well be exercising the virtue of courage. But so might a manager who "knows when to call it quits." It is the reason or judgment underlying the action that will determine whether the agent is truly courageous. Thus, a virtue is not a maximum or a minimum. Unlike rationality in the finance paradigm, practical rationality concerns moderation and balance.

The crucial difference, therefore, between traditional approaches to business ethics and the approach adopted in virtue-ethics theory is that the latter focuses on the character and motivations of the agent, and on the agent's ability to pursue excellence through virtuous acts. As mentioned earlier, Klein succinctly distinguishes between the traditional approach to business ethics and the new virtue-ethics approach by labeling them as "action-based" and "agent-based" respectively. The former tends to focus on moral rules that can be generally applied to contractual situations (e.g., Kantianism and utilitarianism), whereas virtue ethics concerns the aspirations of the agent, and the agent's ability to exercise the moral "virtues." A recent definition of virtue is supplied by MacIntyre: "A virtue is an acquired human quality the possession and exercise of which tends to enable us to achieve those goods which are internal."[27] He distinguishes between internal and external goods as follows:

> It is characteristic of what I have called external goods that when achieved they are always some individual's property or possession. Moreover characteristically they are such that the more someone has of them, the less there is for other people. . . . External goods are therefore characteristically objects of competition in which there must be losers as well as winners. *Internal* goods are indeed the outcome of competition to excel, but it is characteristic of them that their achievement is a good for the whole community who participate in the practice.[28]

The pursuit of external goods, therefore, is no longer recognized as the ultimate end of human endeavor, but rather as a means to the achievement of excellence. Martha Nussbaum defines this excellence as "the end of all desires, the final reason why we do whatever we do; and it is thus inclusive of everything that has intrinsic worth [i.e., internal goods], lacking in nothing that would make a life more valuable or more complete."[29]

A central feature of virtue ethics is its concept of professional development as fundamentally a moral process; MacIntyre says, "one cannot be practically rational without being just—or indeed without the other central virtues."[30] Thus, rather than being some peripheral appendage or constraint on a substance-based professionalism concept, this approach places morality at center stage.

Role of Community

Virtue-ethics theory also has implications for the role of the *firm*. For the virtues to flourish, a conducive infrastructure is required; "one cannot think for oneself if one thinks entirely by oneself . . . it is only by participation in a rational practice-based community that one becomes rational."[31] Thus, rationality in virtue ethics is a shared rationality with a shared conception of what is ultimately desirable in all human endeavor. This shared conception must be supported by, and indeed be the *raison d'être* of, the organizations and institutions that control and direct human activity. This infrastructure is an aspect of what was known in the city-states of ancient

Greece as the *polis*: "the form of social order whose shared mode of life already expresses the collective answer or answers of its citizens to the question 'What is the best mode of life for human beings?'"[32] Such an infrastructure is essential for virtue ethics. Says MacIntyre,

> Aristotle is articulating at the level of theoretical enquiry a thought inherited from the poets when he argues in Book I of the *Politics* (1252b28–1253a39) that a human being separated from the *polis* is thereby deprived of some of the essential attributes of a human being. . . . A human being stands to the *polis* as a part to its whole . . . for the *polis* is human community perfected and completed by achieving its *telos*.[33]

The virtue-ethics approach thus casts the firm in a role that is far more active and intrusive than merely a contractual nexus or wealth-creating machine.[34] The firm becomes a nurturing community, a *polis*. Robert Solomon points out, "Corporations are real communities, neither ideal nor idealized, and therefore the perfect place to start understanding the nature of the virtues." He emphasizes the link between virtue ethics and this expanded role of the firm as a nurturing community: "It [virtue-ethics] is an Aristotelian ethics precisely because it is membership in a community, a community with collective goals and a stated mission—to produce quality goods and/or services and to make a profit for the stockholders."[35] Within the rubric of virtue-ethics theory, therefore, the goals and aspirations of the individual are nurtured and directed by the institutions of which that individual forms a part.

Role of Moral Judgment

Another significant aspect of virtue ethics is its rejection of a rule-based approach to moral education. Acting ethically in a given situation is less a function of rule adherence and more a function of exercising sound moral judgment. MacIntyre makes this very clear:

> What can never be done is to reduce what has to be learned in order to excel at such a type of activity to the application of rules. There will of course at any particular stage in the historical development of such a form of activity be a stock of maxims which are used to characterize what is taken at that stage to be the best practice so far. But knowing how to apply these maxims is itself a capacity which cannot be specified by further rules, and the greatest achievements in each area at each stage always exhibit a freedom to violate the present established maxims, so that achievement proceeds both by rule-keeping and by rule-breaking. And there are never any rules to prescribe when it is the one rather than the other that we must do if we are to pursue excellence.[36]

This does not mean that, say, financial accountants should ignore accounting standards or codes of conduct, but rather that these should be viewed—not as the entire accounting ethic—but as the foundation from which to pursue professional excellence in accounting. In addition to being nurtured by the firm or professional organizations as a *polis* (i.e., a community), this pursuit of professional excellence is guided by the example of *exemplars*.

In a similar vein, in his recent article "Good Works," Michael Pritchard concludes that "beyond discussing codes of ethics, principles of right and wrong, dilemmas . . . and moral disaster stories, we need stories of a different sort—*stories of good professionals whose lives might inspire emulation.*"[37] The critical importance of moral exemplars is further emphasized by cognitive science in its invocation of "exemplar theory." Goldman summarizes the theory as follows:

> Moral theorists often assume that people's usage of moral terms is underpinned by some sort of rules or principles they learn to associate with those terms: rules governing honesty, for example, or fairness. The exemplar theory suggests, however, that what moral learning consists in may not be (primarily) the learning of rules but the acquisition of pertinent exemplars or examples. This would accord with the observable fact that people, especially children, have an easier time assimilating the import of parables, myths, and fables than abstract principles. *A morally suitable role model may be didactically more effective than a set of behavioral maxims.*[38]

In sum, virtue-ethics theory provokes a complete reevaluation of the economic concept of substantive rationality. From a virtue-ethics perspective, the moral impoverishment of the finance paradigm is reflected in both its failure to recognize the virtues, and in its substitution of the pursuit of external goods for the pursuit of internal goods as the agent's ultimate end.[39]

But, albeit logically coherent, is a virtue-ethics-based rationality concept methodologically applicable to finance? How would the theory and method of financial economics appear in this conceptual light? The remainder of this book addresses these questions by identifying three broad implications of modifying finance's substantive rationality construct along the lines suggested by virtue ethics. First, from a conceptual standpoint, finance would be forced to emerge from behind its veil of scientific detachment and to accept a less quantitative and more qualitative approach to modeling human behavior. Second, from a specifically methodological standpoint, the mere contemplation of the possibility of the existence of one or more virtuous agents will have a significant impact on financial market equilibria. Third, as regards the theory of the firm, virtue ethics casts the firm in a role that is more active and morally intrusive than previously contemplated: the firm, in essence, moves from a "contractual nexus" to a "nurturing community."

What should be clear from our discussion so far is that a reconciliation of this 'virtue-based' paradigm shift with the humanizing shift in finance can never be achieved *within* the existing finance paradigm. This paradigm must be extended into an entirely new universe of human behavior: finance must acquire what Amitai Etzioni terms a "moral dimension."[40] But what exactly is the nature of this moral universe, and what metaphysical concept can be invoked that will encompass both the moral universe of virtue ethics, and the material universe of finance?

Robert M. Pirsig has supplied just such a metaphysic, and it is to this that I now turn. Pirsig's attempt to develop a worldview that succinctly encompasses our entire body of knowledge is an ambitious undertaking, perhaps too ambitious. But despite its undoubted shortcomings, Pirsig's approach does provide a simple conceptual framework by which to compare the finance and virtue-ethics paradigms.

Metaphysics of Quality

In his latest book, *Lila: An Enquiry into Morals*, Pirsig continues his fascinating investigation into the nature of "quality," which was begun in his earlier book *Zen and the Art of Motorcycle Maintenance*.[41] To facilitate an understanding of quality as fundamentally a moral concept, Pirsig develops what he calls a "Metaphysics of Quality." In attempting to explain this concept he recounts the following experience.

He and two associates were walking down a dirt road on a Native American reservation with the local tribal chief. A rather scruffy stray dog appeared on the road and trotted along amiably in front of them.

"What kind of a dog is that?" asked one of Pirsig's associates.

After some thought the chief replied, "That's a *good* dog."

As Pirsig notes, the incongruity of the chief's answer to those of us raised in contemporary Western culture stems from a difference in priority. Western culture is *substance* based, and therefore the questioner was enquiring as to the substance of the dog, that is, its breed. Native American culture is *value* based, and therefore the chief naturally assumed that the question related to the moral worth of the dog, that is, whether it was good or bad. In explaining the difference between this substance-based versus value-based approach, Pirsig essentially goes back to square one. Along with other "postmodernists," such as Hannah Arendt, Foucault, and MacIntyre, he shuns the conventions of modern academe, in which subject areas tend to be compartmentalized, and proceeds to build an entirely holistic worldview that encompasses the domain of both the natural sciences and the liberal arts. In a sense, therefore, he reestablishes moral philosophy as the "all-embracing" discipline; a position it held in the classical world view of Plato and Aristotle. In this view, morality permeates *everything*. Interestingly, in his critique of higher education, *Three Rival Versions of Moral Enquiry*, MacIntyre makes a similar plea for the reinstatement of morality at center stage when he bemoans "the barrenness of a [modern] university which had deprived itself of substantive moral enquiry."[42]

In the tradition of much classical Eastern and Western philosophy, Pirsig identifies two distinct and coexistent metaphysical universes, a *Universe of Substance* and a *Universe of Value*, each vying for prominence as a culture's conceptual foundation.

In his Metaphysics of Quality, Pirsig takes the bold step of implying that the aforementioned Native American chief is correct. "Value" in the sense of moral worth, rather than physical substance, is the fundamental reality. Substance is simply a manifestation of value; "substance is a stable pattern of inorganic values."[43] Within this conceptual framework, Pirsig sees the physical processes of evolution as a substantive manifestation of a continual quest to attain a higher level of value. "Quality" is achieved through a progression to heightened levels of value. Thus, the Metaphysics of Quality reflects virtue ethics by placing morality in a very central role.

Evolution is a perpetual quest for this ethereal, absolute moral Quality. Pirsig identifies five stages of evolution, each representing a higher level of Quality: chaotic, inorganic, biological, social, and intellectual.[44] He subdivides quality into Dynamic Quality and Static Quality. "Not subject and object but Static and Dynamic is the basic division of reality. . . . Dynamic Quality is the preintellectual cutting edge of reality, the source of all things, completely simple and always new."[45]

An interesting similarity can be observed between Pirsig's Dynamic Quality and the recent reconceptualization of the market mechanism as a nondeterministic "creative process."[46] This new approach is often identified as "radical subjectivism."

> The basic objection to neoclassical general equilibrium theory is that it embodies assumptions about the knowability of the future that are entirely unfounded, not only in their most extreme variant, the assumption of perfect knowledge, but also in their softer varieties, such as assumptions about rational expectations or Bayesian adaptive rationality.[47]

The authors conclude that "a perceptual vision of the market as a *creative process* offers more insight and understanding than the alternative visions that elicit interpretations of the market as . . . an *allocative process*."[48] Jack Wiseman summarizes this new position similarly: "The essence of the radical subjectivist position is that the future is not simply "unknown," but is "nonexistent" or "indeterminate" at the point of decision."[49] This ties in with

Thomas Kuhn's notion of the evolution of the sciences, where he sees such evolution as a nondeterministic and infinite process in which there is no absolute truth.[50]

Despite this similarity, however, the activity of an agent given radical subjectivism, and the activity of an agent exhibiting Dynamic Quality in the Metaphysics of Quality, are not entirely compatible. The Metaphysics is deterministic whereas the former is not: "If the market is genuinely perceived as an open-ended, nondetermined evolutionary process in which the essential driving force is human choice, any insinuation, however subtle, of a "telos" toward which the process can be predicted to move must be inherently misleading."[51] But in the Metaphysics, as in virtue-ethics theory, there is just such a *telos*, namely Quality. Static Quality provides a value support and maintains the current level of evolution, while Dynamic Quality is the mechanism by which evolutionary change occurs:

> The cells dynamically invented animals to preserve and improve their situation [i.e., to heighten their Quality]. The animals dynamically invented societies, and societies dynamically invented intellectual knowledge for the same reasons. Therefore, to the question, "What is the purpose of all this intellectual knowledge?" the Metaphysics of Quality answers, "The fundamental purpose of knowledge is to Dynamically improve and preserve society."[52]

At the human level, the Metaphysics of Quality is to some extent a synthesis of Aristotelian moral philosophy and the psychological concept of a hierarchy of needs: from physiological needs (Biological Quality) through safety and esteem needs (Social Quality) to self-actualization needs (Intellectual Quality).[53] This Quality notion is similar to Aristotle's *eudaimonia*: the ultimate goal of human existence, attainable only through the exercise of the virtues. Aristotle makes clear that his 'quality' lies beyond, though is inclusive of, material well-being. "What then does the good for man turn out to be? Aristotle has cogent arguments against identifying that good with money. . . . He gives it the name of *eudaimonia*—as so often there is difficulty in translation: blessedness, happiness, prosperity."[54] Indeed, Pirsig's Metaphysics can be viewed as giving descriptive justification to Aristotle's normative moral philosophy. By placing Intellectual Quality atop the evolutionary ladder, Metaphysics of Quality concurs with Aristotle that the ultimate "end of human life is metaphysical contemplation of truth."[55]

Life is thus a purposeful and perpetual quest for Quality. Indeed, one of the pleasant aspects of the Metaphysics is that it supplies a purpose for life consistent with much of classical philosophy while simultaneously supporting a role for science as an attribute of Intellectual Quality. "The greatest benefit of this substitution of "value" for "causation" and "substance" is that it allows an integration of physical science with other areas of experience that have been traditionally considered outside the scope of scientific thought [e.g., ethics and art]."[56] As such, a value-based universe is a much friendlier place than a substance-based one.

> From the perspective of a subject-object science, the world is a completely purposeless, valueless place. There is no point in anything. Nothing is right and nothing is wrong. Everything just functions, like machinery. There is nothing morally wrong with being lazy, nothing morally wrong with lying, with theft, with suicide, with murder, with genocide. There is nothing morally wrong because there are no morals, just functions.[57]

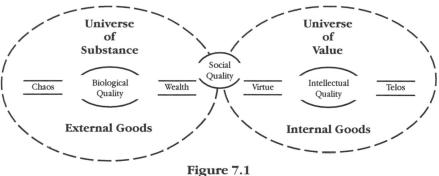

Figure 7.1
The evolution of quality.

Figure 7.1 is my rendition of the Metaphysics of Quality that incorporates also the Aristotelian notions of virtue and *telos*. It provides the foundation for the remainder of this chapter. Pirsig's Metaphysics is embellished here with the classical concept of virtue, and also with MacIntyre's distinction between internal and external goods. My invocation of virtue as the Dynamic-Quality bridge between Social Quality and Intellectual Quality is consistent with the conceptual equivalence of Quality and the Aristotelian concept of *eudaimonia*, which is roughly translated as 'happiness' or 'human flourishing.' Both Aristotle and Socrates believed that the latter could be achieved only through the exercise of the virtues.[58] Pirsig's Metaphysics concurs with Aristotle in that the exercise of the virtues requires an existing foundation of Static Biological Quality, and Static Social Quality. Thus, for example, wealth and social stability must exist before the higher levels of Quality can be attained through virtue. MacIntyre comments:

> We need, so Aristotle argues in the opening passages of Book VII of the *Politics*, to pursue the external goods of the body in order to engage in those activities in which the soul perfects itself. So the life of moral and political virtue exists for the sake of and must be subordinated to the life of contemplative enquiry.[59]

The concept of virtue is, like so many concepts in moral philosophy, elusive. Socrates lists four essential virtues: courage, moderation, justice, and piety (the interpretation of these words is, of course, dependent upon historical context). But one facet of virtue is clear: it is a concept that lies within Pirsig's Universe of Value and is thus concerned with the pursuit of internal goods.

Robert Frank, in *Passions within Reason,* emphasizes the intrinsic nature of internal goods; "satisfaction from doing the right thing must not be premised on the fact that material gains may follow; rather it must be *intrinsic* to the act itself."[60] As figure 7.1 illustrates, the evolutionary link between the static levels of Biological Quality and Social Quality is material wealth: an external good. Static and Dynamic Biological Quality lie entirely within the Universe of Substance, where Substance is taken as being synonymous with MacIntyre's "external goods." Examples of Static Biological Quality are the ecosystem and the perpetuation of physical life and health. Examples of Dynamic Biological Quality are the pursuit of food, shelter, and sex; all of which, in the human realm, are facilitated by material wealth.

The Universe of Substance also contains some Social Quality, namely the portion of Social Quality that is concerned with external goods. Power and celebrity are examples of this external Social Quality, both of which are clearly connected with wealth.

At the other end of the human-evolutionary spectrum, Intellectual Quality lies entirely within the Universe of Value, where Value is taken as being synonymous with "internal goods." Internal goods are by definition more ethereal than external goods and Intellectual Quality is correspondingly elusive. The Aristotelian concept of a "practice" provides an interesting analogy to the Metaphysics' Intellectual Quality. MacIntyre defines a practice as follows:

> any coherent and complex form of socially established cooperative human activity through which goods internal to that form of activity are realized in the course of trying to achieve those standards of excellence which are appropriate to, and partially definitive of, that form of activity, with the result that human powers to achieve excellence, and human conceptions of the ends and goods involved, are systematically extended.[61]

Thus, the scientific method is a form of Intellectual Quality, as is the pursuit of excellence through craftsmanship, sporting, or artistic pursuits, when not predicated on the attainment of external goods. The Universe of Value also contains some Social Quality: the social virtues. The social virtues are distinct from the classical "virtues" as defined above. When Allan Bloom in *The Closing of the American Mind* declares that "a virtue governs a passion," he is defining social virtue.[62] Examples of social virtues are etiquette, table manners, courtesy, and chivalry. They differ from classical virtue in that they are essentially behavioral constraints. But they are not entirely constraints on behavior: for example, chivalry clearly has a flavor of classical virtue in that it may imply the pursuit of some excellence. In a similar vein, MacIntyre considers honesty:

> It is a logically necessary condition for any group of beings to be recognized as a human society that they should possess a language. It is a necessary condition for a language to exist that there should be shared rules. . . . Thus, the recognition of a norm of truth telling and of a virtue of honesty seems written into the concept of a society.[63]

Indeed, it is this moral no-man's-land between the adherence to social virtues and the pursuit of Intellectual Quality through classical virtue that is the dynamic evolutionary force in the progression from Social Quality to Intellectual Quality. When virtues are observed for the purpose of maintaining or attaining social status (an external good), then we are in the realm of Social Quality. When virtues are observed for the purpose of pursuing "those goods which are internal to practices" then we are progressing from Social Quality into the realm of Intellectual Quality.

Within the Metaphysics of Quality human evolution is thus a progression from Biological Quality, through Social Quality, to Intellectual Quality. Each evolutionary stage exhibits both Static and Dynamic Quality attributes. Static Quality provides the support for Dynamic Quality and directs this energy to a higher-Quality evolutionary stage. In a behavioral context, Static Quality provides constraints on morally regressive types of Dynamic Quality and thus directs human behavior toward the *telos* of absolute Quality. An environment of pure Dynamic Quality would be highly unstable with no evolutionary direction in the Metaphysics.

Unlike physical evolution, the evolution of value in the Metaphysics of Quality is not necessarily chronological. Both Neanderthal humans and modern humans possess varying degrees of Biological, Social, and Intellectual Quality as do most mammals and primates. What has been chronologically dependent is the degree to which one or another stage predominates among humanity in aggregate. Thus, in the context of the Metaphysics, "civilization" can be defined as the aggregate triumph of Social Quality over Biological Quality; more specifically, the building of Social Quality on a foundation of Biological Quality. The latter definition emphasizes a fundamental principle of the Metaphysics of Quality, namely that higher levels of Quality are founded on, and require the existence of, the preceding levels. Thus, for Intellectual Quality to predominate, stable patterns of Biological Quality and Social Quality must come first.

Unlike physical evolution, the evolution of Quality is readily and rapidly reversible. The onset of the Dark Ages in Europe, for example, after the Social-Quality triumphs of ancient Egypt, Greece, and Rome, is an instance of such a reversal. In modern history, Pirsig cites the Victorian era—fueled by the Industrial Revolution—as a high point in the dominance of Social Quality. Pirsig notes, however, that individual Victorians—like individuals in ancient Greece—did not in aggregate accomplish the progression from Social to Intellectual Quality: from the pursuit of status to the pursuit of truth. In the case of ancient Greece, this is reflected in the execution of Socrates for "corrupting youth" by intellectually challenging the social norms of his day. In the case of the Victorian era, it is evidenced in the preoccupation with rigid Social Quality and nationalism that culminated in the genocide of the First World War.

In his *Theory of Moral Sentiments*, Adam Smith recognized the predominance of Social Quality in eighteenth-century Europe: "the wise and virtuous chiefly, a select, though, I am afraid, but a small party, who are the real and steady admirers of wisdom and virtue." As compared to the "great mob of mankind [who are] the admirers and worshippers . . . of wealth and greatness" (I.iii.3.2).[64] Thus, modern society seems little removed from that of Smith. We, in aggregate, still await the triumph of Intellectual Quality.

The Finance of Virtue

Although it is an alternative and morally inclusive notion of rationality, does this virtue-ethics approach have any direct bearing on the finance paradigm? What, if any, is the place of the finance paradigm in virtue ethics, and in the Metaphysics of Quality?

Within the Metaphysics, the firm could be defined as Dynamic Quality in the Universe of Substance. The firm is an evolutionary tool by which humans may progress from Biological Quality to Social Quality. As such, the firm provides a material support for human evolution to Intellectual Quality through virtue. In addition to being a source of Dynamic Quality, the firm—in the guise of a corporate culture—is an increasingly powerful source of Static Social Quality also. As was noted earlier, whatever ethnic, religious, or other cultural boundaries may have evolved through history, a global corporate culture is increasingly subsuming these traditional divisions. Thus, the firm has evolved into the transnational corporation and knows no geographic or cultural boundaries. But despite the contemporary firm's size, complexity, and cultural implications, its fundamental *raison d'être*—as a wealth-creating machine—clearly remains intact. "The social responsibility of business is to increase its profits." This may be constrained by what Milton Friedman calls "ethical custom" but, within the finance paradigm, the firm would be unintelligible if it were not an organization concerned solely with the creation of material wealth.[65] But if ethics is merely to be some constraint within the wealth-maximizing rubric, then its role in human affairs becomes very tenuous: we are back with the Confidence School of chapter 4. For ethics to exist at all within such a corporate culture, the colloquialism "good ethics is good business" *must* be believed. If it were not generally believed, then agents would find ethics an entirely unintelligible concept, and they would consequently view the practice of ethical behavior as entirely unjustified. This, sadly, in the interface of 'traditional' moral philosophy and financial economics, may be the current state of affairs.

Part I of this book established that today's business environment essentially comprises a complex web of interrelated interest groups, each distinguishable by its unique set of objectives and constraints. The successful enforcement of this multiplicity of interconnected implicit contracts provides the "invisible hand" that aligns the individual's pursuit of economic gain with that of society as a whole. In conjuring the invisible hand, however, Adam Smith clearly did not envisage economic agents operating in an ethical vacuum. Although he recognized the desire for personal economic gain as an essential ingredient for the efficient allocation of resources, he also observed that "no society can surely be flourishing and happy, of which the far greater part of the members are poor and miserable."[66] Smith's invisible hand, therefore, was both a moral and an economic concept. Rather than pure greed, Smith envisioned individuals driven by enlightened self-interest, where enlightenment took the form of not merely honesty and fair dealing in economic contracts but also empathy for those who, through no fault of their own, were unable to reap appropriate benefits from the free-market system: "economic . . . 'invisible hands' must be complemented by a moral 'invisible hand.'"[67]

But with the exception of Smith in *The Theory of Moral Sentiments*, the 'theory of the firm' has generally evolved within the Universe of Substance.[68] In this chapter I wish to extend the theory of the firm into the Universe of Value. This extension is similar to, though somewhat more radical than, what some social economists refer to as the "new evolutionary synthesis": a "unified view of the world which bridges the gap between the physical and the human sciences."[69] Invoking the firm within this unified context of Substance and Value overcomes the aforementioned impasse between financial economics and moral philosophy. In this broadened context, the firm has a moral, in addition to an economic, role. In addition, these roles need not necessarily conflict. Its economic purpose is to build a foundation of material wealth upon which agents can pursue their moral *telos*: the attainment of higher levels of Quality through the exercise of the moral virtues.

Viewing the finance paradigm within the evolutionary process of the Metaphysics of Quality reveals also the degree to which the role of economic agents is dependent upon historical context. Interestingly, the new view of the market as a "creative process" akin to Dynamic Quality appears to necessitate a similar perspective: "the essential characteristic of the radical subjectivist position that marks its critical departure from a neoclassical framework is, at the same time, the feature that it shares with the new evolutionary synthesis. . . . Its conception of 'a world in which time plays a vital role.'"[70] It is thus to an historical perspective that we must now turn.

A Brief History of the Finance Paradigm

In chapter 1, I quote F.Y. Edgeworth in his *Essay on the Application of Mathematics to the Moral Sciences* as declaring, in 1881, that "the first principle of Economics is that every agent is actuated only by self-interest."[71] Thus, what I have called here the "finance paradigm," characterizing agents as individualistic and opportunistic wealth maximizers, was clearly established by the end of the nineteenth century. It was not until the twentieth century, however, that this conceptualization of the human character became a dominant cultural paradigm. But the writings of Smith and Hume indicate that the finance paradigm has not always been isolated in a Universe of Substance. To see how this happened, indeed to see how the rise of the firm in the guise of a 'corporate culture' helped éclipse the Universe of Value, we need to take an historical perspective. This perspective provides a narrative foundation from which a new and broadened concept of economic rationality can be built.

A central tenet of virtue ethics is the importance of viewing morality in the historical context of a tradition of belief. Says MacIntyre, "Narrative history of a certain kind turns out to be the basic and essential genre for the characterization of human actions."[72] As a manifestation of human action, the firm is thus a phenomenon inseparable from its history. Beneath the many veils of scientific detachment that now surround it, the theory of the firm exists as narrative history.

The relevance of this narrative history in the current context is that it explains how the behavioral assumptions of financial economics, as reflected in the finance paradigm, have unwittingly inherited the role previously played by the behavioral prerogatives of moral philosophy, namely that of cultural progenitor. Hence, we hear the increasing talk of a global 'corporate culture.' A detailed account of the many and multifarious historical developments that led up to this epistemological power shift is beyond the scope of this book. Some narrative background is necessary, however, in order to give logical credence to the extension of the finance paradigm within virtue ethics. What follows is thus a skeletal account of the historical developments that facilitated the emergence of the contemporary finance paradigm as an epistemology.

The Demise of Virtue and the Birth of Corporate Culture

The inception of the Industrial Revolution in eighteenth-century northern Europe marked the emergence of the firm as a cultural force. During this period human life became circumscribed by the factory whistle and the living wage: "In the short span of years between the accession of George III and that of his son, William IV, the face of England changed. . . . Hamlets grew into populous towns; and chimney stacks rose to dwarf the ancient spires. . . . The changes were not merely "industrial," but also social and intellectual."[73]

The Industrial Revolution and the accompanying social and intellectual upheaval—what Polanyi calls "the Great Transformation"—saw the rise of a dynamic entrepreneurial class. T. Ashton says, "The eighteenth and early nineteenth centuries were rich in entrepreneurs, quick to devise new combinations of productive factors, eager to find new markets, receptive to new ideas. 'The age is running mad after innovation,' said Dr. Johnson; 'all the business of the world is to be done in a new way.'"[74]

These entrepreneurs saw wealth as the dynamic mechanism for the attainment of Social Quality. Wealth was a means to an end, and the end was the lifestyle and status of an aristocrat. Those who were not fortunate enough to attain this status through birthright, Ashton observes, could attain it in a couple of generations through wealth:

> Lawyers, soldiers, public servants, and men of humbler station than these found in manufacture possibilities of advancement far greater than those offered in their original calling. A barber, Richard Arkwright, became the wealthiest and most influential of the cotton spinners; an innkeeper, Peter Stubs, built up a highly esteemed concern in the file trade; a schoolmaster, Samuel Walker, became the leading figure in the north of England iron industry. "Every man," exclaimed the ebullient William Hutton in 1780, "has his fortune in his own hands."[75]

These individuals invariably used their wealth as a means to social advancement. Their sons and daughters were groomed for the role of aristocrats, not industrialists. To be engaged in the competitive activity of 'trade' was generally viewed as inferior to the leisurely and contemplative life of the 'gentleman.' It is noteworthy that aristocracy entailed a high level of education, and thus Intellectual Quality was recognized.

The role of the firm as a cultural force during this period was tempered by the preexisting rigid social structure, from rules of common law to rules of etiquette. In the vocabulary of the Metaphysics of Quality, the role of the firm was clear. The firm was Dynamic Quality, the freedom to move within the evolutionary stages of Value. The means was wealth and the end was Social Quality. The evolution to preeminence of Social Quality, which Pirsig notes reached its zenith in England with the Victorians and Edwardians, thus cast the accumulation of external goods as a means to an end. There was a work 'ethic.' Indeed, the idea behind 'self-interest,' as invoked originally in the eighteenth century by Hume and Smith, was not "greed"—as we might equate the two in the contemporary finance paradigm—but rather "prudent thrift" and 'consistent reasonable behavior.' The concept of self-interest was invoked by these intellectuals largely to counteract the disastrous quest for 'glory'. Since the Middle Ages, this quest had lead to many a bloodbath through wars premised on religious fervor or some other ostensibly altruistic and glorious motive. The economic concept of self-interest, therefore, was first conceived, not as a vice, but as a virtue.[76]

The rigid social structure that accompanied the Industrial Revolution as evidenced by the strict adherence to social virtues and etiquette may have provided a rigid moral code, but the ongoing debate among moral philosophers—who were attempting to fill the void left by the demise of classical virtue and organized religion—indicated that it was a moral code without sound and generally accepted intellectual foundations. The social rigidity of the Victorian era, which culminated in the First World War, was an example of what Hegel describes as the impoverishment of the master-serf relationship.

> The serf is indeed deformed, for his aims are so limited by the aims and commands of the Master, that he can do little more than assert himself in the barest possible way; but the Master, insofar as he sees himself as Master, cannot find in the Serf any response through which in turn he could find himself as a fully developed person. He has cut himself off from the kind of relationship in which self-consciousness grows through being an object of regard by others, through finding itself "mirrored" in others. Whereas the Serf can see in the Master something at least that he wants to become. But for both it is true that growth in self-consciousness is fatally limited by the Master-Serf relationship.[77]

This "fatal limitation" was given dramatic illustration in the two world wars of the early twentieth century. But the resulting demise of rigid social structures, which had justified wealth as a means to social status, left the purpose of economic activity unclear. Since social advancement was no longer tacitly accepted as the goal of human endeavor, agents could no longer justify the pursuit of wealth on grounds of social advancement.

From a moral perspective, therefore, the wealth created by the Industrial Revolution was a mixed blessing. It ensured a solid economic base for social advancement, but the accompanying physical and cultural upheaval led to a distortion of the concept of virtue. Classical virtue became merely the social virtues, an attribute of Static Social Quality. For example, "honor becomes nothing more than a badge of aristocratic status" and more generally "virtues are indeed now conceived of not, as in the Aristotelian scheme, as possessing a role and function distinct from and to be contrasted with, that of rules or laws, but rather as being just those dispositions necessary to produce obedience to the rules of morality."[78] So virtue is reduced to little more than mere etiquette and table manners. But why did the Industrial Revolution necessitate this?

The Industrial Revolution was a material revolution. But the generation of material wealth on such a scale necessitated a change in individual psyche: a break with tradition. Whatever traditional values might have held sway became subservient to the individual's capacity for production and consumption of external goods. Ashton comments, "The state came to play a less active, the individual and the voluntary association a more active, part in affairs. Ideas of innovation and progress undermined traditional sanctions: men began to look forward rather than backward, and their thoughts as to the nature and purpose of social life were transformed."[79]

The Aristotelian concepts of 'practices,' 'internal goods,' and, most critically, 'virtue' became lost in a society awash with material externality and change. Says MacIntyre, "Within that culture conceptions of the virtues become marginal and the tradition of the virtues remains central only in the lives of social groups whose existence is on the margins of the central culture."[80]

Virtue was not only redundant within this new "corporate" culture, it was actually antithetical to such a culture. For the Industrial Revolution to establish a corporate culture, albeit within a rigid social structure, necessitated the disappearance of classical virtue. A society based primarily on the acquisition of external goods inevitably conflicts with one based on the acquisition of internal goods through the practice of the virtues. MacIntyre continues, "The possession of the virtues may perfectly well hinder us in achieving external goods. . . . We should therefore expect that, if in a particular society the pursuit of external goods were to become dominant, the concept of the virtues might suffer first attrition and then perhaps something near total effacement."[81]

In addition to eradicating the traditional justification for classical virtue, the psychological and physical upheavals engendered by the Industrial Revolution destroyed the medieval infrastructure which gave credence to classical virtue.

> Moreover the kind of work done by the vast majority of the inhabitants of the modern world cannot be understood in terms of the nature of a practice with goods internal to itself, and for very good reason. One of the key moments in the creation of modernity occurs when production moves outside the household. So long as productive work occurs within the structure of households, it is easy and right to understand that work as part of the sustaining of the community of the household and of those wider forms of community which the household in turn sustains. As, to the extent that, work moves outside the household and is put to the service of impersonal capital, the realm of work tends to become separated from everything but the service of biological survival and the reproduction of the labor force, on the one hand, and that of institutionalized acquisitiveness, on the other.[82]

But there is evidence to indicate that virtue's fate was sealed *prior* to this period. Indeed, it is conceivable that virtue's demise, to the extent that it shifted focus to material self-advancement, facilitated this material revolution. The Industrial Revolution's inception is generally placed in the eighteenth century. But this revolution may just be the physical manifestation of an earlier revolution of ideas, namely the Reformation. MacIntyre says, "Following the age of Luther and Machiavelli, we should expect the rise of a kind of moral-cum-political theory in which the individual is the ultimate social unit."[83] The "theory" that emerged was moral philosophy's Enlightenment project, outlined in the previous chapter.

The Enlightenment philosophers, most notably Kant, Hume, and Smith, endeavored to free humankind from the fetters of tradition.[84] They invoked humans as essentially products of nature with no *telos* but rather motivated by passions and desires. The quasi-religious role of ethics, therefore, was that of a constraint on these passions and desires. This is most apparent in Kant where ethics becomes a "categorical imperative": a rule by which to constrain behavior. By rejecting the notion of a *telos,* whether defined as *eudaimonia*, the internal good, or Quality, this new moral philosophy left no room for virtue since classical virtue's sole justification was as a means through which the *telos* could be achieved.

In attempting to give some logical foundation for ethics in an increasingly 'rational' world, the Enlightenment philosophers endeavored to discern some absolute rationality, independent of time and place, by which to judge human actions. But this endeavor failed and, judging by the current lack of consensus among business ethicists and moral philosophers in general, continues to fail. MacIntyre observes,

> The project of providing a rational vindication of morality had decisively failed; and from henceforward the morality of our predecessor culture—and subsequently of our own—lacked any public, shared rationale of justification. In a world of secular rationality religion could no longer provide such a shared background and foundation for moral discourse and action; and the failure of philosophy to provide what religion could no longer furnish was an important cause of philosophy losing its central cultural role and becoming a marginal, narrowly academic subject.[85]

Thus, by rejecting virtue the Enlightenment philosophers may inadvertently have rung the death knoll of their own discipline. Equipped with a narrow conceptualization of Smith's "invisible hand" and Darwin's "natural selection," corporate culture was ready to receive the baton of cultural hegemony and become the dominant paradigm in human affairs. The dominant rationality becomes that of the market economy: the orderly and continual pursuit of external goods. Untrue to its name, therefore, the Enlightenment actually precipitated a dark age for morality. We increasingly view ourselves as economic agents constrained by morality, rather than as fundamentally moral agents who face economic constraints.

Despite the economic success of the firm during the eighteenth and nineteenth centuries, therefore, its cultural dominance was kept in check by a rigid social structure. This social structure maintained a tradition of virtue, albeit increasingly in the form of the "social virtues" as defined above. But with the disappearance of a *telos*, any justification or rationalization of classical virtue became tenuous. The remnants of classical virtue, namely the social virtues, were themselves justifiable only in terms of the existence of a rigid social hierarchy.

The cultural shock and subsequent disillusionment engendered by the First World War lead to an eventual dissipation of the Static Social Quality perfected by the Victorians. As this social structure crumbled, so did the final justification for virtue. The "emotivist" moral philosophy of the early twentieth century, promulgated by Moore, Keynes and other 'Bloomsburies,' reflected this rejection.[86] Under emotivism, absolute concepts of The Good, *eudaimonia*, or Pirsig's Metaphysics of Quality were utterly rejected: morality became entirely nebulous and humanity was left to follow its material whim. The wealth created by the firm in the previous two centuries had liberated humanity from the yoke of poverty, while the social and philosophical upheavals of the early twentieth century liberated individuals from a rigid social structure and any notion of social obligation or *telos*. MacIntyre says, "For liberal individualism a community is simply an arena in which individuals each pursue their own self-chosen conception of the good life, and political institutions exist to provide that degree of order which makes self-determined activity possible."[87]

In the context of the Metaphysics of Quality, the disappearance of virtue severed humanity's common link to the Universe of Value. Thus, the "good," in "the good life," became definable in terms of external goods only. Individuals adhering to the tenets of the finance paradigm's rationality in which a rational agent is simply one who pursues wealth in a consistent manner became the cultural force of the twentieth century. Disparate political ideologies that existed at the beginning of the century were steadily subsumed by the ideology of the market. Since the inception of the Industrial Revolution, the firm—as a wealth-creating machine—had never faltered, but with the disappearance of any common notion of internal goods—and therefore the loss of any concept of material wealth as a means to attaining internal goods—the survival of the firm necessitated wealth becoming an end in itself. Material "self-interest" had thus evolved from its original invocation as a type of instrumental rationality—as Smith and Hume's "prudent thrift"—to a premise for substantive rationality.

This shift is reflected in ever more omnipresent corporate advertising in the twentieth century, the essential purpose of which is to convince individuals that happiness and the acquisition of external goods are one and the same. Since the young or the uneducated are more likely to believe this deception, advertising tends to focus on these two groups.[88] To paraphrase Aristotle in the *Nicomachean Ethics (NE)*: "The young . . . may reason badly from lack of experience and, even if they reason well, may still be misled by untutored passions, but so also may those who, although no longer youthful, have never developed maturity of intelligence and character" (*NE* 1093a2–10).

Thus, a natural antipathy develops between the interests of the firm and intellectual maturity. In the context of the Metaphysics of Quality, the firm becomes a potentially nefarious organization that is endeavoring to regress humanity toward Biological Quality. This sinister aspect of contemporary corporate culture, resulting from the disappearance of a Social Quality foundation, is noted by Thomas Mulligan: "It is within the power of business to provide products which help make this world safer, healthier, more beautiful, and even smarter. It is also within the power of business not to do so, to opt instead to shovel the world full of junk, distraction, and harm."[89] As figure 7.1 illustrates, virtue is the sole evolutionary link between the Universes of Substance and Value. The disappearance of virtue effectively sealed off humanity from the Universe of Value. *Techne* (technical know-how) effectively eclipsed *phronesis* (Intellectual Quality, ethical know-how) as the foundation of rationality. The Evolution of Quality thus entered its current epoch of lateral drift.[90]

This lateral drift is readily apparent in the substantive rationality premise of the finance paradigm. As discussed in part I, wealth maximization has been adopted as a substantive rationality premise merely because of its mathematical convenience, with no sound philosophical justification. In evolving from the morally inclusive self-interest of Smith and Hume to the morally impoverished self-interest-*qua*-wealth-maximization of today, something has been lost, namely the link between economic *substance* and moral *value*. In the context of the Metaphysics of Quality, the preceding account of the demise of classical virtue implies that if humanity is to resume its evolutionary progression toward Quality it must rebuild the link between the Universe of Substance and that of Value. Classical virtue, as a meaningful concept in human affairs, must be rekindled from the ashes of the Enlightenment project and the Industrial Revolution. Fortunately, glowing embers have recently been supplied by the resurgence of virtue-based philosophies. These embers come in the form of an alternative substantive-rationality premise. This premise encompasses the modern logic of instrumental rationality as essentially consistent behavior *qua* the axioms of von Neumann and Morgenstern. In addition, however, it provides a sound philosophical foundation for substantive rationality; in one word, it provides a *telos*. This 'new' rationality is a modern interpretation of Aristotelian practical rationality. The implications of practical rationality for building a morally inclusive finance paradigm provide the focus of the next chapter.

8

Practical Rationality

In the economic sphere I suggest that utilitarian ideology, in the narrow market-oriented revealed preference form that in fact prevails, simply fails to grapple with the realities of the human situation. Then economics as a properly social, that is to say a human, science is betrayed through a built-in allegiance to the essentially unrestrained market economy. We witness a mutually reinforcing process of what has been called economism, of exaggeration of the domain and application of the economic (narrowly conceived) in theory and in practice. As to theory, note the process of cultural imperialism by which economists seek to explain, not only economic behavior, but also political behavior and family behavior, using the fundamental economic model of constrained, self-interested utility maximization.

—Tony Cramp

A chess championship recently took place in London between the reigning champion, Gary Kasparov, and a British challenger, Nigel Short. The winner of the tournament was to receive some $2 million in prize money. Imagine that one of the players, say Kasparov, is 'rational' in the economic sense as invoked by the finance paradigm, while the other player, Short, is 'rational' in the sense of Aristotelian 'practical rationality' as invoked by virtue-ethics theory. How, exactly, would these two individuals differ in their approach to the chess tournament?

Clearly the *actions* of the two agents may be indistinguishable. They would both be playing chess to the best of their ability, and would both be playing to win. Clearly, also, either player *could* win. The difference between the two players would likely rest entirely on their respective *motivations* for winning. Kasparov's motivation would derive from the *external goods* to be gained from playing chess, namely the $2 million prize money and perhaps also the fame and power that comes from being 'the champion.' Contrarily, Short's motivation would derive from the *internal goods* to be gained from playing chess. These goods are less easily identified in the vocabulary of modern English. They are, as MacIntyre notes, "those goods specific to chess . . . the achievement of a certain highly particular kind of analytical skill, strategic imagination and competitive intensity."[1]

In essence, Kasparov views chess as a means to an end, where the end is wealth, fame, and power. Short, on the other hand, views chess as an end in itself. To the practically rational Short, chess is a "practice"; indeed, an understanding of the concept of a practice is central to an understanding of practical rationality. Barry Schwartz isolates three central features of practices:

1. They establish their own standards of excellence and, indeed, are partly defined by those standards.
2. They are teleological, that is, goal directed. Each practice establishes a set of "goods" or ends that is internal or specific to it, and inextricably connected to engaging in the practice itself. In other words, to be engaging in the practice is to be pursuing these internal goods.
3. They are organic. In the course of engaging in the practice, people change it, systematically extending both their own powers to achieve its goods, and their conception of what its goods are.

What the rationality embedded in virtue ethics makes very clear is that excellence within a practice is *in and of itself* a moral excellence; the pursuit of excellence in a practice necessitates the exercise of the virtues. MacIntyre says, "A virtue tends to enable us to achieve those goods which are internal to *practices* and the lack of which essentially prevents us from achieving any such goods."[2] Thus, a practically rational financial manager would be one who views financial management as a "practice," with goods internal to the activity itself. Contrarily, an economically rational financial manager viv-à-vis the finance paradigm is one who views financial management primarily as a means to the attainment of external goods. This latter financial manager or 'agent' is the one who currently populates the models of agency theory, acting opportunistically in the pursuit of personal wealth with, if necessary, guile and deceit.

Both types of financial manager will pursue what they perceive as their self-interest. In the case of practical rationality, however, the agent's self-interest is defined in terms of the pursuit of excellence within the practice. Furthermore, this pursuit will be undertaken through the exercise of the virtues within a community (the *polis*). MacIntyre says,

> Agents in the Homeric poems can certainly be said always to act in their own interests as they understand them, but the interest of an individual is always his or her interest *qua* wife or *qua* host or *qua* some other role. . . . There is not the same contrast between what is to one's own interest and what is to the interest of others as that which is conveyed by modern uses of "self-interest" and cognate terms.[3]

Thus, practical rationality is an interactive or 'connected' rationality. A practically rational agent pursues happiness or excellence (what Aristotle termed *eudaimonia*) while realizing that this pursuit cannot be successfully undertaken opportunistically: the achievement of happiness requires the exercise of the moral virtues such as honesty in dealings with others.

In contrasting economic and practical rationality, therefore, the central issue is not whether agents act according to their own self-interest or whether they act in some way altruistically, but rather whether they view their own self-interest in a narrow sense—as invoked by the finance paradigm—or in a broader Homeric sense. Economic rationality depicts one subset of self- interest, namely that dealing with the Universe of Substance, as the only conceivable type of self-interest. Since it lies within the Universe of Value, Homeric self-interest is afforded no role in the existing economic-rationality rubric.

But, albeit morally desirable, is practical rationality methodologically feasible? Invoking practical rationality as the substantive rationality premise for financial economics may justifiably cause some concern among financial theorists who value the analytical rigor afforded by a simple behavioral premise of wealth maximization. In this chapter I hope to assuage these fears by illustrating how practically rational agents may be incorporated into one of the most extensive financial-contracting models developed to date, namely Douglas Diamond's model "Reputation Acquisition in Debt Markets." In addition, as discussed in the introduction to this book, the idea of mathematical precision in modeling rationality, even economic rationality, has always been illusory. Consider, for example, the concept of 'utility of wealth' that is used frequently in financial contracting models.[4] We may say that this utility increases with increasing wealth (the sixth axiom), and decreases with increasing risk (agents are assumed to be risk averse), but even though the functional relationship may be approximated by a lognormal or similar utility function, this function can never be measured with precision for any one individual or individuals in aggregate.[5] Rather than a sacrifice, therefore, any loss of quantitative rigor engendered by practical rationality may simply represent the weighing of another of finance's mathematically convenient but unrealistic conceptual anchors, namely the concept of finance as an exclusively descriptive and mathematically precise science. Aristotle, in the third chapter of book 1 of his *Nicomachean Ethics*, recognizes this:

> Our discussion will be adequate if it achieves clarity within the limits of the subject matter. For precision cannot be expected in the treatment of all subjects alike, any more than it can be expected in all manufactured articles. . . . Therefore, in a discussion of such subjects (the noble, just and good) . . . we must be satisfied to indicate the truth with a rough and general sketch. . . . For a well schooled man is one who searches for that degree of precision in each kind of study which the nature of the subject at hand admits. (1094b12–27)

This qualitative broadening need not be at the expense of mathematical rigor where the latter is correctly applied. Clearly, such rigor has a valuable role to play even within the context of rationality, namely in modeling instrumental rationality. But when it comes to assumptions concerning substantive rationality, finance must recognize the value judgments inherent in its wealth maximization premise; specifically, as discussed above, the extent to which positive behavioral assumptions may become normative behavioral prerogatives: finance's "implicit normative agenda." Financial economics must find the ideal balance—the Aristotelian 'mean'—between the qualitative and quantitative analytical extremes; between the Universe of Substance and Value.

Implications for Agency Theory

In part I of this book I showed that agency theory addresses the question of how 'rational' agents behave in imperfect markets, where the market imperfection takes the form of some contractual enforcement problem ranging from the simplest moral hazard to informational asymmetry and adverse selection. I noted also that much attention has been devoted to identifying and analyzing different market imperfections, but that the 'rational agents' part of the agency question has attracted much less attention in the finance literature. This lack is probably due to the presumption that opportunistic agents will drive any type of ethical agents out of the market: in the language of game theory, opportunism is a 'dominant' strategy. But are ethical agents really so weak in a competitive environment when pitted against opportunists?

A first step in answering this question is to identify the behavioral characteristics of an ethical agent. Our discussion so far in this chapter indicates that Aristotelian practical rationality is one feasible way of going about this. Practically rational agents are certainly 'rational' given this expanded concept of rationality. Indeed, von Neumann and Morgenstern's five axioms of instrumental rationality can be readily applied to the practically rational agent: the agent will still act consistently in making preference orderings, for example.[6] Where the practically rational agent clearly differs from an agent within the finance paradigm is in terms of the substantive rationality premise that directs the instrumental rationality. Unlike opportunists who, as Eric Noreen observes, will act with if necessary "guile and deceit," practically rational agents are fundamentally ethical, or more specifically they are 'virtuous.' These agents strive to achieve a certain *telos (eudaimonia)*; they know that to achieve this *telos* requires the exercise of the virtues such as honesty, wisdom, and courage; thus it is rational for these agents to be virtuous.

Returning to the game tree depicted in figure 2.1 of chapter 2, player A would presumably offer trust and thus offer the contract if he believes that the rational move for B is to honor trust. But how can honoring trust be 'rational' for B given that her payoff is maximized by abusing trust? Clearly, unless reputation-effects come into play, for an opportunistic agent it can't be. But what if B's utility is a function of more than just wealth? What if the act of honoring trust *in and of itself* contributes to B's 'utility'? Of course there is nothing new in the idea of broadening utility functions to include factors other than a pecuniary payoff. Welfare economists have developed various utility functions which incorporate deontological or teleological ethical strictures.[7] But, unlike the case of Aristotelian practical rationality, in these approaches ethics is not made instrumental to the rationality concept itself. Ethics is usually some peripheral constraint, adherence to which is hard to justify without resort to Confidence School–type arguments. Basically, these attempts to broaden utility functions within economics have been made within the traditional quantitative and material universe, what Pirsig defines as the Universe of Substance. (See discussion in chapter 7.) But Aristotelian practical rationality is a concept of substantive rationality that lies beyond this universe. It is a value-based concept that places emphasis on the pursuit of internal goods through the exercise of the virtues, as opposed to the sole pursuit of external goods.

Consider a contractual situation in which at least some virtuous agents are generally believed to exist. In such a situation, principals would rationally believe that, when dealing with virtuous agents, contracts can be implicitly enforced with trust. In other words, principals believe that, unlike opportunistic agents, virtuous agents will not act with "guile and deceit." Note well that, by acting virtuously and honoring trust, these practically rational agents are not motivated by altruism. They act in their self-interest as they perceive it: for them any "external good" sacrifice resulting from honoring trust is outweighed by the "internal good" gain derived from exercising the virtue of trustworthiness in preference to the vice of avarice.

But in extant financial contracting models, principals operate on the assumption that all agents are opportunistic. For example, in Stuart Myers's "The Determinants of Corporate Borrowing," principals set the interest rate on the assumption that all agents will act opportunistically and thus will underinvest in certain states.[8] Thus, the interest rate is a function of the probability of underinvestment. Underinvestment here takes the form of agents failing to undertake certain positive net-present-value projects. Thus, underinvestment represents not merely a redistribution of wealth from principal to agent, but rather a deadweight loss to the economy as a whole. The objective of the principal is simply to earn a risk-adjusted rate of return. Thus, if the principal believed that at least some agents would not act opportunistically, a lower interest rate would be charged. This lower interest rate would be a direct result of the known existence of virtuous agents. Note that the lower interest rate would not be detrimental to the principal since the amount of underinvestment would be less. Also, the lower interest rate would increase the payoff to *all* agents, even the opportunists.

Also, the lower interest rate will tend to reduce the number of states in which opportunistic agents will underinvest.[9] Thus, there will be less aggregate underinvestment. At the margin, the existence of some virtuous agents will induce some opportunistic agents not to underinvest.

Perhaps the most extensive agency-theory model developed to date is Douglas Diamond's 1989 model, "Reputation Acquisition in Debt Markets." Diamond's model is more complex than that of Myers in two respects. It invokes agents of different *types* and therefore involves adverse selection as well as moral hazard. Also, it models behavior through many iterations where memory and learning exist. In Diamond's model, there are two investment choices and three types of agents. The two investment choices are a risky project and a safe project. The safe project yields a higher *expected* return but, if successful, the risky project's return is much higher than the expected return from the safe project. Thus, investing in the safe project is akin to placing money in a bank savings account, whereas investing in the risky project could be compared to betting on a horse race or buying a lottery ticket. If the agent chooses the risky project and it is unsuccessful, then the agent is forced into liquidation and the lender (i.e., the principal) receives nothing. Type B agents are able to invest in risky projects only. Type G agents are able to invest in safe projects only. The interesting agents are type BG, since these may choose between investing in either the risky or the safe project. Clearly, the first-best outcome for the lenders and for the economy in aggregate would be for type BG agents to invest in the safe project throughout since this project yields the highest expected payoff. But, being opportunists, type BG agents will not do this since their wealth is maximized by investing in risky projects at least some of the time. Lenders (i.e., principals) expect this and therefore levy a higher interest charge in anticipation of this "risk-shifting" agency problem. Thus, the residual loss in Diamond's model results from type BG agents failing to choose safe projects; this renders his equilibrium—as with all agency-theory equilibria—second best. Type BG agents do not choose the risky project in every iteration. Their choice is a function of the interest rate and the stage of the game. Eric Rasmusen, in his 1989 book *Games and Information*, succinctly summarizes the equilibrium path in Diamond's model:

> The BG firms start by choosing risky projects. Their downside risk is limited by bankruptcy, but if the project is successful the firm keeps large residual profits after repaying the loan. Over time, the number of firms with access to the risky project (the BGs and Bs) diminishes through bankruptcy, while the number of Gs remains unchanged. Lenders can therefore earn zero profits while lowering their interest rates. When the interest rate falls, the value of a stream of safe investment profits minus interest payments rises relative to the expected value of the few periods of risky returns minus interest payments before bankruptcy. After the interest rate has fallen enough, the second phase of the game begins when the BG firms switch to safe projects at a period we will call t_1. . . . Towards period T, the value of future profits from

safe projects declines and even with a low interest rate the BGs are again tempted to choose risky projects.[10]

What effect, if any, would the existence of a cadre of virtuous agents have on this equilibrium? Initially, lenders would offer a lower interest rate (i.e., offer trust to the virtuous agents) since the virtuous agents are expected to undertake the safe project (i.e., to honor the trust vested in them by the lender through the lower interest rate). This would increase the payoff to all opportunistic agents. It clearly would also increase the "safe" phase of the game; that is, the phase during which even the opportunistic agents choose not to act opportunistically. Thus, as in Myers, the existence of some virtuous agents will tend to induce at least some opportunistic agents to act virtuously at least some of the time. As opportunistic agents act less opportunistically (i.e., by choosing the safe project more of the time) then lenders will lower interest rates still further, thus extending still further the "safe" phase of the game. Agency problems may be unraveled, therefore, by even a relatively small cadre of agents whose substantive rationality premise is that of virtue ethics.[11]

In summary, by reducing the size of the residual loss, the existence of virtuous agents increases the wealth of opportunistic agents and increases the wealth of the entire economy. Note that the virtuous agents, by definition, gain utility from honoring the trust vested in them by the principal. They exercise the virtue of trustworthiness. Trust enters into the game because the principals are now offering a lower interest rate in the knowledge of the existence of virtuous agents. Thus, in the context of our game tree from chapter 2, the lenders (i.e., the principals) are now offering trust (the Prisoners' Dilemma has been avoided). The virtuous agents are gaining greater utility from the intrinsic (i.e., internal good) payoff from honoring that trust than they lose from the lost material (i.e., external good) payoff derived from opportunism. But would this always be the case? Might there not be situations in which the material sacrifice is too great to be outweighed by the intrinsic gain from honoring trust? Virtue-ethics theory would answer this question by noting that internal and external goods cannot be traded off against one another. Internal goods are inherently superior to external goods: "We need, so Aristotle argues in the opening passages of Book VII of the *Politics*, to pursue the external goods of the body in order to engage in those activities in which the soul perfects itself [internal goods]."[12]

Thus, the situation of an opportunistic game into which some virtuous agents are introduced is an "all-win" situation: given their broadened utility concept the virtuous agents gain by their virtue, the opportunistic agents materially gain by—in the above scenarios—facing lower interest rates, the principals are no worse off, and by reducing the amount of opportunism *even among opportunistic agents* and thus reducing the residual loss, the economy as a whole gains.

A Model

By focusing attention specifically on Agency's rationality premise as enumerated by the finance paradigm, the model to be developed in this chapter differs from preceding Agency models.[13] Interestingly, the following model indicates that the existence of trustworthy agents in financial markets is not merely desirable from an economic perspective, but actually is *essential* if debt markets are not to fail. Specifically, if lenders do not believe that some nontrivial cohort of trustworthy agents exists, then lenders cease to lend and debt markets cease to function. Also, the greater the proportion of honest agents, the greater the overall level of economic activity; indeed, the existence of some practically rational agents exercising the virtue of honesty will tend to induce at least some of the opportunistic agents to act honestly.

In the following model, a cohort of virtuous agents is introduced into debt markets characterized by informational asymmetry, where lenders are unable to observe borrowers' investment choices. Borrowers have the opportunity to exploit the informational advantage they have over lenders by choosing risky projects, thus illustrating the classic agency problem of risk shifting. In the model, lenders know *a priori* that a certain proportion of borrowers are virtuous. They view a virtuous agent as one who deals honestly with others. Lenders thus set interest rates on the basis of this knowledge.

Borrowers know everything that lenders know. They are aware, therefore, that the interest rate offered is offered in the expectation that the virtuous agents will not indulge in risk shifting, while opportunistic borrowers may shift risk. Borrowers know that lenders know that, given the interest rate, to risk-shift would be uncharacteristic for a virtuous agent since it would represent reneging on the implicit contract offered by lenders. Given these beliefs, lenders offer a lower interest rate than would be offered if they believed no virtuous agents existed, and the virtuous agents display the virtue of trustworthiness by not risk shifting. In summary, the following model will support these three hypotheses.

Hypothesis One: A belief among lenders that some practically rational (i.e., virtuous) agents exist is a necessary condition for financial markets to exist. Rather than a luxury, therefore, "virtue" is a necessity.

Hypothesis Two: The known existence of one or more virtuous agents will increase the material wealth of all opportunistic agents. Furthermore, the economy in aggregate will experience an absolute wealth gain.

Hypothesis Three: The known existence of one or more virtuous agents will induce less opportunistic behavior even among the opportunistic agents. Once accepted as a possibility, the extent of virtuous behavior in the economy may be far greater than that exhibited by the *a priori* virtuous agents only. Even the perceived existence of such agents, therefore, may result in a complete unraveling of agency problems. Virtue is, as it were, contagious.

In the market economy to be modeled here, at least some of the prospective borrowers are virtuous, in that they are not willing to deceive lenders as to their intended use of borrowed funds. But why would such deception necessarily be contrary to the tenets of practical rationality? Clearly, a practically rational agent may rationally deceive: one of the primary characteristics of this type of rationality is its *relativism*, thus it does not ban deception absolutely. Whether or not deception is practically rational depends upon the motivation for the deception. In this case, the motivation for the deception is avarice. The deception would betray the vice of avarice rather than the virtue of prudent thrift because the deception is myopic and ultimately self-defeating; the deception incurs agency costs that are ultimately borne by the agent. Contrarily, being honest in this situation—as the following model will illustrate—exhibits not only the virtues of truthfulness, temperance, and community-mindedness, but also that of prudent thrift in that aggregate wealth is maximized.

At this point, readers who are unfamiliar with game theory may wish to skim through the following pages until they reach the "Conclusions" section at the end of this chapter.

In the parlance of game theory, the following model is a supergame: it is a multiperiod, multi-iteration, finite-life model of a market economy. There are two types of investment opportunities available at the beginning of each period: R, which is risky, and S, which is safe. There are three types of prospective borrowers. Type B borrowers can only invest in R. Type BG borrowers and type G borrowers both have the choice of investing in either S or R; however, type BG borrowers are assumed to be opportunists while type G borrowers are assumed to adhere to the tenets of practical rationality. Type G borrowers are thus the "virtuous" agents. In order to honor the trust vested in them by lenders, these virtuous agents will not risk default by risk shifting. Consequently, type G agents will always choose project S regardless of the interest rate or the stage of the game.

Lenders know the percentage of each type of investor in the population, but are unable to distinguish individuals. They may *ask* borrowers which type of investment they intend to make, but they will not be able to *observe* which type of investment is made. At the beginning of each period, a Nash-type equilibrium is established, in which both lenders and borrowers know what the "equilibrium" interest rate will be for that period, and the prospective borrowers all offer that rate. The lenders will accept that rate, if the expected return is at least as great as their cost of funds, r, or else they will refuse to lend that period, and the markets will fail.

A priori, lenders know the proportion of each borrower type. Interest rates are set, therefore, on the assumption that the type G borrowers will choose the safe project. In effect, lenders enter into an implicit contract with type G agents because these agents are viewed as trustworthy. Contrarily, lenders know that the portion of type BG borrowers are opportunists and therefore no trust is offered. The known existence of three types of agents thus results in an interest rate that reflects lenders' willingness to trust the type G agents, while accepting the undetectable presence of the type BG and B agents in the population of borrowers.

Both types G and BG, therefore, have a choice between one unit of a safe investment, with end-of-period payoff $S > r$ (where r is lenders' opportunity cost of funds), for which the risk is zero, and one unit of a risky investment, R, which carries the possibility that the investor will default on the loan used to finance the investment. As in Diamond, the payoff from investment in R is $R > S$, with probability π, and 0 with probability $1 - \pi$. The expected return on R is $\pi R < r$. The investments are indivisible, and borrowers may not invest in both simultaneously. The difference between type G borrowers and type BG borrowers is that type BG borrowers will choose the investment which maximizes their expected material payoff, while virtuous type G investors will not risk default regardless of the expected material payoffs. As in Diamond, the third type of borrowers, type B, can only invest in the risky investment.

All three types of borrowers are assumed to be risk neutral, in the expected-utility sense. They seek to maximize expected consumption between now and time T. This is given by the expression $\Sigma_1^T E(c_t)d^t$, where $d < 1$ is a discount factor, reflecting the assumption that investors prefer early consumption to later consumption.

It could be argued, and certainly would be argued by type BG and B borrowers, that it is not unethical to risk default, since the interest rate, r_t, allows for a certain proportion of defaults. However, this ignores the fact that it is the type G borrowers who are paying the difference between the promised rate r_t and the expected rate r. Thus, any borrower investing in the risky investment is knowingly accepting an interest subsidy from the virtuous (i.e., type G) borrowers.

As in Diamond, the lenders last for only one period, and therefore cannot commit themselves to future actions. They do not know, *ex ante*, what type of borrower they are dealing with, nor do they know what type of investment is actually made. They will only know that an investor has chosen to invest in the risky investment, R, if the project fails and the borrower defaults. The only information lenders have about borrowers is their credit history; therefore, they cannot distinguish between a type G borrower and a lucky type BG borrower. There is an unlimited number of potential lenders, all risk neutral, and an opportunity cost of funds ("storage technology," in Diamond's model) of r, where r equals the end-of-period balance per one unit of deposit, in a risk-free account. There is more capital available at r than investment opportunities, so that competition between lenders will result in their expected return, per unit loaned, being equal to r, and r is assumed constant over time.

Borrowers begin each period with zero endowment, and borrowing against returns from investing in future periods is impossible. They consume only the net return (that is, the residual after paying debt service) from investment each period. Therefore, each time borrowers invest in R, there is a risk that they will default. In the event of default, lenders' only recourse is to seize the investment and liquidate it. Liquidation is assumed to destroy any value of the assets, leaving the borrower with nothing. Therefore, default is only rational if it is unavoidable. In this event, lenders also receive nothing, instead of the promised return for that period, r_t. Therefore, if default (by the borrower) is inevitable, then it does not matter whether the lender seizes the property or not: both parties end up with nothing. Defaults and seizures are public information.

Initially, type G, BG, and B investors represent a fraction f_G, f_{BG}, and f_B of the borrowing population, respectively. Each period that type BG and B borrowers invest in R, the proportion π of them will default, resulting in declining proportions of type BG and B investors who have not defaulted. Therefore, for period t, f_{BGt} and f_{Bt} represent type BG and B borrowers, as a percentage of all borrowers who have not yet defaulted.

Equilibrium in the Final Period

In the final period, there will be five groups of potential borrowers: those type BG and B borrowers who have invested in R and defaulted; type BG and B borrowers who may have invested in R, but have been lucky; and type G borrowers who have only invested in S. All borrowers who have never defaulted are indistinguishable. Therefore, as a result of the competitive nature of the lending market, all borrowers who have never defaulted will be offered the same borrowing rate, r_T. Those with a record of default will effectively be denied credit, as we shall see below.

Borrower Mix and Interest Rates

In any given period, lenders, who are risk neutral, will offer to lend at a rate r_T, which results in their earning an expected return on their loan portfolio of r, the opportunity cost of funds. If the riskless project, S, has a higher expected utility than the risky project, then type G and BG borrowers will invest in S, there will be defaults equal to πf_{BT}, and the expected return will be equal to $r_T^S = r/(f_{GT}+f_{BGT}+\pi f_{BT})$. However, if the risky project, R, produces a higher expected utility, then both type BG and B borrowers will invest in it, and a proportion π of them will default. For period T, the equilibrium interest rate would be $r_T^R = r/(\pi f_{BGT}+\pi f_{BT} + f_{GT})$. As long as there are still type BG investors who have never defaulted in the population of borrowers, $r_T^S < r_T^R$.

The equilibrium rate itself is a function of the relative expected payoff of the two investment alternatives. That is, if the safe project is chosen, then the payoff to the borrower is $(S-r_T)$, while the expected return to the borrower from the risky investment is $\pi (R-r_T)$. Therefore, the safe project is utility maximizing only if $r_T \leq (S-\pi R)/(1-\pi)$. In this case, $r_T = r_T^S$. If, however, the utility-maximizing alternative is R, then $r_T = r_T^R$.

Depending upon the proportion of type BG investors in the population, and the size and probability of R in the risky investment, it is possible that no investment will take place. That is, if $r_T^R > S$, then type G investors will not borrow. The combined proportion of type BG and type B investors that would produce this condition is given by $f_{BG}^* > (S-R)/[S(1-\pi)]$. No–type G borrowers, not wishing to reveal themselves as such, will never offer to borrow at a higher rate than S, so that lenders will make no loans that period, and the markets will fail. As a result, lenders would "store" their endowments, potential borrowers would neither invest nor consume, and the level of economic activity would be decreased accordingly.

A perhaps more interesting set of conditions occurs if the interest rate is such that all types of borrowers will borrow, but only type G borrowers will invest in S, while the other borrowers will invest in R. Since lenders know that this will occur, but not which investors will do this, the interest rate will reflect this possibility, so that $(S-\pi R)/(1-\pi) < r_T^R < S$. In this case, type G borrowers who will be investing in S will be paying r_T^R, even though the riskless nature of the investment would have justified their paying only r. The difference will, in effect, subsidize type BG borrowers, who should be paying r/π, based upon the risk of their investment. Type BG and G borrowers, as a group, may or may not be making a net positive contribution to economic activity, depending upon whether their aggregate *ex post* return is positive ($\pi R > 1$). But even if it is positive, it is still less than they would have contributed if they had invested in S (since $S > \pi R$, by assumption). Thus, type BG and B borrowers are free riders on the system, both from the perspective of type G borrowers, and the economy at large. This brings to mind Bowie's observation, quoted in chapter 1, "It only pays to lie or cheat when you can free ride off the honesty of others. . . . The conscious pursuit of self-interest by all members of society has the collective result of undermining the interests of all."

Investment, Consumption, and Economic Activity

In this section, I consider the effects of investment type on the economy at large. Define 'consumption' as the purchase of goods and services from third parties, who are neither borrowers nor lenders. Assume also that net returns to lenders, whether they store their endowment or lend it, will be consumed. Define 'economic activity' as the aggregate production of goods and services. Assume further that, excepting for the production of consumption goods and services for borrowers and lenders, all economic activity by third parties (nonborrowers and nonlenders) is independent of activities in this sector of the economy. Then, for each unit of endowment invested in S, the borrower will, at the end of the period, consume $S-r_T$, and the lender will consume $r_T - 1$, for a total consumption of $S-1$. Similarly, a unit invested in R will return an average $\pi(R-r_T)$ to the borrower, and an average of $\pi r_T - 1$

to the lender, for a total consumption of $\pi R - 1$. If the endowment is stored, then the lender will consume $r - 1$. Since by assumption $S > r > \pi R$, the maximum level of economic activity will be generated by investment in S. Conversely, each unit of endowment invested in R will, at the margin, return less than a unit stored. We have now established the following lemma:

Lemma 1: *Economic activity is increased by investment in S, and decreased by investment in R, vis-à-vis storing endowments.*

It follows that market failure *may* result in a lower level of overall economic activity than lending to a mix of investor types. That is, assume that utility is maximized by investing in R, so that only type G investors invest in S. Then, the total economic activity resulting from investing a unit of endowment to a mix of borrowers is $(\pi R - 1)(1 - f_{GT}) + (S - 1)f_{GT} = \pi R(1 - f_{GT}) + Sf_{GT} - 1$. If this total is greater than $r - 1$, then overall activity is increased by investment. This can be expressed as: If $R\pi(1 - f_{GT}) + Sf_{GT} > r$, then overall activity is increased by borrowing. But earlier, we found that if the equilibrium interest rate is $r_T^R > S$, the market will fail, and no borrowing will take place. Writing this condition as $S < r_T^R = r/[(1 - f_{GT})\pi + f_{GT}]$, and solving for r, we can derive the condition under which borrowing would have increased economic activity, but the borrowing markets will fail. Since $S < R$, it is possible that these conditions will hold simultaneously. We state the condition as a limit on the range of the proportion of type G borrowers in the market, f_{GT}:

Lemma 2: *If $(S - r)/(S - S\pi) > 1 - f_{GT} > (S - r)/(S - \pi R)$, then the markets will fail, resulting in a lower level of activity than if lending and investing had taken place.*
Corollary: *The belief among lenders of the existence of some non-trivial cohort of virtuous borrowers is a necessary condition for debt markets to exist.*

Proof of Corollary: If f_{GT} is known to equal 0, then $r_T^R = r/[\pi(f_{GB} + f_B) + 0] = r/\pi$. But by assumption $\pi R < r$, so that $r/\pi > R > S$, so that no one would borrow (or lend).

Equilibrium in a Multiperiod Model

In the previous section, myopic decision criteria were developed. In this section, we examine the conditions under which these rules, and equilibrium conditions, might evolve over time. The bases for changes over time are twofold: first, the declining proportion of undetected type BG and B borrowers in the population; and second, the possibility that type BG borrowers might find it optimal to mimic type G borrowers, under certain conditions. These changes will, in turn, affect the equilibrium interest rate, and the level and type of investment in the economy. The following lemmas, which are proven in Diamond, apply *mutatis mutandis* in our model:

Lemma 3: *Lenders will never knowingly lend to type BG or B borrowers.*

Since the only means by which lenders can identify a type BG or B borrower is if the borrower defaults, this means that, once a borrower has defaulted, credit will be denied him or her in the future.

Lemma 4: *If a loan is made at date t, then the face value $r_t \in [r, S]$.*

This merely states that the interest rate will be at least as great as the riskless cost of funds, but less than the return on the safe project. If an investor offered to borrow at a rate greater than S, he or she would reveal him or herself to be a type B borrower, or a type BG borrower intent on investing in R. And from Lemma 3, credit would be denied.

Lemma 5: *Borrowers repay face value r (and avoid liquidation) if their project returns at least r_s, and borrowers with projects that return less than r_t are liquidated.*

That is, a borrower will not default unless it is necessary (Lemma 3), and will never pay more than required, under the debt contract.

Lemma 6: *Any default (payment of less than r_t) by a borrower at a date t leads to no lending for all future dates.*

This follows from Lemmas 3, 4, and 5.

Lemma 7: *At all dates all borrowers offer the lowest interest rate that provides lenders with an expected return of r.*

Borrowers are aware of the competitive nature of the lending market, and stand to gain nothing by offering more than the minimum rate which will produce an expected return of r to lenders.

Project Choice, Interest Rates, and Economic Activity

The decision between risky projects and safe projects in a multiperiod environment, for the type BG borrower, will be based upon the maximization of discounted expected utility over the entire time horizon. Diamond shows that this choice can change over time; that is, it is possible that it will be optimal for type BG borrowers to invest in the risky project in the early periods. As unlucky type BG and B borrowers default, the proportion of type G borrowers in the population of never-defaulted borrowers increases, and interest rates fall accordingly. As interest rates fall, the relative desirability of the safe investment increases, and its present value may surpass the risky investment's present value. Under these conditions, both type G and type BG borrowers will invest in the safe project.

In Diamond's model, this represents the acquisition of reputation. For never-defaulted type BG and B investors, this reputation allows them to borrow at the same rate as type G investors, and the utility-maximizing choice for them during this middle-time period is to invest in the safe project, in order to preserve their ability to borrow in future time periods. However, as the final period, T, approaches, the present value of future borrowing diminishes. At some time t, it again becomes optimal for type BG borrowers to invest in project R. The conditions under which type BG borrowers would invest in project S are given by the following lemma, as derived by Diamond:

Lemma 8: *Type-BG borrowers will select safe projects on some date only if $d(S-r)/(1-d) > d\pi(R-r)/(1-d\pi)$, implying that the present value of financing the safe project at the riskless rate of interest for an infinite number of periods exceeds the present value of selecting the risky project for an infinite number of periods (until the first default).*

Type BG borrowers' predisposition to choose the safe project is therefore a function of the prevailing interest rate. This interest rate is, in turn, an inverse function of the perceived proportion of virtuous (i.c., type G) borrowers (Lemma 7). Thus, the existence of virtuous agents has a direct impact on the behavior of the opportunistic type BG agents.

Diamond then derives one of the more important results of his analysis: conditions under which a type BG borrower, having invested in risky projects in early periods, would (at time $\hat{t}$) switch to safe investments, in order to preserve his or her reputation. Toward the end of the "game," the type BG investor would then revert to investing in risky investments, since the present value of returns on safe investments would be less than the present value of (conditional) returns on the risky investments. This is his or her Lemma 9, with notation modifications:

Lemma 9: *If, for all $t \in [\hat{t}, T]$, $r_t < dS + (1-d)(S-\pi)/(1-\pi)$, then there exists $T < \infty$ such that safe projects are the optimal choice at date t: T such that $r_{\hat{t}} - V_{\hat{t}+1} (S-\pi R)/(1-\pi)$. This bound on future interest rates specifies feasible rates—that is, $dS + (1-d)(S-\pi R)/(1-\pi) > r$—if and only if the necessary conditions (in Lemma 8) for reputation to have value are true.*

An area of interest here, which was not addressed by Diamond, is the effect over time of defaulting borrowers on overall economic activity. Virtuous agents will never default since they never choose the risky project. The proportion of virtuous agents, therefore, may impact the aggregate level of economic activity. Given the conditions in Lemma 9, then over time we would observe an early phase ($t < \hat{t}$) where type G investors would invest in the safe investment, and type BG and B investors would invest in the risky investment. Each time period, the fraction π of type BG and B borrowers would default. Since lenders would know that the proportion of these borrowers, in the population of never-defaulted borrowers, is decreasing, r_t would fall over time. But since the total number of type G borrowers remains constant, while attrition reduces the number of type BG and B borrowers, the investment in S will remain constant, while the investment in R would fall, over time, resulting in increasing activity:

Lemma 10: *For each period when type BG and type B borrowers invest in the risky investment, a proportion π of each will default, resulting in less investment in the risky asset the following period, and hence a higher level of economic activity.*

The second phase begins at time $\hat{t}$, when type BG borrowers would begin investing in the safe project. At the beginning of this phase, the interest rate would drop, from $r_{(\hat{t}-1)}{}^R$ to $r_{\hat{t}}{}^S$, since lenders would know that all borrowers, except surviving type B borrowers, would invest in the safe project. In addition, since type BG borrowers have switched from R to S, the level of activity will experience a quantum increase, equal to $N_{BG\hat{t}}(S-\pi R)$, where $N_{BG\hat{t}}$ is the number of never-defaulted type BG borrowers remaining at $\hat{t}$. But since type B borrowers will continue to borrow and default, economic activity will continue to grow during this period. We state this as a lemma:

Lemma 11: *At the beginning of the phase when it is optimal for type BG borrowers to invest in S, economic activity will experience an immediate increase, and economic activity will continue to grow during this phase.*

The third phase, or 'endgame,' begins when it becomes optimal for type BG borrowers to again invest in the risky project. At this time, τ, interest rates will experience an abrupt rise, to reflect the increased risk to lenders. This will be accompanied by an abrupt drop in economic activity at time τ, equal to $N_{BG\tau}(\pi R-S)$, followed by a resumption of growth in economic activity as both type BG and type B borrowers default. We state this as a lemma:

Lemma 12: *At the beginning of the endgame, the economy will experience a onetime drop in activity due to type BG borrowers switching from the safe project to the risky project. Thereafter, economic activity will continue to grow until time T.*

Summarizing the multiperiod analysis, we see that economic activity (consumption of goods and services) will rise over time, as borrowers who invest in the risky investment default, and are denied credit thereafter. This is coincident with a falling interest rate, as the proportion of type G borrowers rises. If conditions are such that reputation is of value, then total economic activity will experience a onetime increase at the time that type BG borrowers begin investing in the safe project, and will experience a onetime drop at the time that type BG borrowers revert to the risky investment.

Note that the overall level of economic activity is a function of the proportion of agents choosing the safe project. Since virtuous agents always choose the safe project, their existence will tend to increase economic activity and thus move financial-market equilibria toward first-best outcomes with no residual loss due to risk shifting. Furthermore, if the proportion of type G borrowers is too small, then markets will fail altogether, thus virtue—in the guise of trust—is a necessary condition for the existence of financial markets. In addition, the economic efficiency of financial markets is a direct function of the proportion of these practically rational agents.

Conclusions

One might reasonably argue that the model developed above may illustrate the importance of an ethic of trust in financial markets, but it does not illustrate the need for practical rationality *per se*. Could not Kantianism provide this ethic of trust equally well, or even utilitarianism given that trust seems to lead to maximum social welfare? Also, did not the original model developed by Diamond imply that some sort of ethic would arise naturally even within the finance paradigm (some of the borrowers choose the safe project at least some of the time in order to maintain their reputations)? Thus, without introducing *a priori* ethical agents, as is done here, ethics may arise, as it were, "naturally" among self-interested agents. This is essentially the argument made by Gauthier in *Morals by Agreement*, as described in chapter 3.

This notion of ethics as an economically justifiable strategy ties in also with the work of Frank in *Passions within Reason*, also outlined in chapter 3. Frank envisages an equilibrium in which trustworthy and opportunistic agents coexist. Indeed, in Frank's model both types of agent are essential: the known existence of the opportunists is what induces the principals to take the trouble to monitor agents in order to identify the trustworthy ones. Thus, Frank views the world as a place where there always will be, and always should be, both "ethical" agents and opportunists. So what does the concept of Aristotelian practical rationality have to offer over and above these other "rationalizations" of ethical behavior?

I would answer this question by noting that these other accounts of ethics in an economic environment—whether based on Kant, utilitarianism, *Morals by Agreement*, or *Passions within Reason*—are simply *not* rationalizations. The fundamental weakness of these approaches is that they fail to rationalize ethical behavior. The weakness of Kantianism and utilitarianism and other "isms" of the traditional approach were discussed at length in chapter 4. As regards Gauthier and Frank, these models fail to explain why an agent will rationally act ethically. Gauthier's model explains why agents may honor trust some of the time, but his rationale is essentially that of the reputation effect discussed in chapter 3: the underlying *motivation* for these agents' actions is economic not moral. *Morals by Agreement* are not morals at all, but rather a cooperative strategy for economic gain that will presumably be dropped by the agent as soon as it is no longer economically optimal (i.e., in game theory parlance, when the *endgame* is reached). Furthermore, I am not alone in this view. To quote Donaldson in *The Ethics of International Business*: "Do the conclusions generated by self-interested man in the Hobbesian state of nature or in the maximization models used by Gauthier, add up to real morality? I am persuaded that they do not. . . ."[14]

A similar criticism can be made of Frank's rationalization for ethical behavior. Frank gives no *reason* for why an agent would choose to be ethical. In his equilibrium, honest agents and opportunistic agents perform equally well so presumably in choosing which path to follow an agent may flip a coin—"heads I'm ethical, tails I'm not"! In short, in Frank's "commitment model" some agents simply *are* ethical, and some are not. Frank, like Gauthier, does not *rationalize* ethics.

Herein lies the strength of Aristotelian practical rationality. As discussed earlier, practically rational agents act ethically *because it is in their self-interest to do so*. For such agents economic objectives are recognized and valued, but they are not valued as ultimate objectives. The ultimate objective is *eudaimonia* (i.e., the goods internal to the practice), and material wealth is of use merely as a means to that end. For a practically rational agent, therefore, the underlying motivation is moral not material: this is a rationality based not on *substance* but on *value*. In modeling the behavior of economic agents, therefore, virtue-ethics theory provides a solid logical foundation for the existence of agents who act honestly *because* this is the rational choice.

In essence, through the concept of practical rationality, virtue-ethics theory rationalizes honesty. Thus, in Diamond's model, or indeed in any agency model, a virtuous agent's choice to honor trust is not premised on any physical parameter of the contractual situation. These agents will honor trust (e.g., invest in the safe project in Diamond's model) regardless of the expected payoff or the stage of the game, or any other strategic consideration. Far from being complex and elusive, therefore, from a modeling perspective the actions of a virtuous agent are both predictable and eminently rational.

9

Some Gender Implications

The contribution of feminist theory to business ethics is a perspective of self in relation to others. Organizations that have been designed in the image of men now need to incorporate some of those features that represent women's ways of thinking and relating. What are these features? They include listening, responding on the basis of others' needs rather than on the basis of one's own needs, building strong relationships, making decisions on the basis of responsibility to others, giving feedback, nurturing, building cooperation rather than confrontation.
—Robin Derry

Another paradigm shift underway in moral philosophy is the growing recognition of possible gender differences in attitudes toward ethical decisions. The extent of and, indeed, the very existence of these gender-based differences is still hotly debated, but one additional attribute of the virtue-ethics approach adopted here is that this approach to applied ethics—with its focus on community and not on abstract rules—is generally recognized as a particularly 'feminine' approach to ethics.

A seminal work in this area is Carol Gilligan's book *In a Different Voice*, which claims to present evidence of significant gender differences in moral orientation. She identifies "two voices," one predominantly female and the other predominantly male, which represent two distinct moral selves. The autonomous self separated from others in a hierarchical world is predominant among men. Ethics for this self adopts a gamelike quality; the moves that are acceptable and unacceptable are clearly defined before the game, disputes are refereed impartially according to the abstract principle of fairness, and setting a precedent becomes worrisome.

The self that is predominant among women is the connected self, joined to others in a web of relationships. The ethical outlook derived from this connected self is more situational and contextual than that which a "separate" self produces. Instead of the male orientation to "rules of the game," the dynamics and expectations involved in relationships are central. Women tend to conceptualize moral questions as problems of care involving empathy and compassion, while men conceptualize them as problems of rights.

In one study, a sample of men and women were asked five questions relating to unethical behavior. The study revealed that men were more than twice as likely to be willing to engage in actions regarded as less ethical. The study also revealed that men are more likely to work long hours and break rules because men view achievement as competitive.[1] Another study asked over one thousand business students to evaluate the ethical acceptability of each of ten different scenarios. In four of the ten responses, there was no significant difference between the male and female responses. The results of the other six questions, however, support the above findings of significant gender differences in ethical orientation. Once again, the male responses tended to be rule based, and to view the problem as that of a game. The female responses tended to be more compassion based and more contextual.[2]

But Gilligan's dichotomy between male and female moral orientation is far from generally accepted.[3] Harriet Baber, for example, has recently argued that "the thesis of gender differences in moral reasoning hypothesized by Carol Gilligan . . . was early shown to be false on empirical grounds. Nevertheless, like a number of other 'scientific fictions,' . . . the myth of women's way of knowing took on a life of its own within the literature."[4]

It may well be that these purported gender differences are in fact differences due to some other factor. Carol Tavris, for example, notes that "new studies find that the behavior that we link to gender depends more on what an individual is doing and needs to do than on his or her biological sex."[5] Even acknowledging these caveats, however, Gilligan's central message is viewed by many as possessing a kernel of truth. Males and females do often view an ethical decision from different perspectives.

In light of these possible gender differences in ethical orientation, the account in part I of what—according to the finance paradigm—constitutes reasonable business behavior clearly exhibits a male gender bias. This concept of business behavior has been noted as one in which "work is a game with rules and customs geared to reward traditional *male* behavior."[6] Similarly, a recent article in *Newsweek* magazine summarizes the views of various observers that "traditional business-school teaching methods are male-oriented."[7] Specifically, three central attributes of the financial-economic concept of rationality favor the male orientation:

1. The narrow focus on wealth maximization as the ultimate and sole end of all human endeavor.
2. The increasing use of a game-theory methodology and conceptualization to model business environments. As Daniel Hausman and Michael McPherson note: "[game theory] does not rule out altruism or sympathy . . . but it does rule out a collective perspective, a perspective that considers what *we* should do and what the consequences will be for *us.* "[8]
3. The fundamentally rigid mathematical axiom approach to developing a concept of rationality reflecting a rule, rather than contextual, orientation.

Thus, the very foundation of business education, its rationality assumption, may actively deter female participation. Possible evidence for this comes from enrollment trends in MBA programs. A disquieting trend is apparent in America's business schools. Although the number of professional women in the workforce continues to grow, the percentage of women enrolled in MBA programs has fallen dramatically in recent years.[9] At Northwestern University's Kellogg Graduate School of Management, for example, female enrollment has dropped 37 percent since 1986, and similar trends can be observed at other major universities.[10] These trends are particularly alarming when one considers the dramatically *increasing* percentage of women on corporate boards of directors and in management positions at all levels. Ishmael Akaah observes that "one of the most significant socioeconomic trends of the past two decades is the unprecedented increase in the number of women in the labor force, particularly that of women holding executive/management positions in business organizations."[11]

This would imply a *greater* incentive and need for women to enter business education, yet the opposite appears to be the case. In addition, these trends show no sign of abating in the 1990s: during 1992 both Indiana University and UCLA experienced 17 percent drops in female enrollment in their respective MBA programs.

Several nonethical reasons have been proposed to account for this declining female enrollment. There is evidence that women have traditionally been excluded from senior management positions by a 'glass ceiling,' and therefore they have less incentive to pursue a business career. But the aforementioned increase in the number of women in senior positions over the last few years tends to contradict this argument. The high cost of MBA programs has been proposed as another reason, although why cost should deter women more than men is not clear. Other suggested explanations include the tendency for MBA programs to favor candidates in their late twenties and early thirties which, for women, are prime childbearing years. Statistically, there is some evidence that the increasing numbers of students from foreign countries, most of whom are men, tend to be skewing the enrollment trends.

Although all of these suggested reasons undoubtedly have some validity, they do not explain fully either the scale of the gender shift or the fact that the shift appears to be a fairly recent phenomenon. In light of Gilligan's work, it seems at least possible that women may be increasingly avoiding graduate business programs because they find the value system promulgated therein not merely morally impoverished but also inherently hostile.

If the extant financial-economic approach to developing a rationality concept were the only feasible one, then the above evidence of male bias would seem inevitable. Indeed it would imply that, in reference to Gilligan's "two voices," men are more rational than women. In the previous two chapters, however, an alternative approach to modeling rationality has been identified, namely Aristotelian 'practical rationality.' As the foundation of virtue-ethics theory, this concept encompasses a logically coherent and morally inclusive substantive rationality premise. Moreover, as mentioned earlier, virtue ethics has been recognized as a particularly gender neutral—perhaps even feminine—notion of rationality.[12]

In light of these gender differences, an interesting way of viewing the difference between rationality within the finance paradigm and rationality within virtue ethics may be in terms of gender orientation. The traditional "theory of the firm" in financial-economic theory may in fact be a theory of the archetypally *masculine* firm. What virtue ethics offers through practical rationality is a theory of a different firm, a *feminine* firm.

Is this masculine firm as invoked by the finance paradigm economically optimal, or even desirable? Financial economic theory implies that it is not. Most interestingly, the inefficiencies of the masculine firm stem from precisely those value characteristics that identify the firm as masculine.

As discussed earlier, the contemporary theory of the firm, as reflected in the financial contracting models of financial economics, invariably engenders equilibria that are *second best*. Specifically, these equilibria are optimal (i.e., wealth maximizing) neither for the agent concerned nor for the economy in aggregate. Note that agency costs stem essentially from an inability on the part of agents to reliably enforce contractual agreements: even though it is self-defeating, opportunism holds sway. Indeed, any notion of a value system other than that of narrowly defined self-interest is summarily dismissed by financial economists as no more than a "'Nirvana' form of analysis."[13] This invocation of economic *man* is an invocation of Gilligan's "separated self," reflecting the archetypally male values of competition, individualism, and game and rule orientation; an autonomous self separated from others in a hierarchical world. The idea that a different yet equally plausible type of agent—a more feminine, relationship-oriented, "connected self" type of agent—would ameliorate these agency costs seems appealing. Indeed Richard Thaler predicts just such a future shift in economists' concept of rationality when he predicts a new theory of economic behavior that will "retain the idea that agents try to do the best they can, but these individuals will also have the human strengths of kindness and cooperation."[14] As we've just seen, these "human strengths of kindness and cooperation" have been linked explicitly to a feminine value system. Thus, no doubt inadvertently, Thaler is singing the praises of economic woman over economic man.

The economic superiority of what might be called a more "feminine" firm, therefore, derives from its broadened concept of what constitutes rational behavior, as invoked by virtue-ethics theory. To trust for trust's sake, to be virtuous for virtue's sake, now becomes entirely rational and indeed desirable for an agent pursuing moral excellence. Unlike the masculine firm invoked in financial-economic theory, therefore, the feminine firm will exhibit a tendency to nurture cooperation and a recognition of communal—in addition to merely individual—objectives. This tendency will dissipate the agency problems that plague financial-economics' theory of the firm. In essence, within the feminine firm, *trust* becomes a rational and feasible implicit contractual enforcement mechanism.

The ideal firm, therefore, from both a moral and an economic perspective, may be feminine: where a "feminine firm" is one in which an individual's moral orientation is that identified by Gilligan as the predominantly feminine "connected self," as opposed to the predominantly masculine "separated self."

The moral and economic superiority of the feminine firm is implied by Thomas White's provocative essay "Business, Ethics, and Carol Gilligan's "'Two Voices.'" White applies Gilligan's work on gender differences in moral orientation to organizational behavior. He notes that these gender differences may explain why various empirical studies find women relatively more sensitive to ethical dilemmas in business.

> On this matter it is crucial to note Kohlberg's claim that only one in four people advances to the highest stage of moral reasoning. The vast majority of men, then, probably employ "conventional" moral thinking—an outlook that puts a premium on laws, rules, norms or conventions. The apparent ethical superiority of the women in the studies may suggest that ethical dilemmas in business register more strongly with the average possessor of an ethic of care [the connected self] than they do with someone at the conventional stage of an ethic of justice [the separated self].[15]

Thus, at the conventional levels of ethical reasoning, the connected self is more adept at moral deliberation in business than is the separated self. But White's observations are not limited to the moral worth of the firm. In addition, he suggests that a feminine moral orientation may enhance a firm's *economic* worth. He suggests that the feminine ethic may be more attuned to the essential nature of the firm as a nexus of relationships. A feminine firm, therefore, is both morally *and economically* superior. Given this essential nature of the firm as a nexus of communal relations, the exclusion of the feminine firm levies both a moral and an economic cost on our corporate culture. By establishing a sound logical conceptualization and justification for the feminine firm within the business disciplines, a more balanced portrayal of the financial milieu could be achieved.

But consider, for example, the following recent description of a feminist firm:

> A corporation run by feminist principles would oppose the exploitation of employees and the environment. A value on community welfare—and the collective—would foster concern with making the corporation a more habitable, hospitable, and equitable work environment. . . . Feminist management would protect the physical environment through recycling, cleaning up, or detoxifying industrial wastes, complying with regulations and

rules that protect workers and the ecosystem, and using biode-
gradable materials. It would promote the public interest and return profits to workers and the community (in addition to
officials and shareholders). Feminist managers would resist closing factories as tax write-offs or moving them to Third World
countries, where cheaper labor is found. Feminist managers
would cooperate with and improve, rather than dominate and
degrade, the community and environment.[16]

Such a feminist corporation may undoubtedly be morally desirable, but
I see no reason why it would be particularly economically efficient in a competitive market economy. Indeed, a firm that spent more on pollution control than its competitors, and did not produce where labor costs were
lowest, would presumably tend to be uncompetitive. As Thomas Gilmore
observes, "to build a smokeless factory when no competitors are incurring
the cost is individual firm suicide."[17]

Of course, if stakeholders were willing to pay a premium for such a
'green' firm then it might compete, but then such actions would become
economically optimal. Indeed firms today are keenly aware that environmental sensitivity can be a powerful marketing tool. For example, Robert
Solomon, in his book *The New World of Business: Ethics and Free Enterprise
in the Global 1990s,* notes that "whether or not a corporation designates a
portion of its yearly giving to the Environmental Defense Fund or the Sierra
Club, it is no doubt keenly aware that being green is a good way to bring in
the green."[18] Similarly, in his *Harvard Business Review* article, Craig Smith
identifies possibly the true underlying motivation behind corporate philanthropy; "the strategic use of philanthropy has begun to give companies a
powerful competitive edge."[19]

So, economically motivated firms may in some activities masquerade as
virtuous firms. But perhaps there is still hope here. What if all stakeholders
were virtuous—not just management, but also stockholders, bondholders,
employees, etc. In other words, what if the corporate community were a real
polis, qua virtue-ethics theory? Might not then a virtuous firm flourish?

Conclusion

In essence, the above discussion implies that, to the extent that these gender
differences exist, a virtue-based approach may be an effective way of integrat-
ing them into a new finance paradigm. Broadening the theoretical foundation of business theory and education along lines suggested by virtue ethics
theory will help engender an educational and practitioner environment that
does not present itself *a priori* as hostile to female moral orientations.

In the context of education, business schools can be seen as sculpting
the attitudes and values of individuals who inherit and perpetuate our cor-

porate culture.[20] The business school is, in essence, the crucible of corporate culture. It is currently where disparate and undeveloped ideologies and values are cast or recast in the mold of economic rationality. It is thus up to the contemporary progenitor of corporate culture, namely the business school, to fan the "virtue" embers supplied herein and rekindle virtue as a meaningful concept.

By adopting this broadened concept of what constitutes rational behavior, business schools could rebalance the extant gender imbalance caused by an exclusive preoccupation with the financial-economic notion of rationality. This is another reason to move beyond the finance paradigm.

10

Toward a New Finance Paradigm

We can count, but we are rapidly forgetting how to say what is worth counting and why.

—Robert Weizenbaum

A central theme of this book has been a broadening of the finance paradigm to encompass a moral dimension, a dimension supplied by virtue-ethics theory. To some extent, this broadening is a reflection of the considerable cultural impact of the contemporary firm in the form of the transnational corporation. To some extent, it is a reflection of increasing debate in the business, ethics, and business ethics literature concerning the essential nature of the firm: is the firm an atomistic decision unit, a contractual nexus, or a nurturing community? But, most fundamentally, it is a reflection of the fact that the firm is a *human* organization, implying that, in addition to economic relationships, "business should be seen as consisting of sets of moral relationships . . . what Rawls refers to as a social union."[1]

Rather than being an aberration, therefore, this book's invocation of the finance paradigm in a still broader arena of human interaction is perhaps an inevitable consequence of the increasing impact that financial economics is having on intellectual and practical affairs. This increasing impact necessitates a more holistic conception of human endeavor in economic contexts as being concerned with the acquisition of both external goods *and* internal goods. Part I of this book established the finance paradigm's existence entirely within the Universe of Substance (i.e., that of external goods), and its complete ignorance of the Universe of Value (i.e., that of internal goods). Thus, a recognition not only of the existence of internal goods, but also of their moral superiority, leads inevitably to a moral rejection of this narrow view of economic rationality: "the tradition of the virtues is at variance with central features of the modern economic order and more especially its individualism, its acquisitiveness and its elevation of the values of the market to a central social place."[2]

The 'New' Agent

Earlier, I defined an 'ethical individual' as one motivated primarily by a desire to achieve excellence. Here I use this term in what I believe to be its true—and certainly its original—context, namely the context of *moral* excellence, conjuring the image of ethics as something toward which we strive, rather than something which constrains us. As MacIntyre notes, "the whole point of ethics—both as a theoretical and practical discipline—is to enable man to pass from his present state to his true end."[3]

The pursuit of internal goods, in preference to external goods, is what defines the ethical individual. Interestingly, the concept of the 'internal good' is very similar to the concept of "quality" in the increasingly popular "Total Quality Management" literature, and to the concept of "excellence" in the in-search-of-excellence-type management motivational literature. All these concepts have to do with the pursuit of some ethereal goal that is not external or finite, but that is universally recognized and acclaimed as desirable. According to practical rationality, the pursuit of this quality/excellence/internal good entails adherence to certain behavioral ideals, commonly called the *virtues*. MacIntyre continues,

> The virtues therefore are to be understood as those dispositions that will not only sustain practices and enable us to achieve the goods internal to practices, but which will also sustain us in the relevant kind of quest for the good, by enabling us to overcome the harms, dangers, temptations and distractions which we encounter, and which will furnish us with increasing self-knowledge and increasing knowledge of the good.[4]

Consider the four critical virtues enumerated by Socrates: wisdom, justice, courage, and temperance. Justice, for example, would include a sense of fairness, which would generally entail being honest and trustworthy. But note my tentative wording. I say "would generally entail being honest" rather than "*will* entail being honest" because in the pursuit of moral excellence there are no absolute ethical rules. There are times when circumstances may dictate that the ethical agent conceal the truth. For example, while experiencing negative cash flow, a CFO may choose to borrow funds in order to maintain timely dividend payments. Such action could be construed as deceptive in that the payment of dividends is generally taken by outsiders as a signal of a firm's ability to generate sufficient internal cash flow. But the CFO may genuinely believe that such deception is for the greater good; it is consistent with the pursuit of moral excellence. If the CFO is confident that the firm is only temporarily insolvent but is unsure of his ability to relay this confidence to investors, and if he believes that the announcement of a dividend omission would cause unnecessary concern—if not outright panic—among investors, then this deception is entirely ethical. His motivation is practically rational and virtuous, even though his action is arguably deceptive.

But what about a CFO who chooses the same action, namely borrowing to maintain the dividend, but who has no expectation regarding the firm's future earning potential. Rather, the CFO's motivation is to maintain the stock price temporarily in order that she may exercise some stock options. Clearly, this agent's fundamental motivation is personal material gain. The deception is not motivated by the pursuit of moral excellence. This CFO is not exercising *sound moral judgment*. She is not exercising the virtues of justice or wisdom because, as the classical philosophers make very clear, a wise individual (i.e., one who has been exposed to the concept of moral excellence) will realize that it is only through virtuous behavior and the pursuit of internal goods that one can live the good life.

And what is the good life? Once again, this question brooks no simple answer. The good life is the life that any virtuous individual would choose. It involves adherence to the virtues, and the pursuit of quality/excellence/internal goods. It entails placing virtue and moral excellence above external goods as a source of primary motivation in life. Only the agent who is so motivated and acts in this manner is able to flourish and achieve true happiness. Thus, the pursuit of moral excellence is not self-sacrificing. It is entirely consistent with the pursuit of personal self-interest. An ethical individual simply possesses a heightened concept of self interest viv-à-vis the interests of the community (what Aristotle calls the *polis*)—a concept nurtured by moral education (the virtue of wisdom), but not nurtured by the narrow materially opportunistic behavioral assumptions of the finance paradigm.

An economic agent, that is, one motivated primarily by economic gain, may act in a trustworthy manner, but this has nothing to do with virtue since the *motivation* is not moral excellence. The moral agent, that is, one motivated primarily by the pursuit of moral excellence, will also generally act in a trustworthy manner and will therefore reap the economic—as well as the moral—benefits of a reputation. As virtue-ethics theory makes clear, however, the fact that ethics pays should not be the motivation behind our ethical actions. Even if ethics does not pay off in an economic sense, which clearly in some circumstances it does not, classical moral philosophy gives us ample reason to act ethically: short-term material gain through unethical behavior is inevitably at the expense of long-term happiness and the good life.

The concept of the financial manager as a *professional* sheds additional light on the difference between the economically rational agent *qua* the finance paradigm, and the practically rational agent *qua* virtue ethics. Consider Ronald Duska's statement that "to be an agent in business is to be a professional. . . . One doesn't simply do what one is told, one has expertise, one reads and anticipates the needs and interests of the principal and operates for the principal's good. Managers, Financiers, Accountants, Ad Executives, Sales Representatives, are all agents. Agents are, qua agent, committed to good, i.e., the good of their client."[5]

This invocation of the agent in business is clearly at odds with the individualistic wealth-maximizing opportunist of the finance paradigm. Agency theory certainly does not view the agent as possessing a "professional" attitude. Duska's notion of the agent as one "committed to good" is clearly more in line with practical rationality than it is with economic rationality. The practically rational financial manager can thus be viewed as the consummate professional, or the moral exemplar.

The importance of moral exemplars in an organizational setting is emphasized by cognitive science in its involation of "exemplar theory." Goldman summarizes the theory as follows:

An insight into the nature of professionalism as it relates to virtue-ethics theory is provided by Jack Sammons in a fascinating account of the role that Albert Speer played as Adolf Hitler's chief architect in Nazi Germany. Although in this case the profession was architecture rather than management, the lessons that Sammons draws from the experiences of Albert Speer are universally applicable to the professions.

First, Sammons uses the experiences of Speer to illustrate the infeasibility of the traditional approach to professional ethics. As Sammons sees it, the central weakness of the traditional approach is its notion of a "neutral standing ground" from which professionals—whether they be accountants, managers, or architects—can self-reflect and apply moral rules or principles.

> To reflect from the broadest, and therefore, the least limiting, perspective possible, the authentic self must not identify itself with any role. This moral rebel could not be Speer the German, nor Speer the Christian, nor Speer the citizen, nor Speer the father or husband, nor Speer as *a* Speer nor even Speer as Speer, because these are just other blinding roles, equally relativistic, reflection limiting, choices of a way of life—especially so, for some of them, in Nazi Germany. . . . If we have learned anything at all from postmodern philosophy . . . it is that our reflections always come from a particular perspective and both imply and need a teleology.[7]

In essence, therefore, there is no neutral standing ground from which a professional may morally adjudicate. Every perspective is relativistic. "We are not looking back over our lives from outside our roles or our stories, but from within them."[8] Consequently, ethics and professionalism are not separable; being a "good" professional must entail being a moral professional in the sense that a true professional seeks excellence in a given profession through the exercise of the virtues. Albert Speer's failing, therefore, and the reason why he diligently and unquestioningly designed the great edifices of the Third Reich, was because he did not regard architecture as a *true* profession: "we are failing, as Speer failed, because we do not take our professions seriously enough."[9] In the context of a virtue-ethics-type distinction between external and internal goods,

> [Speer] defined success as an architect only in terms of the external goods it could provide, the ones that have little to do with the

> craft itself. . . . Speer became an architect obsessed with a single,
> immensely powerful and violent client whose pleasure defined
> success for him. Necessarily, as he sought self-respect as an archi-
> tect from Hitler's praise, he rejected his craft.[10]

Had Speer remained true to his craft—his profession of architecture—
he would have recognized the moral impoverishment of Hitler's world vision as it was manifested in the grossly ostentatious and demonstrative
buildings that Hitler cherished.

Speer did finally awaken to the grotesque implications of Hitler's worldview. This awakening occurred when Speer heard of Hitler's plan to raze
Warsaw. Speer writes in his memoir that he saw Hitler "wantonly and without cause annihilating the city which he himself had called the most beautiful in Europe." As Sammons observes, "Finally Speer was learning the lesson
his mentor [Tessenow] had offered so many years before—the difference
between Tessenow's architectural need to spell out truthfully the German
culture and the German people and Hitler's use of the ideas of a culture and
a people for personal political power." Speer finally recognized, therefore,
the difference between Tessenow, the true professional who sought the internal goods of his craft, and Speer, the quasi professional who sought primarily the external goods of status and praise.[11]

Tessenow's pursuit of excellence in architecture was as much a moral
pursuit as an architectural one. As the "true" professional Tessenow pursued
the internal good of excellence over and above any external objective. As virtue-ethics theory illustrates, this pursuit of excellence necessarily entails adherence to the virtues—such as honesty, fairness, perseverance, and integrity.
The virtues become central to the role of a professional within a profession or
a 'practice.' A manager who pursues excellence as defined within virtue ethics will thus realize that sound moral judgment is an integral part of this pursuit. In essence, virtue ethics enhances any discussion of business ethics by
showing that ethics can be an ideal and not merely a constraint.

In comparing the new "virtuous" agent in finance to the old "opportunistic" agent, therefore, we may draw on the comparison between Speer and
his mentor Tessenow. The motivations exhibited by Speer characterize the
traditional agent in the finance paradigm, engaged in the pursuit of external
goods; in this case, power and the approbation of Hitler. Tessenow characterizes the 'new' practically rational agent, engaged in the pursuit of the
goods internal to the practice of, in this case, architecture.

Like Tessenow, the 'new' agent in a practical-rationality-based finance
paradigm will be one who pursues the goods internal to, in this case, financial management. As the evidence summarized in chapter 7 makes clear, this
new agent is no less realistic—and certainly more desirable from both an
economic and a moral perspective—than the old agent. With the introduction of these new agents, agency theory will no longer be driven solely by the
'Sirens' song' of opportunism.

The 'New' Firm as *Polis*

Perhaps the polis is, as Plato and Aristotle thought, the only form of community in which human beings can flourish, rather than merely endure.

—William Prior

Accepting the premise that there is no absolute substantive rationality, what factors determine whether agents in practice become virtuous or opportunistic? Virtue-ethics theory answers this question very concretely. For the virtues to flourish, a conducive infrastructure is required. As was made clear in chapter 7, practically rational Aristotelian agents cannot operate in a vacuum. This form of rationality assumes not only that agents believe in the existence of a *telos*, but also that an infrastructure exists that is structured in recognition of, and in order to attain, the *telos*.

An interesting analogy can be drawn between the role of the *polis* in directing human endeavor, and recent research that highlights the importance of institutional infrastructure in guiding human activity.[12] Douglas North, for example, notes that the entrepreneur within the firm (North uses the term 'organization') represents Dynamic Quality, constrained and directed by the institutional infrastructure. But he also notes that "the subjective perceptions (mental models) of entrepreneurs determine the choices they make."[13] And it is the infrastructure, the *polis*, that helps sculpt these mental models: "It is the institutional framework that dictates the kind of knowledge perceived to having the maximum pay-off."[14] The firm, therefore, as an attribute of the *polis* is instrumental to Aristotelian rationality. Its role is to guide and assist agents in their pursuit of the *telos*: the absolute Quality.

Broadening the role of the firm in this way prompts a definition of the firm that extends that which is implicit in the finance paradigm by recognizing the firm's role as an integral part of the organizational infrastructure, necessary for the pursuit of the *telos*: *Firms facilitate and nurture individual and collective material acquisition as a means to the attainment of excellence through virtue.*

Note that this definition invokes the firm as more than merely Dynamic Quality, or entrepreneurial activity. As part of the *polis* the firm adopts Static Quality attributes. As facilitator, the firm provides an external-good support for the pursuit of excellence through the exercise of the classical virtues. As a nurturer, the firm provides an organizational structure premised on the superiority of *phronesis* over *techne*, of internal goods over external goods.

Invoking the firm as a constituent of the *polis*—as a true corporate culture—clearly broadens its role considerably. Indeed, one likely criticism of this invocation of the firm is that, despite its current size and power as reflected in the transnational corporation, the firm—even as it exists in Japan—still remains a primarily *economic* organization.[15] Even if desirable, is it plausible to invoke the concepts of *polis* and *telos* in the contemporary world of liberal individualism? MacIntyre believes that it is: "if at least those features of the *polis* which are minimally necessary for the exercise of justice and of practical rationality can be exhibited by forms of social order other than those of the *polis*, then the grounds for that charge of irrelevance may fail."[16]

Whether or not the charge fails will clearly depend to a large degree on the infrastructure in which individuals learn about and practice business. As North notes: "If the highest rates of return in a society are for piracy, then organizations will invest in knowledge and skills that will make them better pirates."[17] In an educational context, we must accept the "indoctrination" aspect of business education, that is, we must accept that "is" implies "ought." Therefore, economic rationality must be rejected on the grounds that it fails to recognize the Universe of Value and hence virtue and indeed morality in general. Thus, we reject economic rationality, not on the basis of its descriptive accuracy (albeit questionable), but rather on the basis of its prescriptive undesirability (of course, if 'is' implies 'ought,' then the two become inseparable). If we further accept the ultimate desirability of an Aristotelian-type notion of rationality, with its accompanying notions of *telos* and *polis*, then we must accept the theory of the firm as more than merely a passive description of an organization and human activity therein. The theory of the firm becomes much more than this. It becomes moral dogma: a theory not only of what the firm is but of what the firm *should* be. Bowie echoes the sentiments of many when he states that "business education and research into business must take into account the ethical paradigm as well."[18] Our discussion here implies that business education and business-ethics education are entirely inseparable, thus the meaningful question is not, Should business education consider ethics? but rather, Which moral philosophy should financial economics adopt?

The contemporary flirtation with psychological egoism in the form of the "six axioms" is misguided in the sense that it fails to identify the true *telos*. MacIntyre notes that Aristotle identifies this as an educational failure; "one mark of educational failure will be a tendency on the part of individual citizens to identify as *the* good and *the* best some good which is merely an external by-product of those activities in which excellence is achieved—money or honor, for example (*Politics* 1257b40–1258a14; *NE 1095b22–31*)."[19] Thus, the failure of business education has been not so much a manifestation of a "closing of the American mind," as Allan Bloom suggests, but rather a misdirection of the American mind and indeed the minds of all those immersed in contemporary corporate culture: a confusion of means and ends.[20] This misdirection has led MacIntyre to characterize the modern student as "someone whose education has been as much a process of deprivation as of enrichment."[21] In the current context, this enrichment entails merely the recognition of the firm as a human organization, and that those goods that are ultimately desirable in all human endeavor—whether they be defined as *eudaimonia*, Quality, excellence, or internal goods—are only attainable through the exercise of moral virtue. Thus, the theory of the firm is a moral theory because the firm is a moral organization. Consequently, the business school must be a fundamentally moral institution. Given the Metaphysics of Quality, a theory of the firm devoid of morality is also devoid of Quality. This is indeed a deprivation for, as Pirsig notes, "Quality is the primary empirical reality of the world."[22]

In summary, the finance paradigm invokes the firm as solely a conduit through which agents pursue wealth. Virtue ethics recognizes a more interactive role for the "new" firm as a nurturing community in which individuals may flourish morally as well as materially. In addition to being a powerful economic force as discussed earlier, this "new" firm will also be a powerful *moral* force. Individual virtue—by minimizing agency costs—supports the economic role of the firm, while the structure of the firm itself as a nurturing community encourages individual virtue: the relationship is reciprocal.

Some Concluding Thoughts

In concluding their seminal work on the theory of the firm, Michael Jensen and William Meckling note that "whatever its shortcomings, the corporation has thus far survived the market test against potential alternatives."[23] This statement has since been further vindicated by recent developments in eastern Europe and the republics that once comprised the Soviet Union. We exit the twentieth century with the market system increasingly omnipresent, auguring a global corporate culture. Thus, when viewed within the Universe of Substance, the story of the firm is undoubtedly a story of success.

But there is another universe, a morally superior universe: the Universe of Value. In the Metaphysics of Quality, as in Aristotelian moral philosophy, its superiority is absolute because humanity's *telos* exists within it. Success in the Universe of Substance is merely a prerequisite for entry into the Universe of Value through virtue. Unfortunately, this truth has been obscured by the finance paradigm where "excellence" is equated with efficiency in achieving solely material ends. It is a paradigm that is oblivious to the Universe of Value: there is no virtue, no internal good, no craftsmanship or excellence save in the name of effectiveness. Truth becomes subservient to profit: universities serve firms. Sherwin Klein notes, "In the *Republic*, Plato implicitly and explicitly argues that materialism is the source of many of our moral ills. If one's value system is essentially materialistic, it encourages us to cheat, lie, steal, and the like, for if we can get away with such actions, we will be materialistically better off."[24]

When Aristotle described life's ideal as one of 'intellectual pursuit' or 'contemplative enquiry,' he accepted that the material wealth of *his* society was sufficient for only a small fraction of its inhabitants to realize this ideal. The triumph of our age is that the wealth generated by the firm through the market system has freed the majority of humanity from the fetters of material servitude. But the victory has been Pyrrhic. As virtue disappears from our cultural milieu, the fetters of material servitude are merely being replaced by those of moral ignorance. The tragedy of contemporary corporate culture is thus the tragedy of King Midas. In creating the means for unlimited material acquisition, we have prevented ourselves from acquiring that which we should most desire.

Notes

Preface

1.   Some educators may hesitate to use a business ethics 'text' that does not include case studies. With the possible exception of chapter 5, however, I have intentionally avoided including case studies in this book. Although the case-study approach to business ethics education has been popular in the past, it is coming under increasing (and I feel fully justified) criticism. This book's focus on virtue ethics highlights the essential weakness of case studies as the sole or even primary educational tool in business ethics. This is not to say that cases have no merit, but virtue ethics recognizes that, to be meaningful, ethics must permeate right to the core of human activity. It must indeed become the *raison d'être* of what we do. Case studies can never capture the full complexity of actual life situations. As such, students exposed solely to the case-study approach to ethics tend to view ethics too simplistically. This text emphasizes that ethics is a way of life, not merely a contextually specific behavioral constraint as case studies tend to imply.

2.   See also Williamson (1964), Jensen and Meckling (1976), and Myers (1977), also Diamond (1989), and Kreps and Wilson (1982) on reputation effects.

3.   See also in particular Arrow (1975, 1984), Kahneman et al. (1986), Schiller (1986), and Sen (1987).

4.   These generally come under the heading of *virtue-ethics theory* (Taylor, 1991; Solomon, 1992).

5.   Ashton (1966), Holmes (1990), and Pirsig (1991) also provide invaluable historical background on the economic and moral impacts of the firm during the Industrial Revolution.

6.   In particular—in the context of this book—the work of Bowie (1991), De George (1986), Etzioni (1988), Klein (1988, 1989), and Sen (1987).

Introduction

1.   Friedman (1970), 153–156. Sherwin (1983) sums up Freidman's argument as follows: "Friedman categorically disqualifies managers taking social action on two grounds: first, in complex situations, business managers will probably not know the correct action to take to achieve the desired result and, second, by taking social action, managers would be acting as unauthorized civil servants."

2. The first quote is from Bowie (1991) and the second is from De-George (1986).

3. The first quote is from Byron (1988) and the second is from Barach and Elstrott (1988).

4. Miller, 1986, p. 452.

5. Ponemon, 1992, 242.

6. Jensen and Meckling, 1976, p. 310

7. Jensen and Meckling, 1976, 328.

8. On agents' behavior choices and aspirations, see Axelrod (1984), Baumhart (1961), Etzioni (1991), Ghorbade (1991), Kahneman, Knetsch, and Thaler (1986), and Thaler (1992). On structure of the firm, see Milgram (1974), Marwell and Ames (1981), and Poneman (1992).

9. Bowie, 1991, p. 4.

10. Leland and Pyle (1977), for example, in their seminal capital structure signaling model, state that "the entrepreneur is presumed to maximize his expected utility of wealth" (373).

11. A lognormal utility function of the form $U(W)=\ln W$, where W is wealth, implies that the agent gains progressively less of an increase in utility from steadily increasing increments of wealth. For a discussion of lognormal and other utility functions in finance, see Copeland and Weston (1988), chapter 4. For an interesting discussion of rationality assumptions concerning groups versus individuals, see Kavka (1991), "Is Individual Choice Less Problematic Than Collective Choice?" In essence, Kavka concludes that any attempt to model human preference orderings—whether individual or collective—is extremely problematic.

12. Klein, 1989, p. 241

13. The essential difference between deontological and teleological moral theories is that the former are nonconsequential in the sense that the decision of which action to take is not premised on the likely consequences of the action but rather on some universal decision criterion (for example, Kant's "categorical imperative" in which one should take only those actions that one would wish to become universally applied). Contrarily, teleological moral theories do consider consequences as central to the moral decision (for example, utilitarians endeavor to choose those acts that will maximize aggregate social welfare). See Hoffman and Moore (1990) for a concise summary of these traditional approaches to ethics in a business context.

14. Taylor, 1991, p. 4.

15. Allen, 1988, p. 118.

16. MacIntyre, 1988, p. 401.

Chapter 1

1. Edgeworth, 1881, p. 16.

2. First quote is from Copeland and Weston (1988), 80. Second quote is from Noreen (1988), 359.

3. Even Edgeworth did not believe that nineteenth-century individuals necessarily fitted this caricature of pure self-interest. See Sen, 1978, 317–44.

4. Holmes, 1990, 268.

5. Hume, 1751, p. 5.

6. Smith, 1759, p. 5.

7. Homer, c. –900, pp. 227-228.

8. Myers, 1977.

9. Bowie, 1991, p. 14.

10. von Neumann and Morgenstern, 1947, p. 31.

11. For a summary of these five axioms see Copeland and Weston, (1988), 79–80.

12. Copeland and Weston, 1988, 80.

13. Copeland and Weston, 1988, 80 emphasis added.

14. Leland and Pyle, 1977, p. 373; John and Nachman, 1985, p. 867; Diamond, 1989, p. 833.

15. MacIntyre, 1984, p. 254.

16. Jensen and Meckling, 1976, p. 328.

17. One reason often cited for this popularity is the similarity between economic rationality and the biological ideas of natural selection and the selfish gene. Recent evidence indicates, however, that genes may not be entirely selfish. Some form of tacit cooperation, in other words a morality, may exist even at the molecular level (*Economist*, 21-27 March, 1992, 93–94).

18. Thaler, 1992, p. 2.

19. Moore, 1991, p. 63.

20. Noreen, 1988, p. 359.

21. A study by Robert Frank, Thomas Gilovich, and Dennis Regan, 1993, finds that students who have been exposed to economics classes are more mercenary than students who study other disciplines. Their evidence strongly supports the idea that economics education, indeed business education in general, is a type of indoctrination into a very narrow conceptualization of 'rational' behavior a conceptualization that discourages cooperation. Far from purely a theoretical construct, therefore, in the classroom setting and probably elsewhere, the finance paradigm has an implicit normative agenda.

22. Thomas Copeland and Fred Weston (1988), 790, for example, characterize these markets as ones in which there are numerous buyers and sellers, no information or transaction or transportation costs, no barriers to trade of any kind, and in which the future is known with certainty by all market participants—clearly a contrived environment, to say the least.

23. Chung and Smith, 1987, 146.

24. Jensen and Meckling, 1976, 311.

25. Jensen and Meckling, 1976, p. 311.

26. Fama and Jensen, 1983, p. 315.

27. For example, Ralph Walker and Michael Long (1984) find that, in defending their companies from hostile takeovers, managers tend to look

after their own interests in preference to the interests of shareholders.

28. 1986, p. 20.

29. See UN Center on Transnational Corporations (1985).

30. See Getz (1990).

31. 1970, p. 153.

32. As an interesting aside, Vivienne Brown (1991) discusses the apparent philosophical inconsistency between *The Theory of Moral Sentiments* and *The Wealth of Nations*, which has led some observers to doubt whether both books could have been written by the same hand. Brown does not directly address this question of authorial integrity, but rather emphasizes the importance of historical context in revealing each work's "textual identity" (189).

33. Buchanan and Vanberg (1991), 179. (1979), 38. the "new evolutionary synthesis" described by Wicken (1987, 3), and in an economic context by Allen (1988) in "Evolution, Innovation and Economics": a "unified view of the world which bridges the gap between the physical and the human sciences" (118).

34. MacIntyre, 1984, p. 208.

35. Bowie, 1991, 11–12.

Chapter 2

1. Furubotn and Pejovich, 1972, 1138.

2. See Jensen and Meckling, 1976, 307–308.

3. Alchian, 1969, pp. 2-3.

4. Coase, "The Nature of the Firm" (1937).

5. Cornell and Shapiro, 1987, 6.

6. King, 1988, p. 480.

7. King, 1988, p. 362.

8. Jensen and Meckling, 1976, 308.

9. The nomenclature "moral hazard" may cause some confusion among readers unfamiliar with agency theory since the name itself implies some form of moral evaluation of the contractual relation. The label is misleading in this regard because there is no moral evaluation in agency theory. Indeed, the rationality assumptions of agency theory expressly exclude any moral dimension, as discussed above.

10. See Miller and Rock (1985).

11. See Flannery (1986); also Ross (1977), and John and Nachman (1985).

12. See Allen and Faulhaber (1989); also Beatty and Ritter (1986), and Carter and Manaster (1990), on the IPO underpricing conundrum.

13. See Spence (1977).

14. Jensen and Meckling (1976).

15. Kreps, 1984, p. 12.

16. Formally, this is the unique Nash equilibrium, in which each player's move is 'rational' given the move of the other player.

17. Williamson, 1983, p. 23.

18. Hart, 1983, 23.

19. As an interesting corollary, note that a belief on the part of player A that there is a chance that B might act ethically will lower the amount A is willing to pay for legal enforcement. For example, if A believes that there is a 50-50 chance that B will act ethically and honor trust, then the maximum A will be willing to pay for legal enforcement drops from $10.00 to $7.50 (assuming A is risk neutral): if A offers trust he now has an expected payoff of $2.50 ($10.00 – $5.00 / 2) versus a guaranteed payoff of $10.00 given legal enforcement. Of course, if A were sure that B would act ethically, then he would have no need for legal enforcement. Our simple game, therefore, illustrates the oft-noted inverse relation between the general ethical standards of a society and the amount of litigation in that society.

20. Dybvig and Spatt, 1985, 5

21. Williamson, 1983, pp. 519–520.

22. Gauthier's argument is discussed further in chapters 4 and 8.

23. Gauthier, 1988, p. 96.

24. See Thaler (1992), for a review of these studies.

25. Axelrod, 1984, p. 10.

26. Bull, 1983, p. 658.

27. Telser, 1980, 43.

28. Akerlof, 1970, pp. 488-500.

29. Klein and Leffler label this price premium as the "quality assuring price" (1981).

30. Hart, 1983, 23.

31. Kreps and Wilson, 1982, pp. 863–894.

32. See Milgrom and Roberts (1982).

33. Selten, 1975, pp. 25–55.

34. Dybvig and Spatt, 1985, 4.

35. Kreps and Wilson, 1982, pp. 863–894.

36. Dobson and Dorsey, 1993, pp. 143–152.

37. A different explanation for this abandonment delay is supplied by Mier Statman and David Caldwell (1987), who invoke psychological factors such as "regret aversion" and a general unwillingness on the part of project managers to admit defeat. Perhaps the classic example of this was Lockheed Inc.'s failure to abandon its L-1011 aircraft project in the face of ever-mounting losses, losses that eventually necessitated a government bailout.

Chapter 3

1. Holmstrom, 1981, p. 46; Hart, 1983, p. 23.

2. 1985, 863-877.

3. See, for an example in a finance context, Dejong, Forsythe, and Lundholm (1985).

4. Allen Fuchsberg, *Fortune*, 1988, p. 44.

5. DeAngelo and De DeAngelo, 1987, p. 102.

6. DeAngelo and De DeAngelo, 1987, p. 103.

7. Cornell and Shapiro, 1987, p. 6, pp. 8–9.

8. See Allen and Faulhaber (1989).

9. To see the logic of this argument, consider the game is to be repeated ten times. In the tenth and final repetition, player B would clearly abuse trust. Knowing this, player A will not offer trust in the final repetition. Knowing this, player B will rationally abuse trust in the penultimate (ninth) repetition. Knowing this . . . etc. The game "rolls back" to the first play in which player A will rationally not offer trust given that player B will rationally abuse trust if it is offered.

10. See Smith (1986).

11. Beatty and Ritter, 1986, p. 215.

12. Tinic, 1988, 790.

13. Rock, 1986.

14. Tinic, 1988, p. 819.

15. p. 180.

16. The reputability of underwriters is generally measured from the order in which they appear in financial-newspaper "tombstone announcements" that list the name of the firm going public, the offer price, and all the underwriters in decreasing order of significance.

17. See, for example, Arrow (1975) and Thaler (1992).

18. Noreen, 1988, p. 367.

19. Jenson and Meckling, 1976, p. 328.

20. Frank, 1988, p. 258.

21. Jones and Quinn, 1993, p. 7.

Chapter 4

1. This latter scenario is demonstrated in the model of debt markets developed by Ken Riener and myself: "The Rationality of Honesty in Debt Markets" (1995), as yet unpublished.

2. This is demonstrated in the models of Diamond (1989), Rasmusen (1989), Kreps and Wilson (1982), and Milgrom and Roberts (1982).

3. Smith, 1992, p. 3.

4. Smith, 1992, p. 3.

5. Quote appears in Dobson, 1993, p. 40.

6. Dobson, 1993, p. 40.

7. A recent example of Confidence School–type arguments can be found in Jennifer Moore's article "What Is Really Unethical about Insider Trading" (1990).

8. Klein, 1988, p. 63.

9. Okai, 1991, 4.

10. Okai, 1991, 5.

11. Campbell, 1986, p. 361.

12. Fry, 1989, p. 44.

13. Fry, 1989, p. 44.
14. Bowie, 1970, p. 153; 1991, p. 20.
15. Noreen, 1988, p. 362.
16. Essentially, the period known as the "Enlightenment" occurred in Europe in the seventeenth and eighteenth centuries and was marked by a decline in the power of organized religion and a rise in all avenues of reason-based intellectual enquiry.
17. For a discussion of these theories in a business context, see Hoffman and Moore (1990).
18. Hart, 1983, p. 23.
19. See MacIntyre (1984).
20. Derry and Green (1989).
21. Myers, 1977; Jensen and Meckling, 1976.

Chapter 5

1. Baneish and Chatov, 1993, p. 29, emphasis added.
2. Pastin, 1986, p. 474.
3. Allmon and Grant, 1990, p. 811.
4. Williams and Murphy, 1990, p. 26.
5. Hoffman and Moore, 1990, p. 636.
6. Ladd, 1991, p. 173.
7. Raiborn and Payne, 1990, p. 888.
8. Gioia, 1992, p. 388.
9. Gioia, 1992, p. 388.
10. Dean, 1992.
11. Dean, 1992, p. 287.
12. Dean, 1992, p. 287.
13. Dean, 1992, p. 288.
14. Nystrom, 1990, 971.
15. Business Roundtable, 1988, p. 4.
16. Hoffman and Moore, 1990, 109.
17. Hoffman and Moore, 1990, 109.
18. Klein, 1988, p. 63.
19. Rion, 1982.
20. Rion, 1982.
21. Statman and Caldwell, 1987, 7.
22. Strict utilitarians may balk at the idea of the firm as the "relevant universe." If the invisible hand concept is accepted, however, then the maximization of total economic value can be taken as roughly synonymous with the maximization of individual firm value. Given the invisible hand, therefore, utilitarianism dovetails neatly with standard financial analysis.
23. See Kanodia, Bushman and Dickhart, 1989.
24. Specifically, see a paper by Robert Dorsey and myself (1993).

25. Similar logic would apply to the ethicality of a decision by managers to borrow in order to maintain a dividend payment. Superficially, the payment of the dividend may appear to represent a false signal, in that the funds were borrowed. If managers' underlying motivation is firm value maximization, however, then the signal is not necessarily deceptive. Indeed, the ability of the firm to borrow under such circumstances could be construed as a positive signal.

26. This scenario is similar to that discussed by Myers and Majluff (1984) and Miller and Rock (1985) in the context of dividend signaling.

27. See Statman and Caldwell, 1987, 6. Similar arguments have been presented by Thaler (1980), psychic accounting, Laughhunn and Payne (1991), framing, and Staw (1981). For example, Staw and Ross (1987) note that a certain personal and social esteem accrues to those individuals who "stick to their guns" (59) in the face of adversity.

28. Murdoch, 1971, p.52.

29. See Cottrill (1990) for a review.

30. Swanda, 1990, pp. 752–757.

31. Swanda, 1990, p. 753.

Chapter 6

1. In a recent study, Uric Dufrene and I found that all major stock markets react similarly to news concerning the outcome of U.S. presidential elections. This lends further support to the idea of a single global securities market.

2. Reich, 1990, p. 79.

3. See Shrybman (1990), 30.

4. UN (1985).

5. Bartlett and Ghoshal, 1989, p. 5.

6. One could argue that certain regulations, such as pollution control laws, actually stifle commercial activity rather than foster it. But over the long term, even these types of regulations could be viewed as fostering commercial activity through fostering a stable and healthy environment.

7. Francis, 1986, p. 737.

8. Donaldson, 1989, p. 27.

9. See Dobson (1992a).

10. See Bannock, Baxter, and Rees (1972) for a summary of the contributions made by these individuals to the doctrine of classical economics.

11. Dunkel, 1991.

12. Shrybman, 1990, p. 1.

13. *Economist,* 1991, p. 65.

14. Peng, 1990, p. 211.

15. Peng, 1990, p. 212.

16. Hall, 1986, p. 204.

17. Goldsmith, 1990, p. 204.
18. Keohane, 1989, p. 145.
19. See Keohane, 1989, 145.
20. See Thomson and Dudley (1989), 219.
21. Thomson and Dudley (1989), 219.
22. At the time of Aristotle (384–322 b.c.), the Greek Empire stretched east into Asia Minor.

Chapter 7

1. Kuhn, 1970, p. 208.
2. Rasmusen, 1989, p. 13.
3. See, for example, Statman and Caldwell (1987), and Simon (1986).
4. Hutchenson, 1986, p. 51.
5. MacIntyre, 1988, p. 9.
6. MacIntyre, 1988, p. 367.
7. Sen, 1987, pp. 1–2.
8. Plott, 1986, p. 302.
9. Simon, 1986, p. 223.
10. See DeJong, Forsythe, and Lundholm (1985) and Axelrod (1986).
11. Thaler, 1992, pp. 4–5.
12. Sen, 1987, p. 79.
13. Frank, Gilovich, and Regan (1993).
14. Bowie, 1991, p. 9.
15. Bowie, 1991, p. 19.
16. Milgram, 1974, p. 6.
17. Bowie, 1991, p. 9.
18. See Marwell and Ames, in Bowie, 1991, 9.
19. Duska, 1992, p. 149.
20. MacIntyre, 1984, p. 74.
21. Jensen Meckling, 1976, p. 328.
22. As always, attaching labels to various schools of moral philosophy is fraught with peril. I choose Klein's labels because they are simple and descriptive for the current purposes. The traditional action-based approach to moral philosophy might also be named the 'modernist' or 'enlightenment' or 'encyclopedic' approach. I take the new agent-based approach to be synonymous with virtueethics, but it might also be labeled by some as the 'postmodernist' approach.
23. Sammons, 1992, p. 77.
24. Derry and Green, 1989.
25. Annas, 1995, p. 250.
26. Goodpaster, 1994, pp. 54–55.
27. MacIntyre, 1984, p. 191.
28. MacIntyre, 1984, pp. 190–191.

29. Nussbaum, 1991, p. 38.
30. MacIntyre, 1988, p. 137.
31. MacIntyre, 1988, p. 396.
32. MacIntyre, 1988, p. 133.
33. MacIntyre, 1988, pp. 96-97.
34. Jensen and Meckling, 1976; Miller, 1986.
35. Solomon, 1992, pp. 325, 321.
36. MacIntyre, 1984, p. 31.
37. Pritchard, 1992, p. 170.
38. Goldman, 1993, p. 341.
39. For accounts of virtue ethics theory, see Taylor (1991), MacIntyre (1984 and 1988), Prior (1991), Foot (1967), Hutchison (1976), and Solomon (1992).
40. Etzioni, 1988, p. 1.
41. First published in 1991 and 1972, respectively.
42. MacIntyre, 1990, pp. 235–236.
43. Pirsig, 1991, p. 101.
44. The idea of morality at the molecular level may seem, at first blush, somewhat whimsical. There is recent evidence in the field of evolutionary biology, however, that competition among animal genes may exhibit a form of tacit cooperation and not merely outright competition as the "selfish-gene" idea implied (see Dawkins, 1972). To the extent that tacit cooperation can be construed as a moral order, Pirsig's may—to some extent at least—be vindicated (for a concise recent summary of some of this literature see the *Economist*, 21-27 March, 1992, 93-94).
45. MacIntyre, 1988, p. 115.
46. Buchanan and Vanberg, 1991, 167.
47. Buchanan and Vanberg, 1991, 170–171.
48. Buchanan and Vanberg, 1991, 183.
49. Wiseman, 1989, p. 230.
50. As an interesting aside, Kuhn notes that a similar point of view was the underlying cause of the moral firestorm surrounding publication of Charles Darwin's *Origin of Species*. Darwin's theory was viewed as a threat, not because he claimed that man was descended from apelike creatures, but because his theory implied that evolution was a nondeterministic process, and therefore by inference a purposeless process.
51. Buchanan and Vanberg, 1991, 180.
52. Pirsig, 1991, 300.
53. For a review of the hierarchy-of-needs concept, see Schoell and Guiltinan, 1992, 153.
54. MacIntyre, 1984, 148.
55. MacIntyre, 1966, 82.
56. Pirsig, 1991, 105.
57. Pirsig, 1991, 278.

58. For Aristotle virtue was a necessary condition; for Socrates it was sufficient (Nussbaum, 1991).

59. MacIntyre, 1988, 143.

60. Frank, 1988, p. 254.

61. MacIntyre, 1984, p. 187.

62. Bloom, 1987, p. 129.

63. MacIntyre, 1966, 77.

64. See Brown, 1991, 205.

65. Friedman, 1970, pp. 153–156.

66. See Heilbroner, 1982, 438.

67. King, 1989, 46.

68. Brown discusses the apparent philosophical inconsistency between *The Theory of Moral Sentiments* and *The Wealth of Nations* which has led some observers to doubt whether both books could have been written by the same hand. Brown does not directly address this question of authorial integrity, but rather emphasizes the importance of historical context in revealing each work's "textual identity" (189).

69. Described recently by Wicken (1987, 3) and in an economic context by Allen (1988) in "Evolution, Innovation and Economics" (118).

70. Buchanan and Vanberg (1991), 179.

71. Edgeworth, 1818 p. 16.

72. MacIntyre, 1984, p. 208.

73. Ashton, 1968, 1–2.

74. Ashton, 1968, 9.

75. Ashton, 1968, 13–14.

76. See Holmes (1990).

77. MacIntyre, 1966, 201.

78. MacIntyre, 1984, 232.

79. Ashton, 1968, 2.

80. MacIntyre, 1984, 225.

81. MacIntyre, 1984, 196.

82. MacIntyre, 1984, 227.

83. MacIntyre, 1966, 130.

84. For a concise summary of the Enlightenment project and why it failed, see MacIntyre's (1984) *After Virtue*, chapters 4 and 5.

85. MacIntyre, 1984, 50.

86. See, for example, Moore's *Principia Ethica* (1903).

87. MacIntyre, 1984, 195.

88. This focus is accentuated by the increasing affluence (i.e., spending power) of young people for whom Biological Quality has a strong appeal. Hence, the continual attempt in advertising to link sexual gratification, as opposed to, say, intellectual enlightenment (Intellectual Quality), with material acquisition.

89. Mulligan, 1990, p. 95.

90. See Bella and King, 1989, 428.

Chapter 8

1. MacIntyre, 1984, p. 188.
2. Schwartz, 1990, p. 191, (emphasis added).
3. MacIntyre, 1988, p. 20.
4. For example, Leland and Pyle (1977), in their capital structure signaling model, state that "the entrepreneur is presumed to maximize his expected utility of wealth" (373).
5. For an interesting recent discussion of rationality assumptions concerning groups versus individuals, see Kavka (1991), "Is Individual Choice Less Problematic Than Collective Choice?" In essence, Kavka concludes that any attempt to model human preference orderings—whether individual or collective—is extremely problematic.
6. von Neumann and Morgenstern, 1947.
7. See Arrow (1975).
8. Myers, 1977.
9. This is represented by $s_b - s_a$ in Myers's (1977) figure 2.
10. Diamond, 1989, p. 289 (notation changes).
11. The extent of this unraveling (i.e., the extent to which *all* BG agents will choose the safe project) will depend upon the initial proportion of virtuous agents and the length of the game. If these virtuous agents cause interest rates to be sufficiently low, then even in the final repetition of the game—the repetition in which opportunistic BG agents are most likely to choose the risky project—these agents will choose the safe project. Thus, the agency problem would completely unravel.
12. MacIntyre, 1988, 143.
13. I am greatly indebted to the assistance of Kenneth Riener in developing this model.
14. Donaldson, 1989, p. 28.

Chapter 9

1. Betz (1989).
2. Ruegger et al., 1992.
3. See, for example, the October 1994 issue of the *Monist*, which is devoted entirely to this debate over feminist epistemologies.
4. Baber, 1994, p. 404.
5. Tavris, 1992, p. 63.
6. Collins (1988), emphasis added.
7. Mary Pierce, *Newsweek,* 1992, 98.
8. Hausman and McPherson, 1993, p. 718.
9. Fuchsberg, 1992.
10. This trend does not appear to be limited to the major schools. For example, California Polytechnic State University in San Luis Obispo, which operates a relatively small program with a provincial focus, has experienced

a drop in female enrollment from 34 percent of the total graduate intake in 1988 to 30 percent in 1992.

11. Akaah, 1989, 375.
12. See Pearsall (1986).
13. Jensen and Meckling, 1976, 328.
14. Thaler, 1992, p. 5.
15. White, 1992, p. 57.
16. Anonymous.
17. Gilmore, 1986, p. 31.
18. Solomon, 1994, p. 5.
19. Smith, 1994, p. 105.
20. The term 'business school' is used here to denote the academic community who develop and disseminate ideas concerning individual activity within the corporate milieu (economics departments, wherever physically located, are therefore included in this invocation of the business school).

Chapter 10

1. Bowie, 1991, 19.
2. MacIntyre, 1984, 254.
3. MacIntyre, 1984, p. 54.
4. MacIntyre, 1984, 219.
5. Duska, 1992, p. 164.
6. Goldman, 1993, p. 341.
7. Sammons, 1992, p. 92.
8. Sammons, 1992, p. 97.
9. Sammons, 1992, p. 81.
10. Sammons, 1992, pp. 87–88.
11. 1992, pp. 113, 91.
12. See, for example, Douglas North (1991) and Paul Romer (1990).
13. North, 1991, 5.
14. North, 1991, 10.
15. A great deal has been written about Japanese corporate culture as distinct from that in the West. Japanese corporations tend to provide lifetime employment and therefore adopt a paternal role. For example, a Japanese firm is often likened to an extended family and therefore "company loyalty functions as the motivating force" (Bowie, 1991, 18). As such, the behavioral assumptions that underlie economic rationality may be even less appropriate in a Japanese setting.
16. MacIntyre, 1988, p. 99.
17. North, 1991, p. 4.
18. Bowie, 1991, p. 19.
19. MacIntyre, 1988, p. 127.
20. Bloom, 1987.

21. MacIntyre, 1988, p. 400.
22. Pirsig, 1991, p. 67.
23. Jensen and Meckling, 1976, p. 357.
24. Klein, 1989, 62.

Bibliography

Akaah, Ishmael P. 1989. "Differences in Research Ethics Judgements Between Male and Female Marketing Professionals." *Journal of Business Ethics* 8; 375–381.

Akerlof, George. 1970. "The Market for Lemons: Quality Uncertainty and the Market Mechanism." *Quarterly Journal of Economics* 84, 3 (August) 488–500.

Alchian, A. 1969. "Corporate Management and Property Rights." In *Economic Policy and the Regulation of Corporate Securities,* ed. H Manne. Washington, D.C.: American Enterprise Institute for Public Policy Research.

Allen, F., and G. Faulhaber. 1989. "Signaling by Underpricing in the Initial Public Offering Market." *Journal of Financial Economics* 23: 303–23.

Allen, Peter M. 1985. "Towards a New Science of Complex Systems." In *The Science and Praxis of Complexity*, S. Alda et al. Tokyo: United Nations University.

———. 1988. "Evolution, Innovation and Economics." In *Technical Change and Economic Theory*, G. Dosi, C. Freeman, R. Nelson, G. Silverberg, and L. Soele. London: Pinter Publishers Limited.

Allmon, Dean E., and James Grant. 1990. "Real Estate Sales Agents and the Code of Ethics." *Journal of Business Ethics* 9, no. 10.

Ambarish, R., K. John, and J. Williams. 1987. "Efficient Signaling with Dividends and Investments." *Journal of Finance*, 42, no. 2: 321–44.

Annas, Julia. 1995. "Prudence and Morality in Ancient and Modern Ethics." *Ethics* 105, no. 2:

Aristotle. 1991. *The Nicomachean Ethics.* Oxford: Oxford University Press.

Armstrong, Mary Beth, and John Dobson. 1994. "An Application of Virtue Ethics to the Accounting Profession." Working Paper. San Luis Obispo California Polytechnic State University.

Arrow, Kenneth. 1975. "Gifts and Exchanges." In *Altruism, Morality, and Economic Theory,* ed. E.S. Phelps. New York: Russell Sage Foundation.

———. 1984. "The Economics of Agency." Research Paper. Stanford University

Ashton, T. S. 1966. *The Industrial Revolution, 1760–1830*. London: Oxford University Press.

Axelrod, Robert. 1984. *The Evolution of Cooperation*. New York: Basic Books.

Baber, Harriet. 1994. "The Market for Feminist Epistemology." *The Monist* 77, no. 4 (October): 403–23.

Ball, Donald, and Wendell H. McCulloch, Jr. 1990. *International Business: Introduction and Essentials,* 4th ed. Homewood, Ill.: BPI-Irwin.

Baneish, Messod D., and Robert Chatov. 1993. "Corporate Codes of Conduct: Economic Determinants and Legal Implications for Independent Auditors." *Journal of Accounting and Public policy* 12: 3-35.

Bannock, G., R. E. Baxter, and R. Rees. 1972. *The Dictionary of Economics.* London: Penguin Books.

Barach, J., and John B. Elstrott. 1988. "The Transactional Ethic: The Ethical Foundations of Free Enterprise Reconsidered." *Journal of Business Ethics*, no. 7: 545–52.

Barnea, A. R. Haugen, and L. Senbet. 1980. "A Rationale for Debt Maturity Structure and Call Provisions in the Agency Theory Framework." *Journal of Finance* 35 (December): 1223–34.

Baron, C. and B. Holmstrom. 1980. "The Two-Tiers of Informational Asymmetry." *Journal of Finance* (September): 1223–34

Bartlett, Christopher A., and Sumantra Ghoshal. 1989. *Managing Across Borders.* Cambridge, Mass.: Harvard Business School Press.

Baumhart, Raymond C. 1961. "How Ethical Are Businessmen?" *Harvard Business Review.* (January): 14–17.

Beatty, R. and J. Ritter. 1986. "Investment Banking, Reputation, and the Underpricing of IPO's." *Journal of Financial Economics* (March): 213–32.

Bella, David, and Jonathan King. 1989. "Common Knowledge of the Second Kind." *Journal of Business Ethics* 8: 415–30

Bellah, Robert N., Richard Madsen, William M. Sullivan, Ann Swidler, and Steven M. Tipton. 1985. *Habits of the Heart: Individualism and Commitment in American Life.* New York: Harper and Row.

Betz, Micheal, and Lenahan O'Connel and Jon Shepard. 1987. "Gender Differences in Proclivity for Unehtical Behavior." *Journal of Business Ethics* 8: 321-24.

Bloom, Allan. 1987. *The Closing of the American Mind,* New York: Simon and Schuster.

Bowie, Norman E. 1991. "Challenging the Egoistic Paradigm." *Business Ethics Quarterly* 1: 1–21

——, ed. 1992. *Ethics and Agency Theory,* and R. Edward Freeman. New York: Oxford University Press.

Brennan, Timothy J. 1989. "A Methodological Assessment of Multiple Utility Frameworks." *Economics and Philosophy* 5: 197–99.

Brown, Vivienne. 1991. "Signifying Voices: Reading the 'Adam Smith Problem.' *Economics and Philosophy* 7: 187–220

Buchanan, James M., and Viktor J. Vanberg. 1991. "The Market as a Creative Process." *Economics and Philosophy* 7: 167–86.

Bull C. 1993. "Implicit Contracts in the Absence of Enforcement and Risk Aversion." *American Economic Review* 73, no. 4 (September) 658.

Business Roundtable. 1988. *Corporate Ethics: A Prime Business Asset.* New York: Business Roundtable

Byron, W. J. 1988. "Twin Towers: A Philosophy and Theology of Business." *Journal of Business Ethics* 7: 525–30

Campbell, D. 1986. "Rationality and Utility from the Standpoint of Evolutionary Biology." *Journal of Business* 59, no. 4 (October): 355–65.

Campbell, S. and C. Kracaw. 1986. "Why Do Financial Intermediaries Exist." Working Paper. University of Pennsylvania.

Carter, R., and S. Manaster. 1990. "Initial Public Offerings and Underwriter Reputation." *Journal of Finance* 45: 1045–67.

Chakravarthy, B. 1986. "Measuring Strategic Performance." *Strategic Management Journal* 7: 437–51.

Chung, K. S., and R. L. Smith, II. 1987. "Product Quality, Nonsalvageable Capital Investment and the Cost of Financial Leverage." In *Modern Finance and Industrial Economics*, ed. Thomas E. Copeland New York: Basil Blackwell, Inc.

Coase, R. H. 1937. "The Nature of the Firm." *Economica*, New Series 4: 386–05. Reprinted in *Readings in Price Theory* Homewood, Ill.: Irwin.

Collins, N.W., Gilbert, S.K. and Nycum, S. H. 1988. *Women Leading: Making Tough Choices on the Fast Track*. New York: Stephen Greene Press/Viking.

Copeland, Thomas, and Fred Weston. 1988. *Financial Theory and Corporate Policy,* 3d ed. New York: Addison-Wesley.

Cornell, B., and A. C. Shapiro. 1987. "Corporate Stakeholders and Corporate Finance." *Financial Management* 16, no. 1, (Spring): 5–14.

Cottrill, Melville, T. 1990. "Corporate Social Responsibility and the Marketplace." *Journal of Business Ethics* 9, no. 9: 723–29.

Cramp, Tony. 1991. "Pleasures, Prices, and Principles." in *Thoughtfull Economic Man,* Gay Meeks ed. Cambridge: Cambridge University Press.

Crockett, J., and I. Friend. 1986. "Corporate Dividend Payout Policy." University of Pennsylvania Working Paper.

Dann, L., and W. Mikkelson. "Convertible Debt Issuance, Capital Structure Change and Financing-Related Information: Some New Evidence." Working Paper. University of Chicago, Graduate School of Business.

Dann, L. 1980. "The Effect of Common Stock Repurchases on SecurityHolders Returns." *Journal of Financial Economics* 6 (June): 297–330.

Darrough, Masako N., and Neal M. Stoughton. 1986. "Moral Hazard and Adverse Selection: The Question of Financial Structure." *Journal of Finance* 41; 501–14

Darrough, M. N. 1987. "Managerial Incentives for Short-Term Results: A Comment." *Journal of Finance*, 42, no. 4 (September): 1097–1102.

Dawkins, Richard. 1972. *The Selfish Gene.* Oxford: Oxford University Press.

Dean, Peter J. 1992. "Making Codes of Ethics Real." *Journal of Business Ethics* 11: 285–90.

DeAngelo, H. and L. DeAngelo. 1987. "Management Buyouts of Publicly Traded Corporations." In *Modern Finance and Industrial Economics*, ed. Thomas E. Copeland. New York: Basil Blackwell, Inc..

Dees, Gregory J. 1982. "Principals, Agents, and Ethics." In *Ethics and Agency Theory*, ed. Norman E. Bowie and R. Edward Freeman. New York: Oxford University Press.

DeGeorge, Richard T. 1986. *Business Ethics*, 2d ed. New York: Macmillan.

DeJong, D. V., R. Forsythe, and R. J. Lundholm. 1985. "Ripoffs, Lemons, and Reputation Formation in Agency Relationships. A Laboratory Market Study." *Journal of Finance*, 40, no. 3 (July).

Derry, Robin, and Ronald Green. 1989. "Ethical Theory in Business Ethics: A Critical Assessment" Paper delivered at the Business Ethics Society's annual meeting in Atlanta.

Derry, Robin. 1996. "Toward a Feminist Firm: Comments on John Dobson and Judith White." *Business Ethics Quarterly* 6 (January): 101–10.

Diamond, Douglas W. 1989. "Reputation Acquisition in Debt Markets." *Journal of Political Economy* 97: 828–61

Dielman, T., and H. Oppenheimer. 1984. "An Examination of Investor Behavior during Periods of Large Dividend Changes." *Journal of Financial and Quantitative Analysis* 19, no. 2 (June): 197–216.

Dobson, John. 1990. "The Role of Ethics in Global Corporate Culture." *Journal of Business Ethics* 9: 481-488

———. 1991. "Reconciling Financial Economics and Business Ethics." *Business and Professional Ethics Journal* 10, No. 4 (Winter).

———. 1992. "Ethics in Financial Contracting." *Business and Professional Ethics Journal* 11, Nos. 3 & 4 (Fall/Winter): 93–128.

———. 1992a. "Ethics in the Transnational Corporation." *Journal of Business Ethics* 11: 21-27.

———. 1992b. "The Importance of Corporate Reputation in Transnational Business." *School of Business Journal, San Francisco State University* 1: 79–86.

———. 1993. "Financial Ethics: What Practitioners Really Need to Know." *Financial* (November/December).

———. 1996. "Ethics in Finance II." *Financial Analysts Journal*, forthcoming.

———, and Mary Beth Armstrong. 1995. "Application of Virtue-Ethics Theory: A Lesson From Architecture." *Research on Accounting Ethics*, Vol. 1, 187–202.

———, and Robert Dorsey. 1993. "Reputation, Information and Project Termination in Capital Budgeting." *Engineering Economist* 38, 2: 143–152.

———, and Uric B. Dufrene. 1993. "The Impacts of US Presidential Elections on International Security Markets." *Global Finance Journal*, 4(1): 39-47

———, and Kenneth Reiner. 1995. "The Rationality of Honesty in Debt Markets." *Managerial Finance* 20–36.

———, and Judith White. 1995. "Toward the Feminine Firm." *Business Ethics Quarterly* 5(3) (July): 463–478

————, and Cheryl MacLellan. "Women, Ethics, and MBAs."*Journal of Business Ethics*, forthcoming.

Dolecheck, Maynard M., and Carolyn C. Dolecheck. 1989. "Ethics: Take It from the Top." *Business* (Jan-Feb-Mar): 12–18.

Donaldson, Thomas. 1989. *The Ethics of International Business*. New York: Oxford University Press.

Dunkel, Arthur. 1991. "GATT's Last Chance" *The Economist* 1–7 June: 13–14.

Duska, Ronald F. 1992. "Why Be a Loyal Agent? A Systematic Ethical Analysis." In *Ethics and Agency Theory,* ed. Norman E. Bowie and R. Edward Freeman. New York: Oxford University Press.

Dybvig, P. H., and C. S. Spatt. 1985. "Does It Pay to Maintain a Reputation?" Working Paper. Yale School of Organization and Management.

Dyl, E., and M. Joehnk. 1979. "Sinking Funds and the Cost of Corporate Debt."*Journal of Finance* 34 (September): 877–93.

Edgeworth, Francis. 1881.*Mathematical Psychics*: An Essay on the Application of Mathematics to the Moral Science. London: Kegan Paul.

Eisenhardt, Kathleen M. 1989. "Agency Theory: An Assessment and Review" *Academy of Management Review* 14: 57–74.

Ekins, Paul. 1989. "Trade and Self-Reliance." *The Ecologist* 19, no. 5.

Etzioni, Amitai. 1988. *The Moral Dimension*. New York: The Free Press.

————. 1991. "Reflections on Teaching Business Ethics." *Business Ethics Quarterly* 1, no. 4 (October): 355–66.

Fama, E. 1980. "Agency Problems and the Theory of the Firm." *Journal of Political Economy* (April): 288–307.

Fama, E. F., and M. C. Jensen. 1983. "Separation of Ownership and Control." *Journal of Law and Economics* 26 (June): 301–25.

Flannery, M. 1986. "Asymmetric Information and Risky Debt Maturity Choice."*Journal of Finance* (March): 19–38

Foot, Philippa. 1967. *Theories of Ethics*. Oxford University Press.

Francis, J. C. 1986. *Investments: Analysis and Management*. New York: McGraw Hill.

Frank, Robert. 1988.*Passions within Reason*. New York: W. W. Norton & Co.

Frank, Robert, Thomas Gilovich, and Dennis Regan. 1993. "Does Studying Economics Inhibit Cooropation?"*Journal of Economic Perspectives* (Spring).

Friedman, Milton. 1970. "The Social Responsibility of Business Is to Increase Its Profits." *New York Times Magazine*, reprinted in *Business Ethics* W. M. Hoffman and J. M. Moore.New York: McGraw-Hill, 1990.

Fry, Earl H. 1989. "Is the United States a Declining Economic Power?" *Business In The Contemporary World* 1, no. 4 (Summer): 44.

Furubotn, E. G., and S. Pejovich. 1972. "Property Rights and Economic Theory."*Journal of Economic Literature* 1137–60.

Fuchsberg, Gilbert. 1992. "Female Enrollment Falls in Many Top MBA Programs." *The Wall Street Journal* (September 25): p. B1.

Gauthier, David. 1988.*Morals by Agreement*. Oxford: Clarenden Press.

Gellerman, Saul. 1986. "Why Good Managers Make Bad Ethical Choices." *Harvard Business Review* (July-August): 85–90.

Getz, Kathleen A. 1990. "International Codes of Conduct: An Analysis of Ethical Reasoning." *Journal of Business Ethics* 9, no. 7 (July): 14–18.

Ghorbade, Jai. 1991. "Ethics in MBA Programs: The Rhetoric, the Reality, and a Plan of Action." *Journal of Business Ethics* 10: 891–905.

Gilligan, Carol. 1982. *In a Different Voice.* Cambridge, Mass.: Harvard University Press.

Gilmore, J. Thomas. 1986. "A Framework for Responsible Business Behavior." *Business and Society Review* no. 58 (Summer): 31–34.

Gioia, Dennis A. 1992. "Pinto Fires and Personal Ethics: A Script Analysis of Missed Opportunities." *Journal of Business Ethics* 11: 379–389.

Goldman, Alvin I. 1993. "Ethics and Cognitive Science." *Ethics* 103: 337–60.

Goldsmith, E. 1990. "The Uruguay Round." *The Ecologist* 20 (November/December): 202–4.

Goodpaster, Kenneth E., and John B. Matthews. 1982. "Can a Corporation Have a Conscience?" *Harvard Business Review* (January-February): 132–41.

Goodpaster, Kenneth E. 1991. "Business Ethics and Stakeholder Analysis." *Business Ethics Quarterly* 1: 54–73

———. 1994. "Work, Spirituality and the Moral Point of View." *International Journal of Value-Based Management* 7, no. 1: 49–62.

Grossman, S. J., and O. D. Hart. 1982. "Corporate Financial Structure and Managerial Incentives." In *The Economics of Information*, John J. McCall. Chicago: University of Chicago Press.

Haley, C. W., and L. D. Schall. 1979. *The Theory of Financial Decisions.* New York: McGraw-Hill.

Hall, B. 1986. *Who Owns Whom,* New York: Dow Jones Inc. Winter ed. (quote taken from *The Ecologist*, see Goldsmith).

Harris, M., and A. Raviv. 1985. "A Sequential Signaling Model of Convertible Debt Call Policy." *Journal of Finance* 40 (December): 1263–82.

Hart, Oliver D. 1983. "Optimal Labour Contracts under Asymmetric Information: An Introduction." *Review of Economic Studies* (January): 3–36.

Hausman, Daniel M., and Michael S. McPherson. 1993. "Taking Ethics Seriously: Economics and Contemporary Moral Philosophy." *Journal of Economic Literature* 31 (June): 671–731.

Heilbroner, R. C. 1982. "The Socialization of the Individual in Adam Smith." *History of Political Economy* 14:3.

Hoffman, Michael W., and Jennifer Mills Moore. 1990. *Business Ethics.* New York: McGraw-Hill.

Hollis, Martin, and Steven Lukes. 1982. *Rationality and Relativism.* Oxford: Basil Blackwell.

Holmes, Stephen. 1990. "The Secret History of Self-Interest." In *Beyond Self-Interest*, ed. Jane J. Mansbridge. Chicago: University of Chicago Press.

Holmstrom, B. 1979. "Moral Hazard and Observability." *Bell Journal of Economics* 10 (Spring): 74–91.

———. 1981. "Contractual Models for the Labor Market." *American Economic Review* (May): 307–13.

Homer. *The Odyssey.* Trans. R. Fitzgerald. Garden City, N.J.: Anchor Press/Doubleday.

Hu, Henry T. C. 1991. "New Financial Products, The Modern Process of Financial Innovation and the Puzzle of Shareholder Welfare." *Texas Law Review* 69 (May): 1273–1317.

Hume, David., 1955. "Writings in Economics." Ed. Eugene Rotwein. Madison: University of Wisconsin Press. (Quote in text is taken from essay "An Enquiry Concerning The Principles of Morals" originally published in 1751).

Hutchinson, D. S. 1986. *The Virtues of Aristotle.* London: Routledge and Kegan Paul.

Ingersoll, J., Jr. 1977. "A Contingent Claims Valuation of Convertible Securities." *Journal of Financial Economics* 4 (May): 289–322.

Jarrel, G., and S. Peltzman. 1985. "The Impact of Product Recalls on the Wealth of Sellers." *Journal of Political Economy* (June): 512–536.

Jensen, M. C. 1989. "The Eclipse of the Public Corporation," *Harvard Business Review.* (September-October).

———, and W. H. Meckling. 1976. "Theory of the Firm: Managerial Behavior, Agency Costs and Ownership Structure." *Journal of Financial Economics* 3, no. 4 (October): 305–360.

John, K., and J. Williams. 1985. "Dividends, Dilution and Taxes." *Journal of Finance* 40 (September): 1053–1070.

John, K., and A. Kalay. 1985. "Informational Content of Optimal Debt Contracts." In *Recent Advances in Corporate Finance*, ed. E. Altman and M. Subrahmansam Homewood, Ill.: Irwin.

John, Kose, and D. Nachman. 1985. "Risky Debt, Investment Incentives and Reputation in a Sequential Equilibrium." *Journal of Finance* 40: 863–77.

Jones, Thomas M., and Dennis P. Quinn. 1993. "Taking Ethics Seriously: The Competitive Advantage of Intrinsic Morality." Working Paper. University of Washington.

Kahneman, D., Jack L. Knetsch, and Richard H. Thaler. 1986. "Fairness and the Assumptions of Economics." *Journal of Business* 59: 285–300.

Kalay, A. 1980. "Signaling, Information Content and the Reluctance to Cut Dividends." *Journal of Financial and Quantitative Analysis* 15 (November): 855–63.

Kanodia, Chandra, Robert Bushman and John Dickhaut. 1989. "Escalation Errors and the Sunk Cost Effect: An Explanation Based on Reputation and Information Asymmetries." *Journal of Accounting Research* 27, no. 1: 59–77.

Kavka, Gregory S. 1991. "Is Individual Choice Less Problematic Than Collective Choice?" *Economics and Philosophy* 7: 143–165.

Keohane, Kieran. 1989. "Toxic Trade-Off: The Price Ireland Pays for Industrial Development." *Ecologist* 19, no. 4 (July/August): 144–46.

King, J. B. 1988. "Prisoners' Paradoxes," *Journal of Business Ethics* 7, no. 7: 475–88.

———. 1989. "Confronting Chaos," *Journal of Business Ethics* 8, no. 1: (January).

Klein, B. and K. B. Leffler. 1981. "The Role of Market Forces in Assuring Contractual Performance." *Journal of Political Economy* 87: 615–641.

Klein, Sherwin. 1988. "Is a Moral Organization Possible?" *Business and Professional Ethics Journal* 7, no. 1 (Spring).

———. 1989. "Platonic Virtue Theory and Business Ethics." *Business and Professional Ethics Journal* 8, no. 4.

Kreps, D. 1984. "Corporate Culture and Economic Theory." Working Paper. Stanford University.

Kreps, D., and R. Wilson. 1982. "Sequential Equilibria." *Econometrica* 7, no. 4: 863–94.

Kreps, D., P. Milgrom, J. Roberts, and R. Wilson. 1982. "Rational Cooperation in the Finitely Repeated Prisoners Dilemma." *Journal of Economic Theory* 24 (August): 245–52.

Kuhn, Thomas S. 1970. *The Structure of Scientific Revolutions*. Chicago: University of Chicago Press.

Ladd, John. 1991. "Bhopal: An Essay on Moral Responsibility and Civic Virtue." *Journal of Social Philosophy* 22:1 (Spring): 73.

Lasch, Christopher. 1991. *The True and Only Heaven: Progress and Its Critics*. New York: W. W. Norton.

Laughhunn, D., and J. W. Payne. 1991 "The Impact of Sunk Outcomes on Risky Choice Behavior." *Canadian Journal of Operations Research and Information Processing*, forthcoming.

Leland, Hayne E., and David H. Pyle. 1977. "Informational Asymmetries, Financial Structure, and Financial Intermediation." *Journal of Finance* 32: 371–87.

Lukes, Steven. 1977. *Rationality and Relativism*. New York: Columbia University Press.

MacIntyre, Alasdair. 1966. *A Brief History of Ethics*. New York: Macmillan.

———. 1984. *After Virtue*. 2d ed. Notre Dame: University of Notre Dame Press.

———. 1988. *Whose Justice? Which Rationality?* Notre Dame: University of Notre Dame Press.

———. 1990. *Three Rival Versions of Moral Enquiry*. Notre Dame: University of Notre Dame Press.

Marwell, Gerald, and Ruth E. Ames. 1981. "Economists Free Ride, Does Anyone Else?" *Journal of Public Economics* 15: 295–310.

McGuire, J., T. Schneeweis, and A. Sundgren. 1986. "Corporate Social Responsibility and Firm Financial Performance." *Academy of Management Journal* 31: 845–72.

Milgram, S. 1974. *Obedience to Authority*, quote can be found in Art Wolfe, 1991; "Reflections on Business Ethics . . . " *Business Ethics Quarterly* 1: No. 4 (October): 409–440

Milgrom, P. and J. Roberts. 1982. "Predation, Reputation and Entry Deterrence." *Journal of Economic Theory* 27: 280–312.

Miller, Merton H. 1986. "Behavioral Rationality in Finance: The Case of Dividends." *Journal of Business* 59: 451–68.

Miller, R. E., and F. K. Reilly. 1987. "An Examination of Mispricing, Returns, and Uncertainty for Initial Public Offerings." *Financial Management* (Summer).

Miller, Merton H., and Kevin Rock. 1985. "Dividend Policy Under Asymmetric Information." *Journal of Finance* 40 (September): 1031–52.

Mishra, B. 1984. "Informational Asymmetry in Finance: Three Related Essays." Ph.D. Dissertation. New York University.

Modigliani, Franco, and M. H. Miller. 1958. "The Cost of Capital, Corporation Finance, and the Theory of Investment." *American Economic Review* 68 (June): 261–97.

Moore, Jennifer. 1991. "Autonomy and the Legitimacy of the Liberal Arts." *In Business Ethics: The State of the Art*, ed. R. Edward Freeman. New York: Oxford University Press.

———. 1990. "What is Really Unethical About Insider Trading." *Journal of Business Ethics* 9(3): 171–82.

Moore, Norman H., Stephen W. Pruitt, and K. S. Maurise Tse. 1990. "What Price Morality? South African Divestment Decisions and Shareholder Wealth." Working Paper. Indiana University School of Business.

Morris, J. 1976. "On Corporate Debt Maturity Strategies." *Journal of Financial Economics* 31 (March): 147–75.

Mulligan, Thomas M. 1990. "Justifying Moral Initiative by Business." *Journal of Business Ethics* 9: 93–104.

Murdoch, Iris. 1971. *The Sovereignty of Good*. Cambridge: Cambridge University Press.

Myers, S., and N. Majluf. 1984. "Corporate Financing and Investment Decisions When Firms Have Information That Insiders Do Not Have." *Journals of Financial Economics* 13 (June): 993–1007.

Myers, S. C. 1977. "Determinants of Corporate Borrowing." *Journal of Financial Economics* 5: 147–175.

Narayanan, M. P. 1987. "Mangerial Incentives for Short Term Results: A Reply." *Journal of Finance* 2, no. 4 (September): 1103–1104.

Nash, Laura. 1981. "Ethics Without the Sermon." *Harvard Business Review* (November-December): 79–90.

Newsweek. 1992. "Giving Women the Business," ed. Kantrowitz, Barbara, Debra Rosenberg, Karen Springen, and Patricia King. 16 November, 98.

Noreen, Eric. 1988. "The Economics of Ethics: A New Perspective on Agency Theory." *Accounting Organizations and Society* 13: 359–369.

North, Douglas C. 1991. "Towards a Theory of Institutional Change." *The Quarterly Review of Economics and Business* 31: 3–11.

Nussbaum, Martha C. 1991. "The Chill of Virtue." *The New Republic* 16 and 23 (September): 34–40.

Nystrom, Paul C. 1990. "Differences in Moral Values Between Corporations." *Journal of Business Ethics* 9: 971–979.

Okai, Norimichi. 1991. "Financial Scandals and Their Aftermath." Working Paper. University of Michigan.

Pastin, M. 1986. "Managing the Rules of Conflict—International Bribery." In *Ethics and the Multinational Enterprise: Proceedings of the Sixth International Conference on Business Ethics,* ed. W. M. Hoffman, A. E. Lange, and D. A. Fedo. Lanham, MD: University Press of America.

Payne, Dinah, and Cecily A. Raiborn. 1990. "Corporate Codes of Conduct: A Collective Conscience and Continuum." *Journal of Business Ethics* 9: 879–89.

Pearsall, Marilyn. 1986. *Women and Values: Readings in Recent Feminine Philosophy.* Belmont, California: Wadsworth Inc.

Pettit, R. 1972. "Dividend Announcements, Security Performance and Capital Market Efficiency." *Journal of Finance* 27: 993–1007.

Peng, M.K.K. 1990. "The Uruguay Round and The Third World." *Ecologist* 20 (November/December): 208-13.

Pilotte, E. 1987. "The Impact on Shareholder Wealth of External Financing by Non-Dividend-Paying Firms: An Empirical Examination." Ph.D. Dissertation. Indiana University.

Pirsig, Robert M. 1991. *Lila: An Inquiry into Morals.* New York: Bantam.

———. 1973. *Zen and the Art of Motorcycle Maintenance.* New York: Bantam.

Plott, C. R. 1986. "Rational Choice in Experimental Markets." *Journal of Business* 59: S309–S327.

Polanyi, Michael. 1958. *Personal Knowledge: Toward a Post-Critical Philosophy.* Chicago: University of Chicago Press.

Ponemon, Lawrence A. 1992. "Ethical Reasoning and Selection-Solution in Accounting." *Accounting Organizations and Society* 17: 239–258.

Prior, William. 1991. *Virtue and Knowledge: An Introduction to Ancient Greek Ethics.* New York: Routledge.

Pritchard, Michael S. 1992. "Good Works." *Professional Ethics* 1 (Spring/Summer): 155–178.

Pruitt, Stephen W., and David R. Peterson. 1986. "Security Price Reactions Around Product Recall Announcements." *Journal of Financial Research* 9, no. 2: 113–122.

Raghavan, C. 1990. "Recolonization: GATT in Its Historical Context." *Ecologist* 20 (November/December): 205–07.

Rasmusen, Eric. 1989. *Games and Information: An Introduction to Game Theory.* Oxford: Basil Blackwell Ltd.

Rawls, John. 1971. *A Theory of Justice*. Cambridge, Mass.: Harvard University Press.

Reich, Robert B. 1990. "Who Is Us?" *Harvard Business Review* (January-February): 84–88.

Rion, Michael R. 1982. "Training for Ethical Management at Cummins Engine." In *Doing Ethics in Business: New Ventures in Management Development*, ed. Donald G. Jones. Cambridge, Mass.: Oelgeschlager, Gunn & Hain, Inc.

Ritter, J. R. 1984. "The "Hot Issue" Market in 1980." *Journal of Business* 57: 215–40.

Robbins, E., and J. Schatzberg. 1986. "Callable Bonds: A Risk-Reducing Signaling Mechanism." *Journal of Finance* 41 (September): 935–50.

Rock, K. 1986. "Why new issues are underpriced." *Journal of Financial Economics* 15: 187-212.

Roll, R. 1986. "The Hubris Hypothesis of Corporate Takeovers." *Journal of Business* 59: 197–216.

Romer, Paul. 1990. "Endogenous Technological Change." *Journal of Political Economy* 98: S71–S102.

Rosenberg, R. 1974. "Adam Smith on Profits-Paradox Lost and Regained." *Journal of Political Economy* 82, no. 6.

Ross, S. 1977. "The Determination of Financial Structure: The Incentive Signaling Approach." *The Bell Journal of Economics* 8 (Spring): 23–40.

Rostow, W. W. 1960. *Stages of Economic Growth*, Oxford: Oxford University Press.

Ruegger, Durwood, and Ernest King. 1992. "A Study of the Effect of Age and Gender Upon Student Business Ethics." *Journal of Business Ethics* 11, 179-86.

Sammons, Jack L. 1992 "Rebellious Ethics and Albert Speer." *Professional Ethics: A Multidisciplinary Journal* 1(3&4): 77–116.

Schiller, Robert J. 1986. "Comments on Miller and on Kleidon." *Journal of Business* 59: 501–05.

Schoell, W. F., and J. P. Guiltinan. 1992. *Marketing: Contemporary Concepts and Practices*. Boston: Allyn and Bacon.

Schwartz, Barry. 1990. "King Midas in America." In *Enhancing Business Ethics*, ed. Clarence C. Walton. New York: Plenum Press.

Selten, R. 1975. "Re-examination of the Perfectness Concept for Equilibrium Points in Extensive Games." *International Journal of Game Theory* 4: 25–55.

Sen, Amartya. 1987. *On Ethics and Economics*. New York: Basil Blackwell.

———. 1978. "Rational Fools: A Critique of the Behavioral Foundations of Economic Theory." In *Scientific Models and Men*, ed. H. Harris. London: Oxford University Press.

Sherwin, Douglas. 1983. "The Ethical Roots of the Business System." *Harvard Business Review* (November-December): 183–192.

Shiller, R. J. 1986. "Theories of Aggregate Stock Price Movements." *Journal of Portfolio Management* (Winter): 28–37.

Shrybman, Steven. 1990. "International Trade and the Environment: An Environmental Assessment of the General Agreement on Tariffs and Trade." *Ecologist* 20, no.1: 30–4.

Simon, H. A. 1986. "Rationality in Psychology and Economics." *Journal of Business* 59: S209–S224.

Smith, Adam. 1776. *Wealth of Nations*. New York: Modern Library.

———. 1759. *Theory of Moral Sentiments*. New York: Modern Library.

Smith, Clifford. 1992. "Economics and Ethics: The Case of Salomon Brothers." *Journal of Applied Corporate Finance* 5: 23–28.

———. 1986. "Investment Banking and the Capital Acquisition Process." *Journal of Financial Economics* 15: 3–29.

Smith, C. W. 1977. "Alternative Methods for Raising Capital." *Journal of Financial Economics* (January-February): 273–307.

Smith, Craig. 1994. "The New Corporate Philanthropy." *Harvard Business Review* 72, 3 (May-June) 105-19.

Smith, Kirk R. 1988. "Air Pollution: Assessing Total Exposure in Developing Countries." *Ecologist* 30, no.10 (December): 20.

Solomon, Robert C. 1992. "Corporate Roles, Personal Virtues: An Aristotelian Approach to Business Ethics." *Business Ethics Quarterly* 2: 317–39.

———. 1994. *The New World of Business*. Lanham, Maryland: Rowman and Littlefield Publishers, Inc.

Spatt, C. S. 1083. "Credit Reputation Equilibrium and the Theory of Credit Markets." Working Paper. Carnegie-Mellon University.

"Studies in International Trade, Industrial Pollution Control and International Trade." 1971 GATT: 239.

Spence, A. Michael. 1973. "Job Market Signaling." *Quarterly Journal of Economics* 87, no. 3 (Spring): 355–74.

Statman, M., and D. Caldwell. 1987. "Applying Behavioral Finance to Capital Budgeting: Project Terminations." *Financial Management* 16: 7–15.

Staw, B. M. 1981. "The Escalation of Commitment to a Course of Action." *Academy of Management Review* 6, no. 4: 577–87.

Staw, B. M., and J. Ross. 1986. "Behavior in Escalation Situations: Antecedents, Prototypes, and Solutions." In *Research in Organizational Behavior*, ed. S. Cummins and B. Staw. Greenwich, Conn.: JAI Press.

"Studies in International Trade, Industrial Pollution Control and International Trade." 1971 GATT: 239.

Swanda, John R., Jr. 1990. "Goodwill, Going Concern, Stocks and Flows: A Prescription for Moral Analysis." *Journal of Business Ethics* 9, no. 9: 751–60.

Tavris, Carol. 1992. *The Mismeasure of Women*. New York: Touchstone.

Taylor, Richard. 1991. *Virtue Ethics: An Introduction*. New York: Linden Books.

Telser, J. 1980. "A Theory of Self-Enforcing Agreements." *Journal of Business* 53, no. 2 (January): 27–44.

Thakor, Anjan V. 1989. "Strategic Issues in Financial Contracting: An Overview." *Financial Management* (Summer): 84–88.

Thaler, Richard H. 1992. *The Winner's Curse: Paradoxes and Anomalies of Economic Life*. New York: Free Press.

Thatcher, J. 1985. "The Choice of Call Provision Terms: Evidence of the Existence of Agency Costs of Debt." *Journal of Finance* 40 (June): 549–61.

Thomson, Koy, and Nigel Dudley. 1989. "Transnationals and Oil in Amazonia." *Ecologist* 19, no. 6 (December): 219–24.

Tinic, S. 1988. "Anatomy of Initial Public Offerings of Common Stock." *Journal of Finance* 43: 789–822.

Titman, S., and B. Trueman. 1986. "Information Quality and the Valuation of New Issues." *Journal of Accounting and Economics* 8: 159–172.

UN Center on Transnational Corporations. 1985. *Environmental Aspects of the Activities of Transnational Corporations: A Survey*. New York: United Naitons.

Vitell, Scott J., and Donald L. Davis. 1990. "Ethical Beliefs of MIS Professionals: The Frequency and Opportunity for Unethical Behavior." *Journal of Business Ethics* 9: 63–70.

Von Neumann, J. and O. Morgenstern. 1947. *Theory of Games and Economic Behavior*. 2d ed. Princeton, N. J: Princeton University Press.

Walking, Ralph A., and Michael S. Long. 1984. "Agency Theory, Managerial Welfare and Takeover Bid Resistance." *Rand Journal of Economics* 1 (Spring): 54–68.

Weber, Max V. 1930. *The Protestant Ethic and the Spirit of Capitalism*. London: Allen & Unwin.

Weizenbaum, Joseph. 1976. *Computer Power and Human Reason*. San Francisco: W. H. Freeman and Co.

White, Thomas I.; 1992 "Business Ethics and Carol Gilligan's 'Two Voices'" *Business Ethics Quarterly* 2, No. 1 (January) 51–61.

Wicken, Jeffrey S. 1987. *Evolution, Thermodynamics, and Information— Extending the Darwinian Paradigm*. Oxford: Oxford University Press.

Williams, Oliver E., and Patrick E. Murphy. 1990. "The Ethics of Virtue: A Moral Theory of Marketing." *Journal of Macromarketing* (Spring): 19–29.

Williamson, O.E. 1964. *The Economics of Discretionary Behavior: Managerial Objectives in a Theory of the Firm*. Englewood Cliffs, N.J.: Prentice Hall.

———. 1983. "Credible Commitments: Using Hostages to Support Exchange." *American Economic Review* 73 (September): 519–40.

Wiseman, Jack. 1989. *Cost, Choice, and Political Economy*. Aldershot: Edward Elgar.

Wolfe, Art. 1991. "Reflections on Business Ethics." *Business Ethics Quarterly* 1, no. 4 (October): 409–40.

Wor, C. 1986. "Information Asymmetry and Sinking Fund Provision." Working Paper. Syracuse University.

Index

About the Author

John Dobson is associate professor of finance at California Polytechnic State University, in San Luis Obispo, where he has taught since 1990. He received his Bachelor's degree in economic history from Lancaster University in England. His Master's degree in economics and Ph.D. in finance were received from the University of South Carolina.

He has published articles in various academic journals including Financial Analysts Journal, Global Finance Journal, Journal of Business Ethics, Economics and Philosophy, and *Business Ethics Quarterly*. His primary research interests are agency theory and moral philosophy. He is currently working on a postmodern critique of finance theory.